"This book is a much-needed field guide for overcoming polarization. Combining deep historical analysis, biblical insights, and lived experiences, Shirley Mullen's *Claiming the Courageous Middle* helps to define the current divisive landscape, identify its theological and political root causes, and provide creative and practical solutions that have been field-tested. Mullen's personal history, her scholarship as a historian, her track record as a college president, and her sincere faith in Christ all come together to equip those in the middle to own their space and to lead redemptively."

—**Toni Kim**, director of spiritual care, National Association of Evangelicals

"Mullen, a distinguished historian and college president emerita, has written a prophetic book. It calls for Christians to resist the seductive undertow of the culture wars and claim a courageous middle—a place that listens attentively, admits complexity, and does not fit into binary categories of left and right. The church today desperately needs such courageous voices."

—**Nathan O. Hatch**, president emeritus, Wake Forest University

"This book is a must-read for pastors, professors, students, and individuals who believe there is an alternative to polarization. I was captivated by this book. Mullen is a great storyteller, historian, and philosopher who brings her profound analysis to bear on the everyday realities of misunderstanding and separation that are plaguing communities today. She persuasively makes the case that despite the risks, strong convictions and graciousness toward others are possible and the preferred vision for the future. A commitment to explore a middle space comes with the potential for a more complete vision of truth. This book is hope in the midst of despair."

—**Shirley V. Hoogstra**, president, Council for Christian Colleges and Universities

"Mullen brings a lifetime of wisdom and experience to this meditation on the courageous middle. Mullen's journey into Christian higher education as a student, a teacher, and ultimately, a college president, anchors this important book full of resources, ideas, and practical steps for Christians seeking to faithfully navigate the deep differences in our society."

—**John D. Inazu**, Sally D. Danforth Distinguished Professor of Law and Religion, Washington University in St. Louis; author of *Confident Pluralism: Surviving and Thriving through Deep Difference*

T0339004

"*Claiming the Courageous Middle* is a call for Christians to find more common ground in response to prolonged, pervasive polarization over race, sexuality, politics, economics, and other current issues. From her vantage point as a scholar and educational leader, Mullen correctly identifies courage as the primary virtue that the present cultural moment requires. Keeping our biblical balance is not a form of compromise, Mullen demonstrates, but an act of spiritual courage that advances Christian unity as an urgent priority for the church."

—**Philip Ryken**, president, Wheaton College

"In a vexing time of mean-spirited, self-assured, and rapid-fire pontification, Mullen does something astonishing. She invites us to slow down and savor textured stories of earnest faith and to carefully consider the historical forces that are shoving individuals and institutions, churches and communities into ideological corners. Then she guides us toward a different way. Mullen calls us to live and lead from the courageous middle—not a place of muddled thought and squishy compromise but of curiosity, humility, love for Jesus and others, and a confidence that God is not daunted by our moment."

—**Walter Kim**, president, National Association of Evangelicals

"Mullen invites all who are intellectually, politically, and spiritually lonely to join her and other fellow travelers in the courageous middle. This is a space of nuance, complexity, and humility filled with 'radical redemptive possibilities.' I have been waiting for a book like this for a long time. Mullen's call will resonate with anyone troubled by the era of polarization in which we now live."

—**John Fea**, distinguished professor of history, Messiah University; executive editor of *Current*

Claiming *the*
Courageous
Middle

Claiming *the* Courageous Middle

Daring to LIVE *and* WORK TOGETHER for a More Hopeful Future

Shirley A. Mullen

Baker Academic

a division of Baker Publishing Group

Grand Rapids, Michigan

© 2024 by Shirley A. Mullen

Published by Baker Academic
a division of Baker Publishing Group
Grand Rapids, Michigan
BakerAcademic.com

Printed in the United States of America

Library of Congress Cataloging-in-Publication Control Number: 2023050981
ISBN 9781540967046 (paperback)
ISBN 9781540967329 (casebound)
ISBN 9781493444526 (ebook)
ISBN 9781493444533 (pdf)

Baker Publishing Group publications use paper produced from sustainable forestry practices and postconsumer waste whenever possible.

24   25   26   27   28   29   30   7   6   5   4   3   2   1

To my grandmother
MARGARET GRAHAM DUNLOP
(1904–71)

*who first showed me what it means
to live courageously in the middle*

Contents

Preface

I did not invent the notion of a "courageous middle." It would be truer to say that I discovered it, even before knowing that it had a name. It is the purpose of this book to invite you into the story of the courageous middle in hopes that you will want to become a part of it.

At first, the idea of a courageous middle is a curious one. We do not instinctively think of the middle as a place of courage. It is more often seen as a place of timidity or weakness or fearfulness, a place we wander about until we dare to choose a side. I want to suggest that, in reality, in this polarized moment in our society and in the church, the most courageous choice we can make is to occupy the middle.

I don't mean that we just take up space in the middle or that we wait passively as observers for something to happen or for someone else to do something interesting. Rather, we choose each day and in each situation to work actively in this "middle space" in such a way that we convene a new community of individuals who, together, can imagine a way forward out of the polarization that is dividing our families, our workplaces, our politics, and our churches. Instead of our collective creativity as a society being used to maintain our side—whatever that side is in a particular situation or on a specific issue—we are directing that energy forward in service to the common good.

At first, this work might not sound too exciting. It is not as loud or as confident as the work of the poles, where we have clearly defined the problem and neatly divided the world into our friends and our enemies. On the edges, it is also easier to keep score because one side will be winning and the other losing. The work of the courageous middle is not like that. It is more like being part of an underground resistance movement. You will gradually come to recognize others who are doing the same work—side by side in creative collaboration toward a common goal that is larger and more comprehensive than the goals that keep us divided. It is more like the work of leaven or salt—the images that Jesus used to describe change agents who do not draw attention to themselves but who, in the end, effect the desired outcome of the entire enterprise.

I am grateful for those in my life at every stage who modeled for me what it means to live courageously in middle space—and to dare to bring all of who I am into that space—in the hopeful expectation of making a difference for good for others. It would have been much easier at many points to make myself smaller to fit into one of the readily available boxes on one side or another. I am grateful for God's providential and improvisational grace, which led me finally to understand that this work of the courageous middle is holy work—modeled for us in the Scriptures of the Old and New Testaments and finally in the incarnation of Jesus Christ, who came to be in his person the ultimate convener of radically redemptive middle space.

I am grateful to those alumni and colleagues who responded to the notion of a courageous middle when I first began to speak of it in my work as president of Houghton College. The discussion of this notion generated more response than any other topic I raised in my entire fifteen years as president— always animated and mostly positive, but not entirely positive. Some in the constituency were as intensely negative in their response as others had been positive. In either case, the term provoked curiosity and a desire for further explanation.

As I began to use the term more broadly to describe the calling of at least some of God's people in this moment of cultural paralysis and polarization, I was encouraged to write about it. Not knowing which of these individuals might prefer to keep their encouragement private, at least until knowing the outcome of the book, I will simply say, "Thank you! You know who you are."

I would, however, be remiss not to name several individuals explicitly here. Without their support along the way, the book would never have come to fruition. I am grateful to Betsy Sanford, my chief of staff at Houghton College, who over the years, whenever I used the term, reminded me that I needed to write a book someday on the courageous middle. John Lee, the chairman of the Houghton board of trustees, prompted me to develop the idea more fully and to connect it explicitly to a Wesleyan vision of Christian higher education. Jeff Crosby, president and CEO of the Evangelical Christian Publishers Association, who first heard me use the phrase on a panel he was hosting, took the trouble to follow up after the interview and tell me that the phrase was worth developing into a book. He graciously introduced me to the world of Christian book publishing and coached me informally on how to keep moving with this idea. Robert Hosack, chief acquisitions editor at Baker Publishing Group, shepherded the idea through its initial stages of submission to acceptance. He worked patiently to help me translate my traditional style of academic, disciplinary writing and thinking into a book with potentially broader interdisciplinary appeal. Emily Allen, Emily Mahoney, and Thomas Hallman—three recent graduates from Christian colleges who are all now in seminary—graciously agreed to be a consulting team to represent the intended audience in reviewing the manuscript. Their comments have been invaluable in helping me see from the standpoint of their generation—the future conveners of the courageous middle.

Finally and most important of all, I want to thank my husband, Paul Rees Mills, who has once again—as when I was in the presidency—taken on the work of managing the household so that I can spend my days these past several months in writing. I will be forever grateful that God brought him into my life. He has been my best supporter, my most constructive critic, and the primary reason these past fourteen years have been the most extravagantly joyous years of my life.

I offer this book now in hopes that it will inspire others to reflect on their own journeys and how they, too, are being prepared for particular roles that only they can play in the story of courage and radically redemptive activity in the middle spaces of their own lives.

Introduction

One morning in the early 2000s, Daniel (not his real name) showed up in my office to raise concerns about the college's diversity policy. (At the time, I was provost at one of the country's well-known Christian colleges.) He echoed the puzzlement I had heard before on campus about why we could not just be one in Christ. Why were we adopting the "political correctness" of the larger culture? Why was the administration promoting the divisive value of "diversity"? Why was this all we seemed to care about—in chapel, in the classrooms, and wherever else on campus it could be promoted? (I should mention here that this was all before anyone had heard of George Floyd or "critical race theory.") It soon became clear that even more particularly, he wanted to know why, if we were serious about diversity, it was only students from certain ethnic backgrounds that counted. He was especially frustrated that his own background was not taken into consideration as part of the diversity that received special financial support for underrepresented ethnic minorities. I listened for quite a while.

I asked him first whether he knew of others who felt the same way that he did. Daniel eagerly assured me that there were many on campus who shared his views on the topic. I then followed up by asking whether he was aware that there were also many students who believed that we spoke far too little about diversity and that the administration should be caring much more about the concerns of the campus's underrepresented ethnic minority students. He seemed quite surprised. Apparently, these groups did not eat at the same tables in the dining commons or follow the same social media sites.

We discussed what might be done about this impasse on campus. I asked if he would be interested in knowing why some of his peers took an entirely different view from his own about diversity. He agreed that if I could find three students who would speak for the "other side," he would be glad to find two others besides himself to speak for his point of view.

Out of that conversation came the "Supper Club." Along with the vice president for student life, herself a Japanese American—who cared passionately about campus diversity but would not be considered one of the state's underrepresented ethnic minorities—we agreed to set up a series of dinner meetings in the provost's office to listen to each other. For several weeks, the eight of us gathered together to enjoy the gourmet cuisine prepared personally by the vice president for student life but with a very specific conversational agenda. No small talk. We were there to listen, to ask questions, and to come to understand how others—equally committed to intellectual and ethical integrity—could actually come to conclusions different from our own.

We asked for three commitments: first, to be at all the scheduled meetings; second, to avoid "eye-rolling," as we called it; and third, to be ambassadors on campus to promote greater understanding of why diversity might matter for those who want to follow Jesus Christ. We had to show up—to be fully present at each meeting. We also agreed to do our best to suspend any instant, reactive comment, such as "I can't believe she would think that!" and any inclination to share with those outside the Supper Club who might share one's disbelief. We were committed to staying with the conversation until we truly understood how others had arrived at their opinions and until we could appreciatively articulate to others on campus why someone might draw conclusions different from our own.

The Supper Club helped to change the campus culture, slowly but surely. It took individuals who had the courage to leave the safety and security of their comfortable "sides" and to come to a common middle space where something new could be created—something more vibrant than the bland averaging of their previous views or the abandonment of their convictions—a new and larger community informed and enriched by attentive engagement with those whose experience of the world has been different from their own.

Reflecting on a "Supper Club" Mentality

The "middle" is not a place that we seek out in our tradition—and especially not now. Even when there is good food on offer, agreeing to meet for discussion on common middle ground seems to be a waste of time. We already know what we think. We don't want to be confused or unacceptably compromised in our convictions. We associate middle space with "sitting on the fence" or wimpy, wishy-washy thinking. Those within the Christian tradition have even more reason to be wary of an invitation to middle space. They are no doubt familiar with the dire judgment pronounced in Revelation 3 upon those who are "lukewarm" and "neither cold nor hot" (vv. 15–16). No one wants to be "spit out" for lacking either the courage or the conviction to be definitively one thing or another! Even when there is an official effort to program space for conversations on controversial topics within our communities, universities, and churches, it is just uncomfortable—sometimes downright painful—to disagree with people who are friends and family. One college student recently confessed, somewhat sheepishly, that even after an entire three-day college programming effort dedicated to having "difficult conversations," it was much more likely for students to engage in discussion in a formal setting than to reach out personally to those they knew were on a different place on the political spectrum. Just practically, it takes too much time!

The Pull of the Poles

The pressure to take sides at any moment when something of value is at stake is strong and actually quite understandable. We associate clear thinking with decisive conclusions. Our judicial system requires that someone be judged either "guilty" or "not guilty." When I tried once upon a time to make a plea in a traffic violation that I was "guilty but with explanation," I was told that was not an option. I had only two choices. At a much more serious level, as a society, we saw the political and cultural reactions to the June 2022 Supreme Court decision to overturn the *Roe v. Wade* decision that made access to abortion a matter of federal constitutional right. While there was a range of implications the court might have drawn from its conclusions, it was called to conclude one way or another as a starting point: Was the previous court's conclusion justifiable or not?

More broadly, in any formal debate, we expect the audience to vote "yea" or "nay" at the end. The audience cannot sit on the fence. They are expected to rule that one side was more convincing than another. In most formal meetings in Western culture, we agree to be structured by *Robert's Rules of Order*, a carefully delineated process designed to enable a group of people to arrive at a settled conclusion without resort to chaos or violence. In the classroom, much of our framing of ethical situations takes the form of a seemingly irreconcilable dilemma. One of my former colleagues in the discipline of philosophy shared, by way of confession, that he used to assume that students who did not play along with the binary assumptions of his proposed dilemmas were just lacking in intelligence. Of course, it must be this or that! He had come to see that these students were just seeing complexities—often important ones—that were obscured by the either-or assumptions of the scenario.

In fundraising, we know it is easier to ask for money if there is a clear and present threat that must be combatted—and preferably if it is a direct threat to those who have the capacity to contribute large sums to our cause. A new president of an academic nonprofit recently lamented in our conversation that it is difficult to raise funds if one is attempting to approach issues in an irenic and reasoned fashion. It just does not seem urgent enough. Another colleague noted that if she wants to raise funds for the nonprofit organization she leads, she simply has to announce to her constituency some new statement or action from the religious establishment that seems to threaten the particular constituency she serves. The funds pour in.

We know well that political campaigning thrives on pointing out the danger or threat of a group's opponents, much more than elaborating on a nominee's own virtues. This is embodied in the recent focus on "security moms," who replaced, at least in the minds of campaigners and pollsters, the older and more benign designation of "soccer moms."[1]

Aligning with one side or the other of a binary framework seems to be a prerequisite for acting when something must be done. The more urgent the situation is judged to be, the more pressure to take sides. I once stood helplessly at the sidelines following a serious equestrian accident at our institution's homecoming parade, as five well-trained alumni physicians debated what should be done with the accident victim lying injured and bleeding on the road. Fortunately, an alumnus trained as an emergency medical technician soon appeared. He took charge and things began to happen! It is not those who hesitate or have reservations or see all the uncertainties who get things done, especially when major change is needed or immediate action is required. Those who point to complexities or ambiguities are not likely to be walking the picket lines or risking their lives or their reputations. No one wants to be accused of the logical fallacy of "death by a thousand qualifications."[2]

In short, some degree of polarization seems to be a constant and perhaps even necessary feature of human experience—whether in the context of a university residence hall, a college faculty meeting, the annual meeting of a church congregation, the courtroom, or the halls of the United States

---

1. Michael Wear and Melissa Wear, "The New Security Moms," *Reclaiming Hope Newsletter*, September 13, 2022.

2. The American preference for the two-party political structure in contrast to the more globally common multiparty system has often been defended in terms of it increasing the likelihood of obtaining the necessary votes to make something actually happen.

Congress. All too often, it is taken for granted that within these last twenty years or so, Western culture and American society in particular is more polarized than ever. I frankly doubt if this is the case. My natural skepticism as a historian about any claim that seems to exalt the absolute uniqueness of the present moment was reinforced over the course of this past year by reading such works as Robert Putnam's *Upswing*, Jill Lepore's *These Truths*, and Gordon Wood's *Friends Divided*.[3]

It certainly may be the case that the social impact of polarization in our time is made more vitriolic, immediate, and pervasive by social media. Unlike in earlier times, when the polarization was reflected primarily in local town meetings or pubs, often among the social and intellectual elite, and reported in local newspapers and when news from centers of power took days to spread throughout the country, today's social media assures that a curious mix of fact and opinion is instantly available throughout the world for people of all ages and backgrounds. The information arrives without context and often in the strongest rhetorical terms. The reality of social media is also embedded in technologies controlled by algorithms designed to cater to individual preferences and to favor the sensational, thus both ensuring that one's own biases will be confirmed and constantly reinforced and one's "personal profile" made even more pronounced, on the one hand, and crowding out any space for subtlety and nuance, on the other.

We know what channels or media sites we prefer—and we know the channels and sites of our friends and acquaintances. We also know where "those people" on the other side get their "facts." We are used to charges of "fake news" from all sides. We have felt the anxiety through the recent pandemic created by the different voices of those we had counted on for expert advice. Even the modern confidence in natural science has been eroded and all too often politicized. Workplaces, colleges and universities, churches, and even families are divided by such issues as whether to mask, whether to meet in person with or without masks, and whether to try to accommodate both those who want to continue to meet online or work remotely and those who want to seek to return to some level of prepandemic normalcy. Worst of all, it is not at all clear who can provide information for resolving the tensions who will also be trusted by everyone involved. (You will no doubt have your own personal stories of the surprising and painful divisions of this season!)

3. Robert D. Putnam, *Upswing: How America Came Together a Century Ago and How We Can Do It Again* (New York: Simon & Schuster, 2020); Jill Lepore, *These Truths: A History of the United States* (New York: Norton, 2018); Gordon S. Wood, *Friends Divided: John Adams and Thomas Jefferson* (New York: Penguin Random House, 2017).

The Growing Presence—and Cost—of Polarization

The campus divisions in the 1990s that occasioned the "Supper Club" have only expanded and accelerated in intensity since then. College and university campuses, as well as public school districts, religious denominations and local congregations, political parties, and even our courts, are hotbeds of polarization fueled by simplistic slogans, economic scarcity, fears and uncertainty about the future, the pervasive realities of power politics—both inside and outside the formal political arena—insulated ideological frameworks, and increasing skepticism about common regulative principles for resolving the controversies. Concerns about the civil rights of members of the LGBTQ+ community, along with the persistent and longstanding concerns of gender and racial equity and inclusion, have all been intensified in recent years by a long list of historical circumstances, including the 2008 global economic downturn, the growing dilemmas around immigration, increasingly vitriolic presidential elections since 2008, the shifting alliance structure of international politics, and languishing, unresolved conflicts in the Middle East and Afghanistan—all in the context of increasingly pervasive and potentially invasive information technology. These larger and multifaceted issues have been complicated even further by the arrival in late 2019 of the COVID-19 virus and subsequent global pandemic; racially charged incidents such as the death of George Floyd; various executive and judicial rulings affecting sexual and gender sensibilities, culminating in the overturn of the 1973 *Roe v. Wade* decision on abortion; and finally the 2020 presidential election and its aftermath on January 6, 2021, in Washington, DC.

Given the sheer complexity of concerns facing individuals and organizations as they seek to carry on their daily lives, it is understandable, if regrettable, that we have found refuge in totalizing narratives and self-perpetuating ideological frameworks that help to give shape and meaning to what we see. As a society overwhelmed with torrents of uncatalogued information from often-competing authorities such as government, church, science, academy, and media—all available through our own personal technologies—we are frighteningly vulnerable to anyone who offers clarity and guidance in making sense of it all.

The challenge is that this understandable yearning for a coherent framing narrative has resulted in a polarization of our country into two warring camps—each with its own intellectual and rhetorical weaponry and each claiming to offer a winning strategy for realizing the complex combination of ends that are at the heart of the American experiment. Everyone is for freedom, equality, justice, economic prosperity, opportunity, and the achievement of individual potential—just in different forms and in slightly different relationships of tension with other values. We see this in the tensions that cut across all sectors of the American religious community—between faith traditions;[4] within such mainline traditions as Anglicanism/Episcopalianism and Methodism, both of which have witnessed major splits in recent years; and within broader movements such as evangelicalism.[5] We see it in the ubiquitous election maps of "red" and "blue" states. We see it in the "culture wars" on our college and university campuses—most visibly in the tensions between such historic values as free speech, academic freedom, and freedom of inquiry and the value of protecting those who might be harmed, either physically or emotionally, by the exercise of these freedoms.[6] We see it in the battles over public school curricula—what books ought to be taught and what values ought to be inculcated. We see it in the increasing politicization of the discussions and the voting in Congress. We see it in the appointments of our judges and the battles over their confirmation and in the analysis surrounding their decisions. Slowly but surely, we have brought ourselves to a place of gridlock and paralysis as a culture and a society. We don't trust the very institutions—even our own elections—that have directed our way of life as a democracy.[7]

We have lost even the ability to agree on what it means to speak truth to ourselves in such a way that we can see our way out of this morass. One professional gathering of college presidents, even before the pandemic, was sufficiently concerned about the lack of common rules of evidence within the culture as a result of the recent polarized elections to choose to devote an entire evening to discussing a book with the rather sensational title *Truth*

---

4. Eboo Patel, *Acts of Faith: The Story of an American Muslim, the Struggle for the Soul of a Generation* (Boston: Beacon, 2007); Patel, *Out of Many Faiths: Religious Diversity and the American Promise* (Princeton: Princeton University Press, 2018); Asma T. Uddin, *When Islam Is Not a Religion: Inside America's Fight for Religious Freedom* (New York: Pegasus Books, 2019).

5. Mark Labberton, ed., *Still Evangelical? Insiders Reconsider Political, Social, and Theological Meaning* (Downers Grove, IL: IVP Books, 2019); Michael Graham, "The Six Way Fracturing of Evangelicalism," with Skyler Flowers, *Mere Orthodoxy* (blog), June 7, 2021, https://mereorthodoxy.com/six-way-fracturing-evangelicalism/.

6. Michael S. Roth, *Safe Enough Spaces: A Pragmatist's Approach to Inclusion, Free Speech, and Political Correctness on College Campuses* (New Haven: Yale University Press, 2021).

7. For examples of this concern, see Michael Gerson, "Trump Should Fill Christians with Rage. How Come He Doesn't?," *Washington Post*, September 1, 2022, https://www.washingtonpost.com/opinions/2022/09/01/michael-gerson-evangelical-christian-maga-democracy/; David French, "America's Near-Death Day," *The Atlantic*, January 5, 2022, https://newsletters.theatlantic.com/the-third-rail/61d614df05e48f0021124667/americas-near-death-day/; Peggy Noonan, "Republicans, Stand against Excess," *Wall Street Journal*, February 10, 2022, A15.

Decay.[8] We should not be surprised at the call in an even more recent book by the president of Johns Hopkins University for universities to help restore to our culture some common vision as to what counts as evidence, whether it be in the laboratory or in the news media. It remains to be seen whether such a consensus is even possible![9]

If you or your family identify as part of the Christian tradition, you may feel the polarization even more intensely than your friends and colleagues who do not see themselves as part of this tradition. While the longstanding debate about slavery in this country pitted Christians against each other, both sides drawing on biblical and theological support for their respective positions, it was in part the very common assumption of a Christian cultural framework that drove the discussion. It was assumed that one framing of the Christian narrative was truer and more compelling than the other. This is quite different from the current reality in America, where the cultural divide increasingly places Christian faith on one side of the political spectrum rather than the other and where one's religious convictions seem to be driven more by politics than the other way around. If you have noticed the complicated interrelationship of faith and politics in the current moment, you may want to take note of several recent books that have sought to help us sort out what is happening.[10]

So while political polarization is not new to American politics, there seems to be a new aspect to this particular moment. What role will religion—and Christianity in particular—play in American self-identity of the future? In all moments of polarization, some individuals will feel themselves caught in the tensions of the current cultural and social divisions. They will feel themselves pulled in both directions by their own family history, life experience, and personal convictions. They will feel as if moving toward either side forces them to become smaller or to let go of part of their own identity. In this book, I am focusing on one set of individuals who find themselves caught in the middle in this particular moment, as religion and specifically Christianity are placed on

8. The less flashy subtitle explains what the book is about: Jennifer Kavanagh and Michael D. Rich, *Truth Decay: An Initial Exploration of the Diminishing Role of Facts and Analysis in American Public Life* (Santa Monica, CA: Rand Corporation, 2018).

9. Ronald J. Daniels, *What Universities Owe Democracy*, with Grant Shreve and Phillip Spector (Baltimore: John Hopkins University Press, 2021).

10. You might choose to invite a group of friends to discuss one of the following: Robert D. Putnam and David E. Campbell, *American Grace: How Religion Divides and Unites Us*, with Shaylyn Romney Garrett (New York: Simon & Schuster, 2012); John Fea, *Believe Me: The Evangelical Road to Donald Trump* (Grand Rapids: Eerdmans, 2018); or Kristin Kobes Du Mez, *Jesus and John Wayne: How White Evangelicals Corrupted a Faith and Fractured a Nation* (New York: Liveright, 2021).

one side of the emerging divide of American society—separated, as Putnam argues, from the dominant values of the press, of the academy, of the intelligentsia. They are committed absolutely to the truth of the Christian message and want to remain faithful disciples of Jesus Christ, to be known publicly for that loyalty. On the other hand, they feel as if the cultural stereotypes of Christianity—especially the more conservative label "evangelical"—make it difficult for them to exercise fully the God-given gifts that they have been given to steward in the public arena for the common good. Their personal intellectual and moral integrity is suspect even before they have had the opportunity to contribute.

They include the thousands of students who come each year to colleges and universities belonging to the Council for Christian Colleges and Universities (CCCU). These students choose to attend these institutions because they want their Christian faith to be developed in partnership with their disciplinary expertise so that when they graduate, their understanding of the Scriptures and their theology are as deep and rich as their professional expertise. They want their learning to be informed by their own deepest moral and theological convictions, rather than developed in isolation from those convictions. They want to be on a trajectory of lifelong growth and development so that their faith, together with their academic and professional training, is large enough for the challenges of a lifetime. At this moment, many of these students—including some reading this book—feel the tension of being in institutions whose convictions are seen as backward and perhaps even bigoted by the larger culture. They wonder if their federal or state funding for tuition will be put at risk. They wonder if their professional training will be accredited by agencies that guarantee their right to practice their professions. Some even worry about their regional accreditation. Even in the best of situations, students often find themselves at institutions that are themselves caught in the polarization—seeking to honor and to be perceived as honoring their own theological and biblical commitments, the constituents who count on their loyalty to these commitments, and their responsibility as educational institutions to ensure that these traditions are informed by the gifts of scholarship and learning. It is not easy for institutions in this moment to make space for students—many of whose values have been shaped unevenly by the larger culture, their churches, and their families—to sort out what they themselves actually believe. How do they make room for students to learn what it means to bring together the truth and grace that are embodied in the life and work of the Lord Jesus Christ as they prepare to be agents of God's redemptive purposes in the world? Sometimes students (and faculty) may be caught, as one recent CCCU colleague put it, by the tension between "wanting to make a statement and wanting to make an impact."

The individuals I focus on in this book include the members of the board of the National Association of Evangelicals who looked at each other in puzzlement after the media coverage of the 2016 presidential election, which equated American evangelicalism with support for Trump. Many of those who still embraced the evangelical label did not vote for Trump. This has resulted in much soul-searching among those who call themselves evangelical but who do not fit the media's characterization of the term nor fall within the notorious "81 percent."[11]

This community includes many Christian academics who find themselves caught between their orthodox Christian faith and the assumptions of the academy, which, since the eighteenth century, has been increasingly skeptical about the truth claims of revealed religion grounded in the biblical text and personal experience. This tension is longstanding and complex but well summarized in Nicholas Wolterstorff's *Religion in the University*.[12]

Finally, this "company of the middle" includes a growing number of individuals from other cultures who see their religion as a core part of their identity and do not identify with the Western tradition of privatizing their religious views or compartmentalizing them from other aspects of their identity. Eboo Patel and Asma Uddin, both Muslim Americans, believe that American culture is stronger when we are able to bring ourselves fully into our interaction with others—including our deepest spiritual and ethical convictions—but when we do so in the spirit of the Golden Rule, respecting others' convictions as we want them to respect ours.[13] They have often shared the platform with Christians who seek to preserve in the public spaces of our country an appropriate voice for religion, grounded in the First Amendment to the United States Constitution. As our country becomes more culturally and religiously diverse, they share the conviction that the religious liberty guaranteed by the Constitution was intended to allow religion to flourish in the personal lives and communities of this country as an aspect of our larger cultural richness and diversity, while also honoring the traditional separation of church and state that ensures that no one religion is allowed to be an instrument of

11. See the resources on evangelicalism mentioned in notes 5 and 7 above.

12. This set of reflections—informed by Professor Wolterstorff's own professional journey, spent partly at Calvin College (now Calvin University) and partly at Yale Divinity School—is useful for understanding the complex and potentially changing relationship between the values of the academy and the commitments of orthodox Christianity. Nicholas Wolterstorff, *Religion in the University* (New Haven: Yale University Press, 2019).

13. See note 4 above.

public policy and that one's religious identity does not affect one's standing as a citizen.

Who Is This Book For? The Hidden Opportunity of Middle Space

This book is, first of all, an invitation to revisit the culture's stereotypical view of middle space. It is a call to consider the radically redemptive possibilities available to those who find themselves reluctantly—or by choice—not fitting comfortably on either end of the multiple and overlapping poles in our contemporary society and in the church.

1. You may find yourself in middle space right now because you cannot fit all of who you are in the company of either the "left" or the "right"—however those terms are defined in your particular context. You find yourself pulled in both directions, depending on the issue. On some matters, you are at home with those on the right. But on other matters, you are more comfortable with those on the left.

2. You may find yourself in middle space because you do not share the certitude that seems to characterize the style or posture of those on either end of the spectrum. You believe in truth—and are actively seeking to be loyal to whatever is clear to you—but you are not ready to minimize the complexities and ambiguities that attend some of the issues on which others seem absolutely certain. You want room to raise questions and to struggle further on matters in which both sides seem to have parts of the truth. Furthermore, you are not ready to demonize those who think differently than you do. You find it difficult to believe, just as a matter of practicality, that all the intelligent and good people are on one side of a complicated issue. In short, you want to make space for humility—and to be sure that your commitment to truth is appropriately seasoned with grace.

3. You may find yourself in middle space because on a particular issue, there seem to be goods or truths in tension with each other. You are not ready to be forced into an either-or choice. You want more room to imagine alternatives that can point beyond the binary options that others have seen or that have become standard in the discussion.

4. You may find yourself in middle space because what seems to be true at the abstract level does not easily fit with the needs of the concrete circumstances in which you are called to serve. You are not a relativist—that is, someone who thinks that truth claims are applicable only in particular

contexts. Nor are you a subjectivist—someone who thinks that truth is entirely relative to individuals. But you also know that being loyal to the truth is more than simply throwing out principles in the abstract. You know that your abstract principles of truth need to be mediated into concrete particular situations in ways that can be received.

5. You may find yourself in middle space because various authorities in your life, who have shown themselves to be trustworthy in the past and who have shaped your journey to this point, are not in agreement on matters of significance. You are not sure how to reconcile them. Furthermore, you are not sure how to apply their wisdom authentically, given your own current understanding of the world.

In this book, I am especially seeking to inspire you who are at the forefront of your own spiritual, personal, and professional journey and who may feel caught among the loyalties of family, church, college, and culture. I want you to know that you are not alone.

Second, I am suggesting that precisely because of your middling status, you are distinctly and perhaps even uniquely qualified to play a convening, reconciling, and ambassadorial role in society at this time—to help us see, as a civil society, a way beyond the current paralysis of polarization. At a time when our culture no longer shares a common literacy around religious texts, is even less familiar with theological terminology, and has almost no understanding of the complexity of church history, you are, at least to some degree or another, bilingual. You know—or are coming to know, if you are students—that an evangelical is not the same as a fundamentalist. Chances are, you know—or are in the process of learning—the complexity of America's history, which certainly included a commitment to religious freedom but also often exercised this commitment in ways that favored some groups over others, sometimes even failing miserably to live up to its own fundamental founding commitments in the Declaration of Independence and the Constitution. You know—or are coming to know—that the historical relationship between Christianity and science has had many chapters—and is not dominated in reality by mutual fear and suspicion. For much of history, they were allies, not enemies. You are not intimidated by someone who dismisses Christianity because of a "thin" understanding of the Galileo controversy or the Scopes Trial. In short, you who find yourselves in middle space have the necessary preparation to do the work of translation and to build trust and goodwill across the current cultures of our polarized society.

Third, if you find yourself in this middle space, I hope to challenge you, winsomely but compellingly, not to make the easier choice to simply lament the current state of affairs, or retreat into silence or privatization, or cultivate connection with other "kindred spirits." Rather, I want to encourage you—out of a sense of God-given call to steward your gifts for the good of others, coupled with a sense of civic responsibility—to make the more courageous decision of committing yourself to reclaiming the radically redemptive possibilities of working in the middle. While choosing this role will certainly involve risks of various sorts, it also offers the potential of creating for our world a welcoming, hospitable, vibrant space beyond polarization, grounded in fervent commitment to the truth, seasoned by the virtues of humility, curiosity, and respect for others, and informed by the insights of intellectually and morally serious individuals from across the political divide. It is not an invitation to surrender one's convictions, but rather to bring them into the light of day, to test them in the company of others of goodwill and a pure heart.

Exploring the Creative Work of Radically Redemptive Middle Space

In the first chapter of this book, I will invite you into my own personal journey of coming to see the power and radically redemptive possibilities of middle space. It is a journey of gratitude for the ways in which my family, my education, even my choice of history as a major, and finally the Wesleyan tradition I discovered upon returning to Houghton College in 2006 as president prepared me to see the potential of a courageous middle. In this section, you will be encouraged to consider those individuals and the circumstances of your own journey that have landed you in some version of middle space.

In chapter 2, we will focus on definitions. How can the word *middle*, which is so often associated with bland, tepid, mushy thinking or lack of conviction, take on a countercultural power of creative and convening strength? We will explore more fully how it is that people find themselves in this middle space—reluctantly—without in any way intending to be there. We will consider how this middling space might truly become a place of courage—a place that is embraced for its opportunity to bring about good—rather than occupied in a spirit of frustration or passive timidity or resignation.

In the third chapter, we will explore a biblical foundation for the redemptive possibilities of middle space. Without prooftexting or being anachronistic, this chapter will invite us to consider the range of ways that the Scriptures of both the Old and New Testaments provide resources for thinking about this work of calling our communities beyond polarization. This work may not be for all followers of Jesus Christ, but it seems to be

for at least some of us. By this point in the book, you will have a good idea
if this includes you.

Chapter 4 will discuss the risks and the opportunities of the courageous
middle. Actively choosing to be a host for the imaginative convening work
of middle space in today's polarized culture poses risks to one's reputation,
one's friendships, and one's integrity, as well as one's professional success and
short-term effectiveness at times. It is not for the faint of heart. Nevertheless,
the potential opportunities for inviting communities beyond the current gridlock of divided dinner tables, athletic teams, and church board meetings; for
learning to live boldly amid creative tensions; for inviting the reconciliation
of estranged friends and family; and in general, for promoting a richer and
more hope-filled public square offer compelling reasons to take on this privileged diplomatic challenge of the courageous middle. In this chapter, we will
introduce real-life examples from the past and present to illustrate and inspire
us for the challenges and the opportunities of this work.

Chapter 5 will focus on practical preparation for the work of hosting
productive conversations in middle space that point communities beyond
polarization. Just as ambassadors in the international sphere must prepare
themselves to understand the relevant languages, cultural nuances, historic
tensions, and hot-button points of their particular assignment, so must we
prepare for the bridge-building, convening work of the courageous middle.
We will discover that this particular calling is not so much a job with speci-
fied hours or even a clear career path; rather, it is a way of life. It is about the
kind of people we will choose to be—whether we are among friends, with
our families, in the classroom, on the athletic field, or in the workplace. It
is a seasoning or a flavor we carry with us wherever we are. As we come to
embody this spirit, we will find out that it is contagious. In this moment of
heightened global awareness of the dangers of "catching" something from
those around us, we would do well to remind ourselves of C. S. Lewis's notion
that there are also "good infections" that can spread themselves in a population for healing and joyful flourishing.[14]

The conclusion will summarize the case for the claim that the ambassadorial work of the courageous middle is one form of "faithful witness" at this
time, not an abandoning of one's convictions or one's loyalty to the Christian
faith. It will affirm once again that a strong cadre of individuals committed
to the creative, convening, translating work of the courageous middle has
the potential to lead our society and the church beyond the paralyzing fear
of polarization to a new vision of hope.

14. C. S. Lewis, *Mere Christianity* (New York: HarperCollins, 2001), 172–78.

Questions for Discussion

1. As you reflect on your own experience up to this point, have you ever felt like the young person in the provost's office who was frustrated that everyone in the room—or the church—was caving to political pressure and failing to focus adequately on realities that seemed obvious to you?

2. Do you remember an experience in which you came to new insights from someone unexpected or very unlike you? What were the circumstances of this moment? Was it planned? What prepared you to be a learner in this situation?

3. Have you ever felt pressure in the classroom, in a peer group, or in the workplace to choose one side in the current political or theological divide? In other words, have you felt pressure to engage in "virtue signaling"?

4. How has your Christian faith helped to shape your own views on current political or social issues? Do you find yourself fitting into the picture Robert Putnam and David Campbell paint in *American Grace*, in which your own political views are shaping your understanding of the Scriptures or your view of discipleship rather than the other way around?

5. Have you ever sensed that the whole of who you are does not fit well within the stereotyped commitments of the right or the left?

6. What questions do you have at this point about the notion of the radically redemptive potential of middle space?

1

Catching a Vision for a Third Way of Being in the World

My Own Story

As far back as I can remember, I wanted to be sure that what I believed was true, not just what my family happened to believe. (I recently heard that this desire to know what is true, as opposed to what is good or beautiful, is apparently characteristic of my generation—those baby boomers born in the decade following World War II.) When I was living through this, I had no idea that my experience was typical. It certainly did not seem to me that my peers were in the same sort of existential perplexity. I felt very much alone.

As I came into my high school years, this agony of spirit became particularly acute. I felt I just had to know if my Christian beliefs were true. I could not get the doubts out of my head. They met me when I woke up and accompanied me throughout the day. They occupied my mind in classrooms, when I tried to study, and when I tried to have fun. I spent long hours lying on the couch in the living room at my home just staring at the ceiling. The only thing that soothed me was listening to our one record of the Robert Shaw Chorale singing spirituals. I would do that for hours. For whatever reason, the woeful strains of "There Is a Balm in Gilead" calmed my spirit and enabled me to keep going.

What made all of this worse was that I did not dare to talk to anyone about what I was going through. I was the oldest child of four, and I felt I should be a good example to my three younger siblings. I was also a leader in my church youth group. As Christians, we were conscious of the call to be good witnesses at school. How could I possibly witness to something that I was not sure I believed? I certainly was not going to share my concerns with my high school youth pastor. Furthermore, we lived in a very small town built around a small Christian college. My father taught Bible and philosophy. As "faculty kids," we all felt a special pressure not to let our parents down.

For months that then stretched into years, I was leading a double life, one inside my own head and one that I presented to the world. The only way I knew I could help myself was to read books that addressed the issues. There were not nearly as many popular books on apologetics then as there are now. In scouring the bookshelves of our home, I found something by the British pastor J. Edwin Orr (1912–87). My father returned from a conference with Francis Schaeffer's recently published book, *Escape from Reason*.[1] I devoured it and then sought out anything from Schaeffer I could get my hands on. In the next few years, I read *The God Who Is There, He Is There and He Is Not Silent, The Mark of the Christian, How Should We Then Live?*, and a number of other Schaeffer books along the way.[2] Josh McDowell had not crossed my path at that point, nor had C. S. Lewis. In reading Schaeffer, I knew at least that I was not the only person wanting to be sure that Christianity was true.[3]

I don't know how my parents found out about my secret life. Perhaps it was the Schaeffer books on my Christmas wish list. But one day, much to my surprise, my mother and father asked to speak with me privately. Since this was definitely not an everyday occurrence in our busy family life, I was taken aback. My father was the spokesperson, as he usually was when my

---

1. Francis A. Schaeffer, *Escape from Reason* (Downers Grove, IL: InterVarsity, 1968).

2. Francis A. Schaeffer, *The God Who Is There* (Downers Grove, IL: InterVarsity, 1968); Francis A. Schaeffer, *He Is There and He Is Not Silent* (Wheaton, IL: Tyndale, 1972); Francis A. Schaeffer, *The Mark of the Christian* (Downers Grove, IL: InterVarsity, 1970); Francis A. Schaeffer, *How Should We Then Live* (Grand Rapids: Revell, 1976).

3. By the 1980s, it was fashionable in Christian liberal arts circles to turn up one's nose at Schaeffer, viewing him as too simplistic, too rationalistic, and even perhaps a bit pretentious. By trying to respond in kind to Kenneth Clark's Civilization series, as he did in *How Should We Then Live?* and then in the accompanying video series, many believed that he had stepped beyond the limits of his effectiveness. I came eventually to believe that much of this critique was appropriate. Nevertheless, I never stopped being grateful for his role in my life at a particular moment in time. For me, as a teenager with lots of gnawing questions about the faith, Schaeffer was God's provision for my need.

parents had a word to deliver. He began, "Shirley, we are not sure exactly what is going on, but we sense that you are searching for answers to deep and personal questions. If we can be of any help, we want to do that. If not, we want to give you space. If you need some time away from church, know that we will support whatever is helpful to you in this season." That was it. I was quite shocked. No condemnation. No pressure to keep up the family image in the college or church community. No pressure to come to a quick resolution about my questions. Just the gift of freedom to follow my journey.

If you find yourself in some version of "middle space" today—for any of the reasons we have already identified—you have no doubt been moving toward this space for some time, probably even without realizing it. Maybe you have found yourself caught in the crossfire between friends and colleagues or fellow church members, all of whom you have found to be sources of trustworthy counsel in the past but who now disagree on key matters of doctrine or public policy. Maybe you cannot reconcile the convictions of your upbringing with what you are learning in a new setting. Perhaps you are mired in questions and the ready answers you have been offered to this point do not seem to do justice to the complexities of the situation. They are simply too small.

No one's journey to this space is the same. And no one's preparation for making this space redemptive, rather than merely a space of paralysis and frustration, will be the same. Your capacity to be a host of convening, productive, potentially radically redemptive conversations in this space will be shaped by your own story. If you are called to this work—in one particular context or on one occasion or for a lifetime—your effectiveness will grow out of the person you are. I share with you my story of coming to understand the opportunities of middle space, not because your story will be the same as mine but rather to prompt your own remembering and reflection.

My Childhood Context

I could easily have grown up in a legalistic context where all the answers were clear and certain—similar to the world we associate today with the Christian right. Anyone looking at the framework of my childhood could quite reasonably have assumed that connection. My two grandfathers and my father were pastors in a small denomination called the Reformed Baptist Alliance. It was a break-off group from another small denomination in the Baptist tradition of eastern Canada called the Free Christian Baptists. After hearing the American revivalist preacher Phoebe Palmer (1807–74) during her tour of Canada's Maritime provinces in the late nineteenth century, several of the Free Christian Baptist pastors came to believe in her message of instantaneous sanctification or second-blessing holiness. It was the idea that there was a second experience of God's grace after salvation that could instantly remove from us the sin nature. Not only could we be saved from or forgiven for particular sins that we had committed and confessed, but we could be saved as well from the desire to sin at all—all at one moment.

When these pastors testified to this experience, they were disfellowshipped from the Free Christian Baptists and "re-formed" a new denomination in 1888. They were not, as the name might suggest, part of the Reformed theological tradition of Calvin and Knox. They were Arminian in theology—thus the "Free" (that is, the free will) part—and they believed in adult baptism, which made them Baptists. Most centrally, however, they became part of the North American Holiness movement, which emphasized the power of the Holy Spirit to help Christians live up to their spiritual status of full sanctification. It was a heavy burden to live with as a child. The "heart holiness" (which our group of friends heard mistakenly as "hard holiness") or "perfect love," to which many of the elders in our church or camp meeting circuit testified, did not fit exactly with what we saw in their lives. This was confusing, to say the least.

What we did understand was the importance of being separate from the world—not drinking, smoking, going to movies, or playing cards (at least the face-type variety). It was hard for me to feel fully comfortable at school with the other children. Most of them attended one of the other churches in the small New Brunswick town where my father pastored. My friends included those who attended the Roman Catholic, Baptist, Anglican, and United Church parishes there (the latter of which was a Canadian version of the "mainline" Protestant tradition). They were all "churched," but they all attended movies and seemed much more comfortable in their skin than I did. I remember, as a second grader, having to explain to a friend why I could not attend the movie *Babes in Toyland*. I also was not able to go to one of the local "Brownie" packs (the first stage of becoming a Girl Guide). I confess to feeling envious of my friends who showed up in their neat uniforms one day a week, signaling that they were headed to Brownies after school.[4]

Like today's Christian right, the Reformed Baptist Alliance was predominantly white and, in socioeconomic terms, mostly rural and urban working

---

4. My mother created a version of a children's club at our church called the "Junior Crusaders." She made uniforms for us, and we could even earn badges like the Brownies. But no one else in my class went to this club. And "Junior Crusaders" communicates a message quite different from that of "Brownies." The name said it all.

class. The congregation was composed of self-employed small business families, with fairly traditional (i.e., binary) gender roles—except, of course, on the farms! Above all, they were spiritually and morally serious. There was a "right" way to do everything—or so it seemed. Of course, we were to be honest and kind and stand up for our beliefs. But the importance of rightness seemed to cover everything—how we performed in school, how we argued and expressed our opinions, how we honored the Sabbath, even how we did the dishes. I well remember my father announcing to my brother one Sunday at lunch, after he had ridden his bike to Sunday School, "James, we [note the editorial and magisterial *we*] don't ride our bicycles on Sunday." My grade school brother responded quite understandably, "Don't worry, Dad. It was just for transportation. I did not have any fun." I also remember one evening when, eager to get outdoors to join the neighborhood game of capture the flag, I did the dishes far too quickly—and apparently sloppily. My father—interestingly, not my mother—insisted that I needed to know how to sweep a floor properly and how to do the dishes the "correct" way. I still remember that step-by-step instruction and still, incidentally, do the dishes and sweep the kitchen floor the same way! It was also very important in our circles not only to get things right but to be seen to be right. The clearest message to an oldest child like me, who wanted very much to please those adults around me, was that, whatever our theology proclaimed about salvation—and sanctification—by grace, what mattered most of all was "deserving" approval by getting things right.

A Subterranean Counternarrative

So, yes, my upbringing looked on the surface a lot like the culture of conservative Christianity in our world today, where certitude and easy answers—usually mediated from top-down authoritative voices—all too often hold sway.

But just beneath the surface of my childhood reality was another set of messages, mediated mostly by the very same people from whom I learned about sanctification and holiness and the importance of getting things right—and being perceived to get them right. Alongside and even within the very culture of the Reformed Baptist tradition, I was sensing in several areas that the world and our life of faith was much larger, more complex, and more complicated than I was learning in Sunday School classes.

Intellect as Guide

First of all, my parents and all my grandparents valued learning—both formal and informal. Both of my grandfathers had left the Maritimes in the early 1900s to seek higher education in New England. While neither completed a college degree (mostly for reasons of finance and competing family needs), both were life-long readers. My paternal grandmother had been a village teacher before marrying my grandfather in 1912. My maternal grandmother, who had not been able to complete school because of a bout with rheumatic fever, read voraciously, was an early adopter of the radio, and always knew the latest news about everything from global events to nutrition, even to the best fertilizer for her vegetable and flower garden. My mother went to university to study literature in the 1940s—something none of her friends did. My father went to Boston from New Brunswick at the age of seventeen and worked his way through college, two master's degrees, and a year of doctoral work in philosophy. He left graduate school before finishing his doctoral program to take a professorial position, along with my mother, at the denominational Bible college in Nova Scotia. None of my immediate elders were afraid of hard questions. (You saw that in the introductory story.) They knew that the world was complex. They knew—from personal experience, I would add—that there were no easy answers to the problem of pain and human suffering. They were not at all eager to try to plot the chronology of the "end times," as many in our circles were. (These were, after all, the days of Hal Lindsey's *The Late Great Planet Earth*.)[5] They were not the least bit troubled by questions of origins—confident that the important point about Genesis 1 was that God created the world and everything in it and that the creation was good. Confident of the "why" of creation, they did not need to know the "how," nor were they the least bit bothered by any of the supposed debates between faith and science. Long before I ever heard of Galileo's notion that the same God who gave us the Word also gave us the world, I knew that there was ultimately no conflict between science and religion. If they appeared to conflict, one just had to go deeper. That confidence came from my Holiness parents and grandparents.

In a strange sort of way, my parents and grandparents all lived in a much larger world than many of those in our subculture. They cared about astronomy, genetics (my paternal grandfather loved to graft trees), environmental sustainability (though they did not call it that!), literature, philosophy, the theology of the early church fathers, politics, gardening, breeding chickens, world geography, history, and anything else that offered them a richer and deeper understanding of their experience as human beings in space and time.

Perhaps even more novel in our circles, they were not afraid to pursue the truth wherever it led. (I did not need professor Art Holmes of Wheaton

5. Hal Lindsey, *The Late Great Planet Earth* (Grand Rapids: Zondervan, 1971).

College to tell me that "all truth is God's truth.") My revivalist preacher-grandfather had already modeled that sort of intellectual confidence and freedom. When I left for graduate school at the University of Toronto in 1977, he took me aside and said, "Shirley, remember that if the Christian faith is not true, you want to be the first to know. You may encounter ideas at the university that seem to you to 'ring true' but conflict with your current understanding of the Christian faith. Go with what seems to you to be true, and you will come out right in the end." What a strange invitation! What a frightfully delightful freedom!

Morality as Gift

Whatever the clarity of the moral directives that came to me formally, I saw a far more generous and gracious practical style modeled by my parents and grandparents. They were not legalists—in the sense of feeling that the sky would fall if there were circumstances that seemed to call for a more nuanced behavior pattern than one typically associated with our virtual "holiness" rulebook. While I was often puzzled, I never thought of them as hypocrites. I trusted them and simply took all this under advisement for further reflection.

On one occasion, when traveling home with my grandparents one Sunday evening after my grandfather had preached, he suggested that we stop for sundaes. I was quite surprised, since we did not typically eat out or shop on the Sabbath—which, frankly, was not too much of a sacrifice since most of the stores in our community were closed on Sundays. My grandfather, perhaps sensing my momentary hesitation, volunteered, "You know, we have to eat sundaes on Sundays. That is what they were made for!" Once, when I accompanied my grandmother to a "rummage sale" led by her local branch of the Women's Christian Temperance Union, I noticed that many of her colleagues were smokers. She treated them the same as she did the nonsmokers at her local church. If someone wanted to partner with her in a good cause, which clearly included preventing the abuse of alcohol in our working-class towns, she was "all in" as their colleague and friend.

Perhaps even more influential was the way that my parents instructed us in the moral life. Yes, there were certain clear behavior patterns that we practiced as a pastor's family—and later in the community of our Christian college. But especially as we came into our teen years, there was much more emphasis on the kind of people we were becoming. I did not hear about virtue ethics until much later in my journey. But that was what my parents were cultivating in us as soon as we were able to bear that kind of freedom. We probably had fewer rules than most of our friends. We never had a curfew or boundaries on how much television to watch or any other kind of clear "line drawing." We were not raised on rules that were assumed to apply in the same way in all times and places.

There were a few frequently repeated aphorisms that constituted the bulk of my parents' moral instruction once we turned thirteen. It all started when one of my friends called to invite me to go to see *Gone with the Wind*. We were no longer a pastor's family in eastern Canada, and in our small New York state college town, people seemed to have different convictions about movies. I wanted my parents to tell me what to do. I did not want the burden of making my own decision. After all, I wanted to "get it right." I remember the situation as if it were yesterday. For the first time, I heard the words, "That is a decision you will have to make." What this meant was that there was moral latitude here. While there were certainly some moral absolutes, there were also moral invitations and cautions that were discretionary, that were not obviously or always right and wrong. Growing up as a moral agent involved learning to recognize the difference between those things that are always right and wrong and where discernment is required. Sometimes, there was room to choose, as long as we owned the consequences. There were other guiding principles as well as the one permitting moral discernment. These included: "Don't do anything you don't really want to do"; "Act, don't react"; and my personal favorite, "Remember who you are today."

In short, the moral life was much more than a list of right and wrong actions. Getting things right was not like looking up a recipe, consulting the telephone book for a number (before the days of personal electronic contact lists), or in today's world, asking Siri or Alexa. There were moral decisions in which the right thing to do might not be obvious. Seeking to get things right might actually be full of agony as one sought to act well in the presence of competing goods. (The classic case of this during our growing-up days was the question of abortion. The moral complexity of this issue has not, of course, become easier with time—whatever the legal framework set down by the Supreme Court.) Being a good person was as much about who we were inside as about how we behaved. It included what we desired, what we loved and admired, as much as what we did. The family moral language included not just the words *right* and *wrong* but *appropriate*, *wise*, and *helpful*.

It turned out to be a much larger and freer world than the apparent legalism of the Holiness tradition. I learned early that this freedom was also a much heavier responsibility—and often more burdensome—than a rule book.

Engagement in the World

Despite the formal understanding that we as Reformed Baptists were a people "set apart from the world," and even amid my own childhood struggle with feeling odd or not quite at home in my world, I noticed that my parents' and grandparents' patterns of behavior did not fit the stereotype. My father, as a young pastor eager to be gospel salt and light in our community, sought out opportunities to relate to a wide range of individuals outside the church. He played chess with one of the retired bankers and one of the semiparalyzed veterans of World War I. He developed his coin collection in order to connect with another set of men. He regularly attended the town hockey games, forming relationships that influenced families for generations. At the same time that he was the president of the New Brunswick Temperance Federation (working to advocate against the province's thriving monopoly on licensing the sale of liquor and spirits), he also served as the chaplain of the Canadian Legion, which would hardly qualify as a model of teetotalism and sobriety. It was no accident that, once a year on Remembrance Day (the Canadian version of Veterans Day), the members of the legion showed up in full uniform at the Reformed Baptist Church. I should add that this was not a show of some sort of God and country nationalism. It was about remembering with gratitude the thousands of Canadians who had died in the trenches of western Europe in that strangest of military disasters that we know as World War I.

My father was so confident of his identity as a child of God that he could reach out into the community without fearing a loss of self. He humanized the image of the town's clergy—complicating the stereotypes in surprising ways. He witnessed to a large gospel that welcomed everyone—no matter where their stories had taken them. In a community where denominational loyalties were strong in the 1960s—one might even say rigidly so—he joined with other local clergy in promoting an annual ecumenical "week of prayer." Each night of the week, parishioners from all the congregations were invited to gather in one of the churches for prayer. It warmed my heart on a recent visit to my hometown to learn that a week of prayer is still on the annual town calendar. Even as a Holiness preacher, my father always preached *for* things and not *against* things. I asked him about this one time when I was young. (I recognized even in grade school that my father's style of "holiness" was more expansive than most of his contemporaries.) "Dad, if you believe smoking is wrong, why don't you preach against it?" He responded by introducing me to Thomas Chalmers (1780–1847), a nineteenth-century Scottish clergyman, whose sermon "The Expulsive Power of a New Affection" had inspired his own style of ministry. "Shirley," he responded, "you make people hungry for the gospel by holding up the love and grace of God. The Holy Spirit takes care of whatever particular changes need to be made in their lives." I saw that illustrated multiple times in his pastoral work.

Of course, my father did not carry on the ministry alone. In those days, the pastor's wife was assumed to be part of the informal (and unpaid) staff. My mother played the organ, directed the choir, led the women's and children's ministries—all while doing the sewing and cooking for a growing family of four children and entertaining countless guests at the parsonage. Everyone, from visiting missionaries from far away northern and southern Rhodesia (now Zambia and Zimbabwe) to local homeless people or abused women, was welcomed graciously into our living room. In addition, she was a leader in her own right in several of the local civic organizations, including the parent-teacher association and the provincial organization that advocated for mentally challenged young people.

Perhaps my parents had been drawn to each other because they both had been raised by parents who believed that the gospel was a large tent. Whatever *holiness* meant to our denomination, for them it meant faithful and even sacrificial openness to those who needed the love of God the most. It was not for them to draw lines between those who were in and those who were out. That was God's job—and much above their proverbial pay grade. My favorite story of my maternal grandmother came from the 1940s. (I heard this from my mother, who witnessed it all as a fourteen-year-old.) The family had moved to Nova Scotia in 1942 to live in one of the coastal towns at a time when German U-boats regularly were detected in the nearby Bay of Fundy. The war was on everyone's mind, and the women of the home front wanted to do their bit. When my grandmother, as the new pastor's wife, went to inquire about the local Red Cross and opportunities to serve, she was told that the Reformed Baptists had their own Red Cross. The thought was that since Reformed Baptists were part of a Holiness church, their Red Cross should be separate from the community's Red Cross. My grandmother, without hesitation, announced that she would be joining the community Red Cross and that the laywomen of the Reformed Baptist Church could do whatever they wished. The next week, there was one Red Cross in town. After all, to my grandmother, bandages were bandages. Where good was being done for the community, Holiness people should be involved.

Sheer Joy in Being Alive

It was not just in their reaching out in ministry that my parents and grandparents exhibited a large and more complex vision of the Holiness tradition. They also lived in a much larger world in general, or so it seemed. They saw the world not just as an arena of God's redemptive activity but as a stage of God's ongoing creative activity. They acted as if they, too, like Adam and Eve, had been given the entire garden to work in and to enjoy. The world was a place of permission and not just prohibition. Of course, growing up, I could not have put words to this. In fact, I did not always know what to do with this complexity. I just watched and wondered. My father was the first of the ministers to have a boat at our annual camp meeting. It was a small boat, to be sure. Actually, it was a very modest rowboat. But when attached to a two-and-a-half-horsepower motor, it could transport our family all over the St. John River. Between services at camp, dad took us to go on picnics, to collect driftwood, to see the waterfowl that made their home in various locations around the seemingly vast expanse of water where the St. John met the Nerepis River to travel in one channel to the Bay of Fundy. Dad enjoyed the river—and treasured it—as if he owned it. He was as at home on the water as he was in the pulpit. Over the decades, he has water-skied, canoed, and windsurfed (well into his late 70s), and he continues to swim daily even into his 90s. My parents and grandparents took their role as stewards and docents of creation quite seriously. They treasured the world that God had made and wanted to invite others to enjoy it with them. Especially, they wanted the children around them to see that God was *for* them. I remember Dad rising at all hours of the night during the winter months to flood our backyard garden to create a skating rink for recreational skating and neighborhood hockey games. My parents hosted backyard art shows—providing not only the paint and paper but the exhibiting space on the back wall of our home. It was no wonder that we never had a well-manicured front yard. Between the marble holes and hopscotch blocks, there was no time for grass to grow.

All mixed into the seriousness of a Reformed Baptist view of holiness was an exuberant joy about being alive. My maternal grandfather embodied this complex richness most fully. He was one of the best preachers in our tradition. His sermons on being the beloved children of God (1 John 3), on God's economy of grace (on God's matching suffering with proportionate grace), and on God's large purposes for the church (based on Paul's pastoral epistles) are still referenced by those who heard them. Even this past summer, I heard mention of these sermons and how helpful they have been to those who heard them. Part of their power came because my grandfather preached what he had lived. He knew the sustaining adequacy of God's grace because he had met it in his own life. He lost his wife suddenly when she died in her sleep at age sixty-seven, and two years later his daughter died at age thirty-nine after a long illness. There was no question that my grandfather took his faith and his calling seriously.

There was also no question about his joy. He could tell stories of his child-hood in the itinerant lumber camps of Wisconsin or on the family farm in Millville, New Brunswick, that kept the audience in laughter for hours—not just the slightly nervous kind of laughter that is unsure of itself but raucous laughter that comes from the depths of one's being. His stories could also come from his years as a teenage worker in the Skowhegan offices of Clyde H. Smith, who later became congressman Smith and husband of the much more famous congresswoman Margaret Chase Smith, or from his narrow escape from being sent to the trenches of World War I. He never did figure out why the head of the enlistment office sent him back to help with the harvest on the farm rather than shipping him off for France. His stories always spoke—though more by implication than explicitly—of God's providential grace, which had shaped a life for him that he could not possibly have imagined for himself. He had planned to be a lumberman. God called him to be a minister of the gospel. He had planned to finish college, but his church needed a preacher. He chose to meet the needs of the community at that moment, though he often puzzled about that fork in the road. He knew that sometimes our decisions require God's creative improvisation!

In his last years, my grandfather, my mother, and I took a day trip to visit four of the cemeteries in central New Brunswick where my grandfather had relatives buried. From early morning until late in the afternoon, my mother and I followed Gramp as he wandered through the cemeteries, stopping oc-casionally to put his hand on a gravestone. He would pause and then regale us with the most astonishing stories of the person marked by that stone. One by one, the people came alive before our eyes—with all their gifts and foibles. My grandfather loved them for who they were. It gave me the most vivid picture of resurrection I have ever encountered. It could have been a sober day walk-ing through cemeteries. It was, rather, one of the most extravagantly joyous days of my life. We returned to the cottage hurting from having laughed so much. I have a picture of that day on my desk—my grandfather and me, his hands steadying himself on a tombstone!

In Summary

My family showed me a clear picture of what it looked like to have strong convictions—but to mediate them with graciousness to others. One did not wield the truth like a weapon. It was to be meted out in a way that left people wanting more. My parents and grandparents exhibited a fearless hunger for knowledge based on the wide range of ways in which God speaks to us—through the Scriptures, to be sure, but also through reason and nature and through other people made in God's image, sometimes even when they did not share our Christian faith. My family illustrated for me that applying the truth of one's principles in a fallen world is not always a simple matter. Translating one's principles into practice often requires creativity, imagination, and attention to the particularity of the circumstances. Sometimes there is a tension between two of our beliefs—and sometimes in a fallen world, true goods can be in tension.

In short, my childhood left me with a legacy of the gospel that was complex—sometimes even complicated and confusing. But it was a vision of the gospel that never made the world smaller to fit its preconceived categories or abstract doctrines. If there was an adjustment to be made, it was in the direction of choosing a larger vision of the gospel and a bigger God. If the gospel were true, it had to reckon with the concrete realities of the world. When there were questions without ready answers, we proceeded in the light that we had, confident that additional insight would be given as needed. We sought to allow the clarities of Scripture to drive our behavior rather than fret unendingly about what did not seem clear. We learned that when there were seeming conflicts between authoritative voices, such as science and Scripture, we needed to go deeper rather than dismiss one voice too quickly for the sake of consistency. We would rather live with some mystery and ambiguity than risk making the truth seem smaller than it was. Perhaps most critical of all, we relied on the fact that God was in charge of the world—not us. We took seriously the teaching in the Old and New Testaments that we had nothing to fear when we had thrown in our lot with the One whose purposes for the world would ultimately be realized in the triumph of God's love. In short, this was a faith large enough to grow into.

My Vocational Call as a Historian

The Accidental Historian

I had no idea what I would major in when I went to college. Unlike many of the parents I encountered over my years as a college professor and president, my parents were liberal arts people and were not at all worried about the fact that I had no plans for a major or a career after college. They wanted me to get an education that would prepare me to think and write well and have a large vision of the world. (If I had been pressed to say, when I started college, what I thought my life would look like afterward, I would have responded that I expected to be a pastor's wife, like my mother and grandmothers. A Christian liberal arts education seemed ideal for that!)

Looking back, it might seem inevitable that I would end up in history. The Mullen family, especially, had a deep sense of their family history. One of my uncles studied genealogy and found evidence that we had roots on the *Mayflower* through the line of Stephen Hopkins. Perhaps. I never took that too seriously. More relevantly, there were family stories about my father's upbringing that were told repeatedly at nearly every family gathering. Many of them related to World War II. Clearly, the war years had shaped my father's entire view of the world. He had lost a number of high school friends in the war. He was the main emotional support for his parents when his older brother, who was flying a Spitfire for the Royal Air Force, was shot down over Germany. After believing Uncle Vernon to be dead for six weeks, the family received a call from him when he arrived in London, having been released from a German prison camp at the end of the war. It happened to be Easter Sunday when the call came. (That was ideal material for my father's Easter sermons over the years. The one who was believed dead has returned to life!) And, of course, Winston Churchill was the hero of the Allied victory in our household. The "war books"—a Time Life series about World War II—were a hallowed part of the family library. So I did grow up with a sense of narrative and the importance of story. I just did not connect it with an academic discipline.

It was during my first semester at Houghton College that I decided I had to be a history major. I took the first of a three-part series of classes on Western civilization—The Ancient World to 1500. From the start, I was hooked. While most of my peers dreaded the long and dense readings of the textbook, I read and underlined and reread until I had the information down. One of the unintended consequences of this effort was mastering the art of study. It was actually embarrassing when the first Western Civ test came around. I got a near perfect score, which meant that I could not be part of the community of peers on the fourth floor of East Hall as they lamented their first college Cs and Ds. I walked around the campus until everyone had gone to bed so I did not have to respond to the question "How did you do on the Western Civ exam?"

I did not put words to this at the time, but looking back, I know now what captured my attention. First, I enjoyed trying to make sense of complexity and messiness. One can do that by creating narrative. Dr. Katherine Lindley, the Western Civilization professor, tended to do that by raising a series of questions and then drawing on the material to suggest possible factors in the explanation. It was not at all neat, like logic, but it helped redeem the myriad of facts from randomness. It offered a way to make sense of one's context, whether that be the college campus or the world in 1972. Second, I appreciated the focus on paying attention to sources—recognizing that no one source offered a complete picture of a situation and that various sources offered different degrees of believability and reliability. We learned to ask, for example, "What evidence is there to suggest that the author's testimony is well intentioned?" and "What was the author in a position to observe?" It was like doing detective work to solve a mystery—a skill that would prove especially helpful years later in college administration! Third, I learned early that there were multiple interpretations of everything and that each perspective—unless deliberately framed to deceive—offered valuable insights to the effort to arrive at a complete understanding of a situation. Finally, I appreciated the fact that there was always room for curiosity and more exploration. Nothing about the world was simple and obvious. We had to work—and work hard—at making sense of the world and doing justice to the stories of the individuals involved. My research project was on Luther's ninety-five theses. What I discovered in that one project enlarged and enriched—but also complicated—my understanding of the Protestant Reformation. What an adventure I was on!

I still did not think of doing history as a lifetime profession. When I finished college, still not having found my pastor husband, I had to do something. I thought I had a position as an interim professor at a small Bible college in the Maritimes. In February of my senior year, that fell through. Not having any other brilliant ideas, I went to the library and looked at the graduate schools that would still take applications for financial aid for the fall of 1976 (not a particularly comprehensive way to choose a graduate program!). I got into four schools, and the University of Toronto seemed to be the one that would force me most to go out on my own. Having gone to Houghton College, close to where my family lived, I thought I should take the bold step into the big world (again, not the wisest way to make a choice). I had no idea about the academic reputation of the University of Toronto, nor much else, except that I had a place to be for the next year and a scholarship to cover it.

It was not until three years later, when I found myself in the fall of 1979 in a doctoral program at the University of Minnesota, that I felt I had consciously responded to my vocational calling. I will skip the details of my year at the University of Toronto. I did come out with a master of arts degree in history, but it was without doubt the hardest year of my life. (Mostly at this point, I recall that year when I want to encourage college graduates not to think their whole journey will be like their first year out. In the fall of 1977, I was certain I was finished as a graduate student in history and that the door was closed to any possibility of being an academic.)

I had a lot to learn about myself before I was ready to steward the calling to be a historian and a college professor. Through a series of providential improvisations (God taking my choices and constructing a story that I was quite unaware of at the time!), I became a director of residence life at Bethel College, now Bethel University, in St. Paul, Minnesota. I would not qualify for such a position in the twenty-first century, but the study of student life was just emerging as a professional field in the 1970s. For two years, I lived in residence with college students and learned about their lives as a whole—not just what they presented in the classroom. I also learned that I was more than a cognitive being who could get good grades. No one at Bethel knew that I was "Shirley Mullen, the A student"—and no one cared. I learned to be a whole person during that time. In the second year, I had the opportunity to teach two sections of World Civilization while one of the history professors was on sabbatical. From the moment I began that semester in the classroom, I knew that I was professionally at home. I had learned the importance of seeing students as whole beings, but I also knew that I could contribute most distinctively to their lives in the classroom. I would always see my students as having more to their lives than my subject area. That was a given. I also knew that none of my resident assistants wanted to hear about the French Revolution. I could be more completely myself in the classroom.

I completed my doctoral coursework at the University of Minnesota in the spring of 1982 and began looking for a teaching position while I wrote my dissertation. The providential adventure continued as—quite unexpectedly and, frankly, quite reluctantly—I accepted a position at Westmont College in Santa Barbara, California. Unlike most Americans, I had no desire to live without the four seasons, and nothing drew me to California except that I knew, as certainly as I have known any of the steps of my journey, that God wanted me there. I should add that this kind of certainty was rare in my story—and not to be assumed as the norm!

Becoming a Person of the Courageous Middle

For nearly twenty years, I practiced full-time the work of a historian and a college professor. Through my research and teaching, historical study shaped my way of being in the world. Contrary to much of the stereotyping, the study of history need not simply fill one with a collection of random and useless facts about the world. Rather, it can provide a lens through which one sees the world. It can even make one a certain kind of person. For me, my experience in the field of history was one of the key factors in preparing me for working in middle space.

I would emphatically, not for a moment, suggest that history is the only or even the best preparation for everyone who wishes to facilitate their community's movement beyond polarization. Rather, I would suggest that each of our vocational callings is much more than simply a way of earning a living. Each of our callings provides us with a lens through which we see the world, and each of them shapes us in ways that make us more distinctively effective in the redemptive work of middle space and in the multitude of settings where such work might be needed.

So while historical study is definitely not everyone's road to preparation for convening productive discussions in middle space, it was my road. I will try to capture some of the ways history has shaped me—more than anything, to awaken in you a keener awareness of how your studies and vocational journey have prepared you, or are preparing you, to do this same work but in your own particular way.

First, history calls a person to focus intently on the *particularity* of each situation and each person in human experience. While it has been fashionable at times, especially after major cataclysmic world events such as the First World War, to try to see overall patterns in the history of the world,[6] the large general patterns tend to obscure important differences among events in an effort to make the case for the overall patterns. Some scholars, in an effort to legitimize history as a valid source of knowledge in the Enlightenment tradition, sought to find "laws" in history comparable to the kind of laws that Newton seemed to see in the natural world.[7] But again, while there may be value in analyzing the characteristics that are common and universal to such widespread human experiences as war or economic crises or elections or dictatorships or revolutions, and while there are historians who tend more to this "social science" approach of focusing on what such experiences have in common, what makes them historians is their attention to what makes each situation distinct and utterly unique. Historians, *qua* historians (that is, in their capacity as historians), are committed to *not*

---

6. See, for example, Oswald Spengler, *The Decline of the West*, 2 vols. (London: Allen & Unwin, 1918–22); Arnold J. Toynbee, *A Study of History*, 12 vols. (Oxford: Oxford University Press, 1934–61).

7. See, for example, Carl Hempel's "covering law" model of explanation, asserting that any valid explanation, including historical explanation, must fit the pattern of science. For a summary of Hempel's thinking, see Carl G. Hempel, *Selected Philosophical Essays*, ed. Richard Jeffrey (Cambridge: Cambridge University Press, 2000).

suppressing what is unique about each event in order to make it fit a larger pattern. They are trained to see and to appreciate value in each case or perspective and to acquire wisdom or understanding or a fuller picture (to speak metaphorically) from this careful attention. So, history taught me to give attention to particularity.

Second, part of paying attention to particularity is taking context seriously. As a discipline, history is committed, first, to the assumption that human beings, as rational beings, have reasons for what they do; but it is also committed to the assumption that while they are united by a common rational capacity, the reasons that make a particular action or decision seem reasonable might differ, depending on their time and place. There is a predisposition among those who study history to seek to understand why people do what they do, rather than to assume immediately that individuals are either morally or intellectually flawed if they think differently than historians or behave in a way that seems strange. As historians, we owe our fellow human beings a "second glance" and the self-discipline of not allowing first impressions to determine our final judgments of them—or of any situation in which humans find themselves. While historians over the centuries have debated about how much of our reasoning *ought* to be shaped by a human nature that transcends time and place, it has been assumed that our capacity for reasoning is—for good or ill—affected by our local circumstances.[8] Context does matter as we seek to understand why individuals behave as they do and why certain events unfold as they do. Events do not emerge in a vacuum or randomly—so one must believe if one is to seek to make sense of human experience as a historian. History taught me to extend the benefit of the doubt to others who think differently and, before rendering a judgment, at least to ask, "Can you help me understand how you are thinking?"

Third, historians will, in the final analysis, privilege the concrete over the abstract. This commitment to do justice to the actual realities of particular persons or situations, rather than to suppress elements that do not fit a preconceived category or abstraction, sometimes works against the discipline. In the eighteenth and nineteenth centuries, when the Enlightenment preference for universal laws was the test of validity in making truth claims, this focus on particularity was considered to be a mark against the gospel claims to the truth of the resurrection. This assumption came to be accepted as a given within the community of intellectuals—the notion that "the accidental

8. This debate, between those who believe that there is a "normed" human experience against which all individual experiences ought to be measured, is a key point at issue between the Enlightenment tradition emerging out of the seventeenth and eighteenth centuries and the post-Enlightenment or postmodern tradition with its roots in the late nineteenth century.

truths of history" could never become the basis of the "necessary truths of reason"—or, in short, the foundation of reliable truth. Known as Lessing's ditch,[9] this assumption tarnished irreparably the late-nineteenth-century reputations of the sacred texts of both the Jewish and Christian traditions, as well as the communities shaped by those texts. The battle between the "higher critics" and those who sought to defend the legitimacy of biblical authority cannot be understood apart from understanding this perceived deficiency in the nature of historical study, which focused on concrete particularity rather than the universals of scientific and mathematical abstraction. Much more personally, I remember discussions within my department at Westmont between those of us who believed that it was preferable to begin from a theoretical perspective (e.g., a Marxist, feminist, or critical race perspective) and those who believed that we must begin from the specifics of concrete historical data. Ultimately, such a discussion would require going deep into the following questions and the like: Are there any individual "facts" of history that can be said to mean anything apart from a theoretical construct? Is the very choice of the data to be used already tainted by certain preconceived, even subconscious, elements in the person of the historian? Are the very questions asked to be understood as the choice of a rational, independent agent, or are they also to be deconstructed in terms of class, ethnicity, gender, or some other group identity of which the individual is a member? These are the questions that have racked the academic community at large, historians among them, as the assumptions of the Enlightenment era have been challenged by the various strands of postmodernism. However one ultimately comes down on these questions, for the historian, the concrete experiences of human beings—in all their complexity—and the evidence for such experiences must not be subsumed or dismissed as irrelevant to any abstract generalizations to be drawn about human experience as a whole. History taught me that, whatever the situation, I must not make reality or lived experience smaller to fit some preconceived ideal category. Whatever was considered truth must, in the final analysis, be large enough to accommodate the full range of concrete experience.

Fourth, historians will argue for the legitimacy of narrative as a way of knowing—a way of making meaningful sense of the world and of human experience. They readily acknowledge that telling stories may not provide the same sort of tightness or predictability that one finds in mathematical

9. Gotthold Ephraim Lessing, "On Proof of Spirit and of Power," in *Philosophical and Theological Writings*, ed. and trans. H. B. Nisbet (Cambridge: Cambridge University Press, 2012), 83–88. Original published in 1777.

equations or logical syllogisms. Nor does it fit the pattern of scientific explana-tion that philosophers such as Carl Hempel hoped to find in history. What it can do, though, is provide the kind of explanation that makes sense of why a particular person did what he or she did in a particular set of circumstances. It is a different kind of approach to wresting meaning from randomness.[10] This is also the style of writing history associated with such modern English historians as Thomas Babington Macaulay (1800–59) and George Macauley Trevelyan (1876–1962). This point is critical for historians in the Christian tradition. It speaks to why we believe that the stories of God's interaction with individuals in the Old and New Testaments and the Gospel narratives in the New Testament are avenues for providing significant theological guidance and wisdom on their own terms, apart from any effort to place them within a larger framework of systematic theology.

Historians find the nature of their method and its truth claims falling some-where between the systematic predictability of the methods of science and mathematics and the more explicitly fictional narratives of novels and poetry. David Hume (1711–76), most famous now for his philosophical skepticism, was actually best known among his eighteenth-century Scottish contempo-raries for his work as a historian. For Hume, history—not philosophy—was the realm of life from which we derive our most fundamental beliefs about the world.[11] Hume's notion of this historical dimension includes custom and tradition, experience and "experiments" (what we might call the empirical dimension of life), and the narratives that fall under the more formal category of history.[12] For Hume and for all of us historians, history teaches in a way that balances the clarity of abstraction with the emotive power of sympathy or the "fellow feeling" we have for our human brothers and sisters presented (supposedly at least) without the intrusion of the author's self-interest.[13] His-tory taught me that stories can often capture the uniqueness and complexity

10. For examples of the theoretical discussion behind the notion of narrative as a way of knowing, see Louis O. Mink, *Historical Understanding*, ed. Brian Fay, Eugene O. Golob, and Richard T. Vann (Ithaca, NY: Cornell University Press, 1987).

11. It was this aspect of Hume that inspired me to undertake doctoral work in philosophy later in my career. While the completion of my doctorate in philosophy coincided with my move into college administration, such that I never fully made use of this work on Hume in my teaching and scholarship in the way I had imagined, I will be forever grateful for the depth that his work added to my understanding of the nature of history, as well as for the clarity of thinking that the discipline of philosophy cultivates in one's communication.

12. For a helpful exploration of Hume's thinking on history, drawn from the full range of Hume's writings, see Donald W. Livingstone, *Hume's Philosophy of Common Life* (Chicago: University of Chicago Press, 1984).

13. See, for example, David Hume, "Of the Study of History," in *Essays Moral, Political, and Literary*, ed. Eugene F. Miller (1777; repr., Indianapolis: Liberty Classics, 1985), 563–68.

of how individuals make sense of their lives more fully than explanations that are drawn from the repeated experiments of the scientific method.

Finally, the study of history teaches one to make room for complexity—even when it means holding aspects of reality that do not seem consistent. Rather than ignore something for which there is credible testimony so as to make an account more logically tight, historians will make space for ambiguity and mystery. One cannot do that in a mathematical equation or a syllogism—and less easily in the conclusion of a scientific report. History offers that gift. It reminds us that, at any given moment, we may not always have all the relevant information for a complete understanding of a situation or a person.

Sometimes, reluctantly and perhaps regrettably, we may have to make decisions in the absence of all the information we would like to have. But as much as possible, we must always leave room for more evidence to come in. We see this played out most practically in the justice system. Establishing guilt or innocence is much more like doing the work of a historian than setting up an experiment in the chemistry laboratory or solving a mathematical problem. This is a helpful reminder that a judge or a jury can and sometimes do make mistakes. Fortunately, in ideal circumstances, there is a recourse to right the situation.

My study in history further convinced me of the complexity and, dare I say, messiness of reality. Nothing is exactly as it seems at first glance. We need to pay attention if we want to see fully and clearly. Furthermore, the circumstances and the people in this fallen world of ours do not divide themselves neatly into good and evil. No matter how well intentioned we are (or others are), each of us sees only partially and often mistakenly. Partly, this is because we are finite and thus see the world from one perspective. Partly, this is because we are fallen—and our best efforts to see clearly are tainted in ways of which we may be entirely unaware. We must leave room for new information and practice the humility that acknowledges and allows for mystery. What the study of history added to the experience of my upbringing was a method for exploring and making meaningful sense of this strange world in which I find myself. The historical method allowed for both fervent and earnest pursuit of knowledge about the world, in all its extravagant variety and richness, and acknowledgment of human frailty—whether of capacity or intent—in coming to a full understanding of truth. It gave me a way of allowing for growth in one's understanding of any particular person or situation. It allowed for both confidence in the existence of truth and humility about any one person's effort to capture a full understanding of that truth. In short, it offered a method for navigating the growing tension within our post-Vietnam culture as well as within the church between those who claimed to be absolutists and those who claimed to be relativists. I discovered that this method is equally helpful in navigating productively between the absolutist, polarized, and politicized claims that are being put forward in the culture and in the church of the twenty-first century.

Rediscovering Holiness—This Time as Gift Rather Than Burden

I returned to Houghton College in 2006, thirty years after I had graduated in the spring of 1976 and forty years since I had first arrived in Houghton as a seventh grader with my family. (In 1966, my father had accepted a position there as a professor in the Bible and philosophy department.) No one was more surprised than I was to find myself back in this small college town in western New York—especially as the president. I had no long-term plan to be back at my alma mater. In fact, I had already turned down the opportunity to return as a faculty member in the history department in the 1980s. I had moved on. Furthermore, I had no plans to stay in college administration. I viewed my stint as chief academic officer at Westmont as a temporary displacement from the faculty to meet the short-term needs of that community. My plan was to return to the history classroom and to retire from Westmont College as a faculty emerita.

But when, in the spring of 2005, I began receiving calls to consider the presidency of Houghton, I could not shake the inner voice reminding me of how much I owed the college and how much I had been shaped by the Wesleyan tradition. For months, over an exceedingly complicated, ongoing dialogue with Houghton and Westmont, I sought to determine where God most wanted me to be. (I wanted the kind of clear, unmistakable confirmation I had received to go west of the Mississippi in 1983. That never came.) On the surface, my desire was to remain at Westmont. My friends were there. Two of my siblings and their families were there. My academic "kindred spirits" were there. The Pacific Ocean was there. But underneath, I kept seeing my Wesleyan, Arminian grandparents reminding me that I was not, in fact, from the Reformed tradition or even the neo-Reformed variety that characterized Westmont and much of the world of Christian liberal arts. My roots were in the Holiness tradition—and that was not the same. I also kept being reminded that I would not be where I was without the gifts of a Houghton education. It was there that I found my love for history—and was given my first chance, as a teaching assistant for Western Civilization, to be at the front of a classroom. It was there that I was introduced to the Christian liberal arts tradition and experienced its enlivening and enlarging impact as a Christian believer and as a human being. It was there that I was encouraged to consider graduate school and to imagine a future that I would never have viewed as an option for myself. After all, as a student at Houghton, I didn't even have the courage to speak out loud in class.

The simple way to capture in one sentence what, in reality, was a fairly turbulent journey back to Houghton would be to say that I was thankful for all that Houghton had done for me—and I needed to spend my next season repaying that debt. The confirmation that this was where I needed to be came not at all when I had asked for it but retrospectively. Looking back, I have no doubts that this was where I belonged for the final stage of my formal calling to Christian liberal arts education.

Much like the pilgrim in C. S. Lewis's *Pilgrim's Regress*,[14] a retelling of John Bunyan's *Pilgrim's Progress*, or the character in T. S. Eliot's *Four Quartets*, I arrived—to paraphrase *Four Quartets*—at the end of all my exploring, at the place where I had started and knew the place for the first time.[15] Even in the first few months, as I read the stories of Houghton's founders and early presidents in preparation for addressing the community and connecting Houghton's past with its future, I knew that I had come back home. I recognized, faintly at first and then progressively more clearly, theological themes that were part of my upbringing and that had been missing in the years since I graduated from Houghton and left Wesleyan circles. For thirty years, I had been serving in educational contexts and worshiping in churches that were shaped by the Reformed tradition. I had not even noticed what I had been missing until I found myself back in Houghton.

It was in returning to Houghton that I first found words for the way of being in the world that was modeled by my family and empowered by my training in the field of history. I eventually termed this approach to living in the world the "courageous middle." It felt to me like a notion that I had discovered rather than invented. In fact, it seemed to come to me as a gift as I sought to find a way of communicating Houghton's position in the increasingly polarized and politicized society and culture that were emerging in the early decades of the twenty-first century. This notion of a third way of being—which was neither "liberal" nor "conservative," neither "left" nor "right," but very much Christ centered and very much a place of conviction rather than passive timidity—seemed to be in the very grain of Houghton's existence as a Christian liberal arts college founded in 1883 by the Wesleyan

14. C. S. Lewis, *The Pilgrim's Regress: An Allegorical Apology for Christianity, Reason, and Romanticism* (1933; repr., Grand Rapids: Eerdmans, 2014).

15. T. S. Eliot, *Four Quartets* (1943; repr., New York: HarperCollins, 1968).

Methodist Church. I simply put a name on it. I first used the term in presidential communications as early as 2012, and I then developed the notion over the next decade of my time at the college.

I was not, in fact, the first Houghton president to associate the college's distinctive mission with a "middle." James S. Luckey (1867–1937), Houghton's first president, had, in the 1930s, on the occasion of the college's first full accreditation by Middle States, exhorted the constituency with the following words: "If Houghton College will keep in the middle of the road, will rely wholly on the Lord, and will keep pushing ahead just as heretofore, I believe a great future is before her."[16] I don't know exactly what the sides or "poles" were in President Luckey's mind as he wrote those words. It could reflect the tensions he might have felt as he forged an institution whose vision combined a theology rooted in Wesleyan revivalism and an educational philosophy rooted in the liberal arts tradition he had met in his years at Oberlin and Harvard. It might have been the tensions felt by a Wesleyan Methodist denomination caught in the early twentieth century in the fundamentalist-modernist controversy and wanting to be faithful to John Wesley's high view of Scripture, appreciation for the methods of science, and commitment to social transformation. It was not a tradition that fit easily into the categories of the fundamentalist-modernist controversy.[17]

Luckey did not tell us the poles of the continuum he sought to navigate. What he did recognize was that Houghton College (Houghton University, as of 2022), as an educational institution in the Wesleyan tradition, occupied a distinctive place on that continuum, a place that required careful stewardship and that was part of its particular calling. Houghton was to be authentically a contributor to both the work of the church and the broader world of American higher education. It seemed to me that this calling that President Luckey recognized and named in the 1930s was more relevant than ever in the world of the early twenty-first century.

What I discovered for myself in that first year as Houghton's president was the part of Houghton's story that was truly Wesleyan and not simply a product of the Christian liberal arts tradition more generically. I had known since being a student here in the 1970s that Houghton was a Christian liberal arts college. I had not realized until returning what the Wesleyan tradition added to the larger tradition of Christian liberal arts, nor what a powerful gift this addition was to Houghton's relevance in the twenty-first century.

16. Erma Anderson Thomas, *The Man of the Hour: The Biography of James S. Luckey* (Houghton, NY: Houghton College Press, 1937), 71.

17. For further reading on this controversy, see George M. Marsden, *Understanding Fundamentalism and Evangelicalism* (Grand Rapids: Eerdmans, 1990).

First of all, the tradition of biblical authority in the Wesleyan tradition is much more complex and nuanced than the more familiar framing of inerrancy that one encounters in Houghton's sister institutions in the Council for Christian Colleges and Universities or the smaller association of the Christian College Consortium. The word *inerrancy* had only been added to Houghton's understanding of biblical authority in the 1940s. It is quite understandable historically that this happened in that period, given the college's desire to align itself with those who saw themselves as protecting the authority of Scripture rather than taking their authority first of all from science or progressive ideals of social justice. After all, Stephen Paine (1908–92), who had succeeded President Luckey in 1937, was a founding member of the National Association of Evangelicals in 1942—part of whose mission was explicitly to take a stand on the unquestionable authority of the Scriptures, at least in their original languages. As a classics scholar himself, well acquainted with the original biblical languages, he may even have felt the crisis of biblical authority more existentially than President Luckey, whose field had been mathematics, and therefore perhaps felt more pressure to take a stand on the issue. (I am only guessing at the latter. I have simply speculated here on why Houghton would, in the context of the 1940s under President Paine, articulate a doctrinal position on the authority of Scripture that did not come from its own Wesleyan tradition.)

One of the first signals to me of the distinctiveness of Houghton's story, in comparison to that of Westmont or Gordon or Wheaton—its most-similar sister institutions in the Christian liberal arts tradition—came as I read from the college's institutional history, *And You Shall Remember*. For Willard Houghton, the college's founder, there was no conflict between the commitment to follow the Scriptures and the commitment to "this great work of reforming the world." Nor was there any sense that the words of the Scriptures were self-interpreting, apart from their engagement with our God-given reason, the insights from our experience in the world, and the superintending guidance of the Holy Spirit.[18] For Willard Houghton (and his successor, James Luckey), the understanding of biblical authority was that of John Wesley and the Anglican tradition. The Scriptures contain "all things necessary for salvation."[19] Willard Houghton did not have to take a position on inerrancy. His theology and practice were shaped in a world that predated the fundamentalist-modernist split, the Scopes Trial of 1925, and the subsequent division of the American

18. Frieda A. Gillette and Katherine W. Lindley, *And You Shall Remember: A Pictorial History of Houghton College* (Houghton, NY: Houghton College Printing Press, 1982), 29–30.

19. See article VI of the "Articles of Religion" in Episcopal Church, *The Book of Common Prayer* (New York: Seabury Press, 1979).

Protestant religion landscape into those whose first commitment was to up-
hold the authority of the very words of Scripture and those who allied themselves with the social concerns they saw in the Sermon on the Mount. Willard
Houghton had no such need to choose. He often signed his letters, "Yours
for fixing up this world,"[20] and he sought to build an institution that would
prepare young people to carry on that mission.

Second, for Willard Houghton and others in the Wesleyan Methodist fellowship in the village of Houghton Creek in the 1880s, there was no such thing
as a personal salvation that did not also result in a commitment to working
for social reform. After all, they were part of the recently founded Wesleyan
Methodist Connection (WMC), which in 1843 had separated from the larger
Methodist Episcopal Church primarily over the politics of abolition. Under
the leadership of Orange Scott (1800–47) and four other ministers who shared
his commitment to abolition, the WMC formed around several key issues
that seemed to them central to realizing God's vision for the well-being of
society—the abolition of slavery; an egalitarian view of church leadership,
including a commitment to women's ordination; temperance; and the end of
secret societies.[21] For those in the WMC, there was no "personal salvation"
and a separate "social gospel." The gospel of Jesus Christ promised redemption and wholeness for both individuals and society.

This vision of a gospel that was both personal and social meant that
Houghton College no more fit neatly into either side of the cultural polarization of the 2010s than into the sides of the cultural polarization of the 1930s.
For Houghton College—a liberal arts college in the Wesleyan tradition—we
did not fit into the categories on offer in a world that pitted traditional religious loyalties against the loyalties of the academy and the press, that pitted
issues of supposed personal morality, such as abortion and sexual ethics,
against issues of social morality, like poverty, care of the environment, and
immigration.[22] On some of the issues, Houghton was pulled to the left. On
some of the issues dividing our culture, our political parties, and the church,
Houghton College was pulled to the right.

When parents called my office to express concern that the dean of the chapel
was bringing politics into chapel rather than "sticking to the gospel," I tried

20. See the reference in *And You Shall Remember*, 29.

21. See, for example, Luther Lee, *Five Sermons and a Tract*, ed. Donald Dayton (Chicago:
Holrad House, 1975). This is available in the Wesleyan Church archives at the international
headquarters of the Wesleyan Church, Fishers, Indiana.

22. For a description of this world, see Robert D. Putnam and David E. Campbell, *American
Grace: How Religion Divides and Unites Us*, with Shaylyn Romney Garrett (New York: Simon
& Schuster, 2012).

to explain to them that, as a college in the Wesleyan tradition, we understood the gospel to include the political dimension. The God of the Old Testament, whose Word was embodied in the life and work of Jesus Christ, cared about not just forgiving private sins but bringing about a restoration of the entire creation. God wanted to undo the impact of the fall in this world, not just prepare us for the life hereafter. The gospel of our Lord—manifested in his life and work—included forgiving sins *and* inviting his followers to form a community that each day modeled more and more the justice and shalom of God's kingdom.

If we were to be true to our Wesleyan roots in their entirety, Houghton College had to choose a different way than the polarized alternatives of the right and left modeled in our political parties and increasingly in our churches. Furthermore, it must be a place of conviction—not bland or timid passivity.

Third, for a college in the Wesleyan tradition, there could be no separation between theory and practice or abstract doctrine without concrete embodiment. As followers of John Wesley—the Oxford don who studied the classics, argued fine points of doctrine with his contemporaries, and yet gave priority to the practical unity of the church and formed communities of accountability to care for one another's needs in the name of the gospel—we could not simply be concerned to get our doctrinal principles right; we also needed to be concerned to see their impact on the lives of the community.

Finally, for a college in the Wesleyan tradition, we could not take a view of the world that separated the spiritual dimension of life from all the other dimensions of our humanness—the intellectual, psychological, aesthetic, and social. Yes, John Wesley was a theologian and a preacher whose sermons and theological writings are still worth reading for their instruction in piety and doctrine. But Wesley was also a person deeply engaged in the culture of eighteenth-century England. He was curious about the natural sciences, especially recent discoveries related to electricity. He prepared written pamphlets on the latest medical advice for his parishioners, who might not otherwise be able to access that information. He believed that God's redemptive plan included not only the souls of his fellow human beings but also of the animals and of the entire created order. Wesley was concerned about creation care long before it became a part of the platform of the political left. Perhaps most obviously, Wesley, along with his brother Charles, also understood that we as humans are hungry for beauty and not just truth and goodness. It is no accident that Houghton College was recognized early in its history not only for its commitment to global evangelism but also for its twin curricular strengths in premedical training and choral and instrumental music. For Houghton, as a Christian liberal arts institution in the Wesleyan tradition, the gospel of

Jesus Christ was a very large gospel, encompassing a message of good news for the whole world, the whole society, and the whole person.

In the work of leading the college, my own personal story and the institutional story I had been called to steward came together. The college's leadership and I had been prepared by our histories to occupy a particular place in the world and in the church—a place that was especially needed in times of political and social polarization. We could not be fully at home or fully ourselves on either of the poles of the spectrum. It was not at all that we were timid or without conviction or without courage to take a stand. Rather, our convictions called us to a new place—to a way of being in the world that created possibilities of moving beyond the paralysis of polarization and that invited others to imagine these possibilities for themselves. It called for hospitality, creativity, engagement, humility, and courage. It was not at all a calling that any of us would have chosen. It opened us up to being misunderstood by both sides. But it was our calling. And we wanted to respond to it with all of our mind and with all of our hearts.

Questions for Discussion

1. How did your family or the church of your childhood handle your questions about faith? Or did you have them?

2. Do you associate your upbringing with provisions of freedom or boundaries—spiritually, intellectually, and morally?

3. How have you been shaped to think about the relationships among the competing authorities that claim allegiance in your life—Scripture, science, government, personal experience, conscience?

4. How do you determine the level of credibility and reliability that you give to any one source of information you encounter?

5. How has your particular field of study or your profession shaped you to think about issues of political or ethical significance? Have they pulled you toward one of the poles of the political and cultural spectrum, or have they left you in the tensions of middle space?

6. How do you ensure that freedom is constructive in your life rather than leading to anarchy or relativism?

7. Can you identify the theological roots that have shaped your own assumptions about the relationship of your faith to your life in the world?

8. Are you able to articulate your personal theology of how God's kingdom relates to the world around you? How should you think about being a follower of Jesus Christ and a citizen of political and social entities in this world?

9. How do you think about your own "spiritual" life and its relationship to the rest of the aspects of your being? If you were to draw that relationship, what would it look like?

2

A Gift We Would Not Ask For

Understanding the Origin and the Unwelcome Adventure of Middle Space

t was homecoming weekend at the college—one of my favorite times of the semester. As a member of the history faculty who also taught some of the required classes in general education, I knew a fair number of the students who returned to campus for this festive time. For this reason, I was often asked to do one of the "miniclasses" that were offered to the returning alumni on the Saturday morning program. At the end of one of these occasions, I was delighted to see one of my former history majors stay behind to chat. I looked forward to hearing how she was doing, expecting that she would be making an impact for good wherever she was. I could tell from the expression on her face that she was glad to be back on campus—but also full of stress. Knowing her, I assumed her question or comment would be a thoughtful one and one that came from deep in her heart. I was not disappointed.

"Professor Mullen," she lamented in some frustration, "I just don't fit any-where. When I'm at work, my questions and comments seem too serious and too religious for the taste of my coworkers. They think I'm strange. Then, when I go to church, my comments and questions are viewed as too radical, too liberal, and even skeptical. Some people in my adult education class don't even think I'm a Christian. What am I going to do? I want to fit in. I want to feel at home."

I thought for a moment, and then the words came to me. "Margaret [not her real name], that is your gift to the world and to the church. That is what you have been prepared to do by your Christian education—to not quite fit in any of the neat boxes that the church and the world provide for you. I know that wasn't in the admissions literature when you came here to college. But that is the deeper purpose and opportunity of this kind of education. All of these boxes are too confining and far too small for you—for all of us who want to be as large as the calling that God has for us as members of the royal family of the kingdom. It is a painful gift. But it is a gift. And we have to decide each day if we want to accept it. God is inviting us to be ambassadors of the kingdom of Jesus Christ. You have been given an education that has prepared you to be competent and effective and to excel in the workplace. You know how to communicate, to listen, to build teams, to think deeply with ruthless clarity and honesty, and to solve the problems that your workplace needs to solve. You have also been invited to a large vision of the gospel—one that will stand you in good stead over the course of your lifetime. You have been prepared to face complexities and ambiguities that come to us as believers in the real world. You know that following Jesus is not like pressing the Help icon on the screen. Your gift to both your workplace and your adult education class at church is to be a winsome representative of God's kingdom, asking questions and making comments that allow your colleagues to come into a larger space, to entertain ideas they had not previously dared to consider— precisely because they trust you."

When I later became president of Houghton, I had the opportunity to speak to graduating seniors during commencement weekend. I always shared Margaret's story, both as a warning of sorts—so they would not be taken off guard—and as an invitation. I often connected this to the biblical stories of Daniel, Joseph, Esther, and Paul—also young people who were not only called into strange places where they did not quite fit, but also prepared to know who they were as God's children and equipped to be effective in the contexts in which they found themselves. They were so effective, in fact, that they were recognized as leaders and given opportunities to serve the common good that they could not possibly have imagined. We might think of them as the original hosts of this space that I like to call the "courageous middle."

This "middle space" that invites us to be courageous in the current cultural moment is not a space that most people choose to be in. It is a place in which certain individuals, like our friend Margaret, simply find themselves, often reluctantly. It is a place that circumstances seem to have chosen for them. If you are in this company, you will soon recognize the signs. We have already attempted in the introduction to name some of the situations that make someone feel the tensions of being in middle space. Any time we feel caught in the midst of binary, either-or thinking and the pressure is on to choose one or the other alternatives on offer, we are in what this book identifies as middle space. Often, there is a win-lose aspect to the situation. If one side is "right," then the other side must be "wrong." Furthermore, all too frequently those who are on the opposite side of the continuum are villainized as the "other," "those people" who are out to destroy what it is that our "side" believes in.

Of course, there are issues and situations where there are two sides—one right and the other wrong. There are some things that are true and other things that are false. There are views of the world that are closer to reality than others. In short, there are times that ask us to take a stand on one side rather than another. In those moments, we must not hesitate to do just that— seeking always to do so with that rare balance of boldness and grace modeled by our Lord Jesus Christ. But the contention of this book is that right now in our culture and in the church, the range of issues that are being put into binary categories of true and false and right and wrong is much larger than it needs to be. Furthermore, the villainization of those who do not think as I do, on matters both large and small, seems inappropriately intense. There are many issues on which intelligent and ethically sensitive people disagree. In this moment, though, that assumption is all too often missing in our discussions.

So the middle space we are focusing on in this book is part of our everyday life in the twenty-first century. Despite certain strains of emphasis that persist in popular culture on the social "sin" of being judgmental or on the notion that "my truth" might not be "your truth," the dominant form of contemporary discussion seems to be binary. Those who think like us do not just share our opinion on a matter; they are also "good" and "trustworthy." They are the "in" group. We "belong" with them. Those who do not share our opinion on a matter are "bad" and "other" and to be ostracized as dangerous and untrustworthy.

We see this tendency most obviously in the political sphere. I was struck by a political ad in the recent midterm election where the opposition candidate was characterized as "dangerous." He did not just have a different view on an issue. He was being portrayed as a menace to society. We also see this tendency within our families, in class discussions, in residence halls, in church board meetings, and even in our friendships. It is easier to take our place safely on one of the sides in the company of like-minded individuals who choose to see the world in the same way. But sometimes that just does not feel right. Like

Margaret in our introductory anecdote, we just don't fit. We are persuaded by some of the points of one side—but we also cannot ignore a key insight of the other side. Whether the issue be women's leadership in the church, or critical race theory, or solutions for gun violence, or the Supreme Court decision on *Dobbs v. Jackson Women's Health Organization*, or the government's ruling on LGBTQ+ policies, it seems impossible to fit all the aspects of your convictions on one side.

In this cultural moment, when you find yourself in such a situation, you have a choice to make. You can opt for a side that does not quite fit. You can be silent and hope that no one asks you where you stand. Or you can begin intentionally to prepare yourself to be an agent of hospitality in these moments to invite the community at hand beyond binary alternatives—to imagine that there are spaces of conviction beyond polarization. You have the opportunity to choose to do the brave, adventurous work of helping to change the tension from being paralyzing to being creative—the sort of tension that holds up the perfect arch of a Gothic cathedral rather than dividing the world between "us" and "them."[1]

First Signs of Middle Space: The Modern World of Higher Education

The cultural divide that came vividly into focus in the context of Donald Trump's presidency was a long time in the making.[2] But the divide will be familiar to anyone who has been educated in the high schools, colleges, or universities of our country in recent years. There are "right" ways and "wrong" ways of thinking about political, moral, and ethical issues. Often, these sides are framed in terms of being "progressive" or "traditional." Almost always, the role of religion in informing the discussion is associated with the traditional side.

---

1. There is also an application of this approach to moving beyond polarization in areas of scholarship as well, where all too often traditional and revisionist perspectives become binary and hardened in their mutual opposition. There can be "orthodoxies" both religious and secular within every area of knowledge on most topics. So while we are speaking in this book primarily about the work of the courageous middle as a way of life—or a "procedural process"—the approach can work equally well in particular instances of scholarship or doctrine. A particularly clear example is John Tomasi's work in political economy, in which he seeks to point his field of study beyond the polarized views of John Rawls and Friedrich Hayek. See John Tomasi, *Free Market Fairness* (Princeton: Princeton University Press, 2012). For later development of John Tomasi's imaginative thinking in this field, see his most recent book coauthored with Matt Zwolinski, *The Individualists: Radicals, Reactionaries, and the Struggle for the Soul of Libertarianism* (Princeton: Princeton University Press, 2023).

2. Its roots in the twentieth century are described in painstaking detail in sociological terms in Robert D. Putnam and David E. Campbell, *American Grace: How Religion Divides and Unites Us*, with Shaylyn Romney Garrett (New York: Simon & Schuster, 2012).

But the roots of today's cultural polarization extend back well beyond 1900. The eighteenth-century Enlightenment's limiting of "knowledge" to those matters that could be determined through reason and scientific experiment increasingly relegated matters of religion, ethics, and aesthetics to the realm of subjectivity or private opinion. One might be a religious believer certainly in one's private life, but that belief was not to enter the public square, where it might seem intolerant or infringe on others' freedoms. Most clearly, personal religious belief did not have a place in the work of the academy. Of course, one could make religion an object of study as long as one could demonstrate appropriate professional distance from any personal engagement in the topic. But any personal conviction that was seen to derive from one's Scriptures or religious experience was not to be part of the public debate in the culture or in the classroom.[3]

The modern world's understanding of what counts as knowledge has also played a role in shaping the understanding of the "self" and what it means for us to flourish and be fulfilled as individuals. Our contemporary notion of the self as autonomous and entitled to shape our own values as long as they are not clouded by force or fraud is outlined compellingly for us by Michael Sandel in his notion of the "unencumbered self." While we are not usually asked about our philosophy of the self in the everyday discussions we have about sexual morality, social responsibilities, or political rights, the language we use and the terms of the debates are profoundly shaped by underlying assumptions as to whether we as individuals are free to determine our own values and ends for "authentic" flourishing or whether we have obligations to realities outside of ourselves, whose claims on us we ignore at our peril.[4]

I think back over my own experience in graduate school in the 1980s. I had wanted to study the British Methodists for my dissertation on Victorian England. My advisor, a self-declared Jewish atheist, said to me that he thought I should choose a topic around which I had no commitments. He illustrated

---

3. This modern limiting of knowledge to those realms that can be determined by reason and scientific experiment—together with the ways that this framework has been challenged in the postmodern framework—is outlined helpfully in Nicholas Wolterstorff, *Religion in the University* (New Haven: Yale University Press, 2019).

4. See Michael Sandel, "The Procedural Republic and the Unencumbered Self," *Political Theory* 12, no. 1 (February 1984): 1–96. For further reading on this forming of the modern notion of the self, see Charles Taylor, *Sources of the Self: The Making of the Modern Identity* (Cambridge, MA: Harvard University Press, 1992). For a more recent exploration of these issues, one that ties the formation of the self with the contemporary debates about sexual morality, see Carl R. Trueman, *The Rise and Triumph of the Modern Self: Cultural Amnesia, Expressive Individualism, and the Road to Sexual Revolution* (Wheaton: Crossway, 2020). Or see its more recent, shorter counterpart: Trueman, *Strange New World: How Thinkers and Activists Redefined Identity and Sparked the Sexual Revolution* (Wheaton: Crossway, 2022).

with his own choice to study the nineteenth-century English Roman Catholics. He was much happier when I chose to work on the "Freethinkers," who—from his standpoint and in their atheism or at least agnosticism—were safely distanced from my personal faith commitments. These were the days prior to the advent of labeling things "postmodern" or "identity politics," when much of the academy, even in the humanities, was still holding out some space for the ideal of "objectivity"—a place we would all attempt to stand, untainted by any potential bias of our background or our personal loyalties. While the neatness of this Enlightenment framework has long since disappeared, its preference for arguments coming from logic or scientific evidence remains part of the confusing array of "tests of truth" that characterize the contemporary classroom, in which students of all ages find themselves today.

I well remember one of the students who transferred to the Christian college where I was teaching in the 1990s. She had been accepted at one of the premier, highly ranked California liberal arts colleges that would have been the envy of many of her undergraduate peers. After a few weeks in her new surroundings, she confessed to the great relief it was to be in a place where she could "take out [her] fundamental Christian beliefs and look at them and allow them to be part of [her] overall intellectual and spiritual development as a student." As she put it, in the previous setting, "I was spending all my energy just trying to hang onto my faith. It was just assumed to be irrelevant to my education."

Much later, after I had come into the college presidency in 2006, I attended a national meeting of college and university administrators. I had a delightful conversation with an experienced administrator from another institution about shared governance—that peculiarly academic governing relationship among trustees, administrators, and faculty—and asked the administrator to come as a visiting consultant to my institution to help us work out some of the tensions we were experiencing in this area. The person agreed to come and indicated some anticipation at the prospect. Shortly afterward, I received a call from this individual indicating with some regret that it would not be possible to come. After reading the faith statement of our institution, the individual concluded that we obviously did not believe in free inquiry. We clearly did not share the person's commitment to follow the truth, wherever it led. I took a deep breath and tried to collect my thoughts. (It was not easy since at that moment I was in Washington, DC, in the tunnel under the Congressional office buildings standing just outside the noisy cafeteria!) I responded, "Actually, we absolutely share your commitments to follow the truth, wherever it leads." I spoke briefly about the tradition of our institution and assured the person that there would be a hearty welcome for anything the person wished to share. The visit turned out to be a grand success and very helpful for our institution. Sometime later, I had the occasion to meet with the administrator, and we had the opportunity to share more deeply our own personal journeys. The person had begun university in the United Kingdom as a Christian believer but, as a student in the natural sciences, had been told in no uncertain terms that one must decide between being a Christian and a scientist. There was, supposedly, no room for religious commitment in the science department. I recounted my own journey in the field of history and my own reasons for choosing to spend my professional career in the context of Christian liberal arts colleges that, I believed then (and still believe), hold out the very best possibility in contemporary America of remaining true to the pre-Enlightenment purposes of a humane educational vision that is open to truth from more than simply the rationalist and empiricist traditions. After listening graciously to my brief account of the history of the Western academy, the person responded, somewhat wistfully, "I wish I had known all this when I first went to university. My own story might have been quite different."

The modern academy early on created the conditions for a cadre of people caught in the middle. Undergraduates may or may not understand all the historic reasons for the situation, but they feel the tensions even as they make their college choices. Will they attend a public university, where the concerns of faith are not taken to be part of the furniture of the classroom, and find a parachurch group like InterVarsity or Cru or perhaps a local church group where they will nourish their Christian faith and find friends who share their Christian identity? Or will they choose a private Christian college that seeks to provide an educational framework in which the pursuit of disciplinary study and professional training can be done in dialogue with one's most fundamental spiritual and ethical commitments? In these contexts, they take their Christian faith seriously but also seek to excel in the full range of disciplines in the arts and sciences so that they will be competitive for positions in the country's finest graduate and professional institutions. In these contexts, students study the questions and the conclusions of the German higher critics in their classes in biblical studies and theology, but they do not take these conclusions as the final word on the nature of biblical authority. At these Christian colleges, students are invited beyond the popular cultural assumption, especially after the Scopes Trial of the 1920s, that science and the Scriptures must be at odds. They are invited to join the company of early scientists, including Galileo (1564–1642), Robert Boyle (1627–91), and Isaac Newton (1642–1727), who maintained that the God who created the world is also the God of the Word.

Sometimes in the modern period, young people chose to travel incognito within the larger academy. Increasingly, those who sought to maintain a commitment to the truths of Scripture, reason, and science found themselves in alternative academic settings, such as denominational or interdenominational Christian liberal arts colleges like Wheaton College or Calvin College or Houghton College or Westmont College—or the host of other institutions seeking to affirm the unity of truth that had been prized by Western intellectuals since the beginning of the Christian era.[5]

The world of higher education has historically made space for these alternative faith-based academic settings as part of its commitment to affirming diversity of institutional mission alongside consistent and demonstrated commitment to certain standard educational outcomes. Nevertheless, the tensions remain and, in fact, are increasing in the world in which we find ourselves today. One hears them, for example, in the occasional confessions of surprise from members of visiting accreditation teams upon observing the stellar academic quality, especially in the natural sciences, at creedal-affirming educational institutions. Much more dramatic and painfully divisive are the current debates over whether educational institutions that adopt more traditional values on sexual morality should be allowed to receive federal and state grants and loans—even when those funds are channeled to them by students through their choices rather than coming directly from the federal and state governments. Also divisive is whether accreditation associations will accept the degrees coming from academic institutions that adopt or make room for a wider range of traditional perspectives, particularly on matters of sexual morality. Will a more progressive set of ideals, especially in the area of sexual morality, be adopted as the cultural norm, such that traditional values on the nature of marriage or sexual intimacy could only be dismissed as bigoted and unacceptable in our civil society? These debates affect not only those who come from the more traditional sectors of the Christian faith, but also those who come from recent immigrant communities whose faith backgrounds have more in common with the values labeled as "traditional" than with those deemed "progressive."

The Middle Emerges in the Culture at Large

It took American electoral politics in the first two decades of the twenty-first century to bring the cultural divide over the public authority of religion to the

---

5. For a series of personal accounts of those in the field of philosophy who felt caught in the middle, see Thomas V. Morris, ed., *God and the Philosophers: The Reconciliation of Faith and Reason* (New York: Oxford University Press, 1994).

front and center of everyone's mind. On the one side, we have the mainline Protestant churches, associated with a more open, critical reading of the Scriptures, more flexibility in doctrine and theology, privatized spirituality, and public commitment to issues of social justice, such as poverty alleviation and equal opportunity in the workplace. On the other hand, we have the evangelical and fundamentalist Christians (increasingly merged into one entity in the media), drawing their authority from the Scriptures, often framed in terms of inerrancy, associated with greater rigidity in theology and doctrine, and concerned primarily with moral issues deemed by others to be more "personal" and often tied in some way to sexual ethics. The general social and cultural upheaval of the 1960s came, in the 1970s and 1980s, to focus on the issue of abortion, following the *Roe v. Wade* decision in 1973. Groups such as the Moral Majority sought to link particular moral issues to electoral and party politics. Increasingly, during this period, political commitments on key issues seemed to drive religious loyalties rather than the other way around. It is this trend that, over several decades, has resulted in the Christian nationalism that we see today. The intense public reaction to the Supreme Court decision to overturn *Roe v. Wade* and to return the question of the legality of abortion to the states demonstrates how central this issue remains in the polarization of our country.

In this moment, the political polarization is also occurring in the context of growing skepticism about the existence of objective truth and any authority that claims to be based on objective truth. There once was a confidence in the Western tradition that public debate—and the more of it, the better—would lead to the emergence of the truth. Both John Milton (1608–74), in his seventeenth-century defense of a free press before Parliament printed in the text of *Areopagitica*, and John Stuart Mill (1806–73), in his nineteenth-century defense of the value of free speech *On Liberty*, assumed that truth has a power of its own to emerge out of the verbal free-for-all that often characterizes free public discussion. For Milton, the guarantor of the emergence of truth would have been the Christian God; for Mill, it would have been a less personal Enlightenment "reason." In either case, there was a confidence that the exchange of words was more than just a contest of power. While there may not be as many debate clubs in the high schools and colleges of today, this tradition is still one that provides some of the most active leaders in the student government organizations of our college and university campuses. I have seen that myself in the ways that students who have been involved in debate still set up campus discussions.

The public authority of truth claims grounded in religion had been waning for several centuries, ironically—and somewhat surprisingly—in large part as a result of the collective impact of the sixteenth-century Protestant Reformation's key rallying commitments to the priesthood of the believer, the authority of Scripture alone, and salvation by faith alone. The price of a pluralistic vision of Christianity in the West was its privatization.[6]

Nineteenth- and twentieth-century thinkers such as Marx, Nietzsche, Derrida, and Foucault called us to go "behind" what we see happening on the surface—whether it be the surface of social structures or the surface of authorial intent in written texts—to see the arrangements of power that, according to their view, are in fact driving what is happening in the world and what is being said about the world. Even those outside the academy have become familiar with the claims that "all reality is social construction." That is, it is the constructs of race, class, and gender—undergirded by deeper geographic, economic, and political realities—that drive the world rather than rational or individual agency. More recently, even science itself—which had long been seen, at least in the public's mind, to be the one neutral and reliable source of truth, based only on empirical evidence and thus supposedly free from political and religious bias—has become suspect.[7]

The politicization of the recent COVID-19 crisis has served to erode even further the trust with which large swaths of the public receive news that claims to be scientific. In every church, every college and university campus, every public space, we saw at least hints of one's intellectual loyalties in the decision to mask or not to mask!

The Complexity of the Two Sides

This pitting of Christianity and secularity against each other is certainly not a neat divide. For one thing, there are all sorts of Christianity in America—mainline Protestant denominations, which, since the early twentieth century, have been associated with a "social gospel" that aligns more with the political left; fundamentalist groups, which, since the late nineteenth century, have been primarily concerned to protect the authority of Scripture and its legitimacy in the face of the claims of science; evangelicals, who emerged in the mid-twentieth century (associated with Billy Graham, Carl Henry's

---

6. See Brad S. Gregory, *The Unintended Reformation: How a Religious Revolution Secularized Society* (Cambridge, MA: Harvard University Press, 2015).

7. For a historical treatment of this development, see Steven Shapin, *A Social History of Truth: Civility and Science in Seventeenth-Century England* (Chicago: University of Chicago Press, 1985). For an account of recent concerns, see Jennifer Kavanagh and Michael D. Rich, *Truth Decay: An Initial Exploration of the Diminishing Role of Facts and Analysis in American Public Life* (Santa Monica, CA: Rand Corporation, 2018).

Christianity Today, and such institutions as Fuller Seminary), viewing themselves as loyal to the authority of Scripture but engaging more with culture; the entire tradition of African American Christianity; the Roman Catholic tradition, associated early on with various nineteenth-century immigrant or ethnic groups but modified significantly by Vatican II; and the entire Pentecostal tradition, which, while often associated with the evangelical tradition in America, has increasingly been shaped by global engagement with emerging Pentecostal movements in South America, Africa, and Asia.

Furthermore, the relationship of historic Christianity and American culture is complicated. First, the tradition of the separation of church and state—which, in the twenty-first century, is all too often taken to mean that religion of all kinds should be left out of the public square, thus creating a public square devoid of religion (e.g., witness the debates about crèches during the "winter holiday" season)—originally was meant primarily to prevent the government from dictating a particular kind of religion for all citizens. The intent was to make space for the flourishing of all varieties of religious conviction, their practitioners living side by side in harmony and with mutual respect. In short, the founders were making way for a pluralistic vision of America rather than a secular vision.[8]

It happened that the vast majority of Americans in the eighteenth and early to mid-nineteenth centuries came from parts of the world that practiced some variety of Protestant Christianity, thus leading to the idea that Protestantism was the "norm." The practical reality of the early republic was Protestant hegemony—and frankly, *white* Protestant hegemony—rather than the founders' stated ideal of pluralism. The arrival of Roman Catholic immigrants from Ireland and later Italy and Poland, as well as Jewish immigrants from Russia and eastern Europe, met with the early rise of "nativist" parties like the Know Nothing Party, even during the nineteenth century. This equation of America with Protestant Christianity only became more strained with the growing number of immigrants in the late nineteenth and twentieth centuries from Asia. Even though the notion of the country's values as rooted in the Western European Christian tradition was redescribed in the mid-twentieth century as "Judeo-Christian,"[9] it remained deeply rooted in the popular consciousness that America was "Christian." This emphasis grew from the time of the bicentennial in 1976 through the emergence of the Moral Majority in the 1980s.[10]

---

8. See Martha Nussbaum, *Liberty of Conscience: In Defense of America's Tradition of Religious Equality* (New York: Basic Books, 2008).

9. See Eboo Patel's account of this in *Out of Many Faiths: Religious Diversity and the American Promise* (Princeton: Princeton University Press, 2018).

10. See, for example, Peter Marshall and David Manuel, *The Light and the Glory* (Old Tappan, NJ: Christian School Curriculum, 1977).

It is understandable that eventually—and long before the Trump era—it would seem that the only two options were a hegemonic cultural Protestant Christianity or the "naked public square," as Richard John Neuhaus described the emergence of the ideal of secularity.[11]

Second, the First Amendment commitment to "religious liberty" became, all too often in the eighteenth and nineteenth centuries, a weapon used to justify the rights of white slave owners in their treatment of African American slaves. It is no accident that religious liberty in twenty-first-century America is taken all too often to be a thin veneer for what is, in fact, merely prejudice and bigotry. Thus, African American Christians, despite sharing the same theological commitments as white evangelicals, align more often with the politics of the American left. I asked one of my African American colleagues how to understand his congregation's commitment to more progressive stances on sexual morality in the public arena, even though it shared the same theological convictions privately. He explained that this was part of the African American community's commitment, rooted in its own experience in this country, to never allow anything that could be understood as discrimination to become formal legislation codified into law. American Latinos also do not fit neatly into the current religious-secular divide in American society. As a community, they almost always identify as Christian, usually either Roman Catholic or Pentecostal. Their concerns pull them sometimes to the left, sometimes to the right of the political spectrum. The reality remains that the notorious "81 percent" of evangelicals who voted for Trump were predominantly white evangelicals. This equation of the term *evangelical* with Trump supporters has made it in certain quarters of the society more a political label than a statement of one's theological commitments.

Who Exactly Might We Find in the Company of Middle Space?

Despite the complexities, there remains in this current moment a discernible and deep cultural divide. It is clear in the divergent voting patterns of "red" and "blue" states—evident even at the county and precinct level—resulting in the vitriolic presidential campaigns of 2016 and 2020; the painful manifestation of violence and disorder on January 6, 2021, in our nation's capital; and the subsequent congressional gridlock that we continue to experience. This divide has left a growing number of America's religious community in an awkward middle space. These people do not fit neatly into the categories of red or blue.

11. Richard John Neuhaus, *The Naked Public Square: Religion and Democracy in America* (Grand Rapids: Eerdmans, 1984).

Nor do they fit with the stereotypic divide that puts the press, the academy, the cultural elites, and science on the side of the progressive left and the Bible-believing, church-attending, grassroots American religious believer on the side of the purportedly xenophobic, nationalistic, homophobic Christian right.

This middle group includes many of the 400,000 young people who, each year, have chosen to attend institutions belonging to the Council for Christian Colleges and Universities (CCCU). This association of 185 institutions of higher education worldwide includes over 150 in this country alone, all of which are fully accredited by their regional accrediting institutions. They are committed to preparing their students to compete for places at the full range of graduate and professional schools. Their faculty have been trained in the mainstream of the academy; they publish in the mainstream journals of their professions and engage regularly in their disciplinary guilds. At the same time, the students who choose to attend these institutions know that they also claim to be Christ centered. CCCU institutions affirm the authority of the Old and New Testaments and ask their faculty and staff to affirm an explicit declaration of the institution's learning covenant. They recognize that all institutions of higher education have a set of assumptions that govern the classroom learning context. These institutions want to make their assumptions explicit, in part because they know that their complex set of commitments to both faith and learning are not taken for granted in our time.

The "middle" includes members of Christian communities who, precisely because of their Christian beliefs grounded in both the Old and New Testaments, are active in the work of immigration reform in this country. Rather than sharing the stereotypic conservative Christian suspicion about immigrants—and the mentality of "keeping America for Americans"—these individuals are on the cutting edge of providing legal assistance to immigrants as they seek to navigate the complex paperwork of the Immigration and Naturalization Service (INS). They are actively caring for all immigrants, for the young people caught in the various aspects of the Deferred Action for Childhood Arrivals (DACA) discussions, for newly arrived refugees, for those waiting on the southern borders, and for all those who are seeking the "American dream" for themselves and their families.[12]

12. See the work of Jenny Yang, senior vice president of advocacy and policy at World Relief, or her book coauthored with Matthew Soerens, *Welcoming the Stranger: Justice, Compassion and Truth in the Immigration Debate* (Downers Grove, IL: IVP Books, 2009). See also the website of the Wesleyan Church's Immigrant Connection (https://www.wesleyan.org/discipleship/immigrant-connection) and that of Women of Welcome (https://womenofwelcome.com), a ministry growing out of World Relief that is committed to helping Christians explore a biblical and theological perspective on immigration and refugees rather than simply a political perspective.

The middle includes members of Christian communities who describe themselves as "welcoming but not affirming" toward the LGBTQ+ community. They seek to be loyal to a traditional biblical sexual ethic but are committed to welcoming as persons those individuals who identify as members of the LGBTQ+ community. They include many of the Christians committed to a traditional biblical sexual ethic who have become involved in the NCAA's Common Ground conversation—a movement committed to promoting mutual understanding between evangelical Christians and the LGBTQ+ communities for the purpose of supporting student athletes from both communities who find themselves feeling misunderstood in the context of collegiate athletics. The middle also includes movements such as Revoice, which describes itself as existing to "support and encourage Christians who are sexual minorities so they can flourish in historic Christian traditions,"[13] as well as members of the LGBTQ+ community who choose to continue to subscribe to a traditional biblical understanding of sexual morality.[14]

The middle includes Christians who identify as evangelical but have chosen to become involved in organizations committed to defending the religious liberty rights of all faith communities. They seek to create a truly pluralistic America, where members of multiple and diverse religious communities can flourish within the framework of constitutional protection, rather than an America modeled on the ideals of either the Christian nationalist vision or those who would opt for an entirely secular public arena. This includes those who work with the 1st Amendment Partnership or, in the legal arena, those associated with the Becket Fund for Religious Liberty.[15]

The middle includes those Christians who believe that the gospel of Jesus Christ does not make a clear divide between politics and religion. As a college president in an institution sponsored by the Wesleyan Church, I heard not infrequently from students, parents, and an occasional donor after chapel messages that touched on any of the contemporary controversial issues (e.g., race, women's ordination, sexuality, immigration): "Can't your speakers just preach the gospel?" "Isn't chapel supposed to be about spiritual development?" "Why do you have to take up political issues?" Sometimes I just listened. If I thought it would be helpful, I would explain that, in the Wesleyan tradition, there was not a neat divide between what was political and what was spiritual.

---

13. See https://www.revoice.org.

14. See, for example, the recent books of Wesley Hill, who self-identifies as gay but also seeks to honor the traditional biblical sexual ethic. Wesley Hill, *Washed and Waiting: Reflections on Christian Faithfulness and Homosexuality* (Grand Rapids: Zondervan, 2010); Hill, *Spiritual Friendship: Finding Love in the Church as a Celibate Gay Christian* (Grand Rapids: Brazos, 2015).

15. See https://1stamendmentpartnership.org and https://www.becketlaw.org, respectively.

The denomination, in the tradition of John Wesley, believed that following Jesus also included taking up such concerns as poverty, hunger, welcoming the outsider, and doing justice to those who are marginalized.

This list is certainly not intended to be exhaustive; it's only to suggest some of those who find themselves in this moment not quite fitting (to refer once again to Margaret) in any of the boxes that our polarized society or divided church is making available to them. My hope in offering these examples is simply to point to the contours of the middle we are discussing—and to allow individuals in the company of the middle to identify themselves and to join the conversation. You are not alone.

How Can the Middle Be a Place of Courage?

We have already recognized the cultural stigma of being in the middle in any context. At first glance, the middle is not a place anyone wants to be—at least not initially.

For starters, it is taken to be a place of danger and vulnerability. "You get hit from both sides. Why would anyone deliberately choose to walk the middle of the road?" responded one constituent after I had quoted from an earlier and somewhat iconic president of Houghton College who had advocated in the early part of the twentieth century the wisdom of the college sticking to "the middle of the road." I wish I knew exactly what issues President James S. Luckey was navigating when he made that statement. I can imagine several, but I don't know for certain.

Beyond that, the middle is taken to be a place of timidity. I found it fascinating to receive letters from college alumni constituents on both the right and the left who believed that the college should be more on their side and who readily assumed that the only reason we were not exactly where they were was that the college was afraid. Perhaps we were afraid of the government. Perhaps we were being pressured by large donors. Perhaps it was the need for students. But the common presupposition was that we couldn't possibly be choosing the middle for morally defensible reasons. Even for the most gracious of these constituents, the decision to occupy the nondualistic cultural position consistent with our Wesleyan heritage was considered "regrettable."

The middle is also sometimes taken to be a place of troublemaking and the cause of unnecessary disruption. Early in my time as Houghton's president, sometime between 2006 and 2010, I suggested to the student life staff that we do a "diversity climate audit" to seek to determine the degree to which our campus was truly welcoming to all of our students. Our campus prided itself on being a place where international students and "third culture" students could be at home. But was it a place that students of color from Baltimore or Buffalo could also see as their home? Not only were we still a majority-white student body, but we were in a decidedly rural part of New York. If we were going to recruit students of color, it only seemed right that we would want to make sure they felt that this campus belonged to them as much as it belonged to the white students whose families had been coming for generations. The student life staff were supportive—or at least they did not object! The group that did object were the leaders of the student government who showed up in my office—politely to be sure—but with a clear message that "everything was really fine on our campus related to matters of race." My idea of a survey or an audit would just "trouble the waters." They urged me to reconsider, just to leave "well enough" alone.

The middle is taken to be a place of intellectual sloppiness as well. Sometimes we are in the middle because we have not thought clearly or long enough about the issues. But it is not necessarily that. The middle challenges the all-too-common assumption, especially intense in times of cultural confusion—and more so when something of value is at stake—that there must be one right side and another wrong side. If there is truth to be had, then someone must have it, in which case anyone not sharing that view must be wrong.

It is even more personal for some of the people I have spoken with over the past several years. If Jesus is the truth, then surely Jesus would be on one side or the other. It is hard for many to imagine Jesus in a middle of any kind.

Finally, the middle is taken to be a place of moral and spiritual betrayal. Especially for Christian believers who want to honor God and who have come to identify their own position with God's position (or God's position with theirs!), anyone in the middle must simply not have the courage to stand for what is right. This position is the most sensitive to counter. For surely, God would want things to be clear. The more earnestly believers find themselves on one side, the more important it is to be sure that this is also God's side. Certitude seems critical. Furthermore, the New Testament blessing on those who are persecuted for Christ's sake and the gospel's can easily play into the mindset that the more we are on "God's side," the more we should expect to be "persecuted" by those who are not with us. The blessing can come to mean that when one is mistreated, that is simply confirmation that one is in the right.

The reality is that someone might be in the middle for any of the above reasons. The middle *can* be a place of timidity, intellectual sloppiness, and moral and spiritual betrayal. It certainly is a place of danger. That is, being in the middle is not at all necessarily a place of courage. But the contention of this book is that it *might* be.

There is an obvious sense in which the middle inherently requires a measure of courage. As we have already said, the middle is neither comfortable nor safe. Anyone in the middle *will* be misunderstood by both sides in any context of polarization. None of us likes to be misunderstood or the object of criticism, least of all by those with whom we share a common faith commitment. Sometimes this is simply a matter of personally feeling left out or misunderstood. Sometimes this is a matter of one's reputation in a community or even one's job. We see this in politics, to be sure, whenever one holds elected positions. But it is also part of the reality of boldly speaking out in a classroom setting, in leadership in the church, in higher education, in the nonprofit world, especially when any kind of funding or economic flourishing is at stake. Unfortunately, even for those who choose to brave the dangers of the middle, they know they are not making this choice only for themselves. The cost often is passed on to family members, sometimes directly, sometimes indirectly. As a college student, one is freer to choose this stance for oneself, but if it is to be a commitment of a lifetime—it will involve others one loves.

All of this obvious cost is multiplied exponentially in the world of social media. There is no room for careful explanation. There is no time for developing a complex argument. There is no opportunity for a confined framework of back-and-forth discussion. Clarity and simplicity rule social media. Cybertrust and followers are built around assertions—the stronger, the better. Furthermore, there is a penalty to yielding ground to anyone who challenges one's position. Admitting the validity of a cyberopponent's point only makes one seem weak, usually resulting in the opponent exaggerating this supposed weakness or hesitation for their own aggrandizement.

Going Beyond the Obvious

But the vibrant and animated courage needed for the middle in this moment goes beyond the obvious.

First, it takes courage to hold out to the larger community truths that are not so much controversial as they are inconvenient in a moment of polarization. Hosts who choose to be part of the courageous middle dare to risk being irritants for the sake of the larger good. They are bold enough to remind people of what is all too easy to forget in high-stakes moments, when it seems as if one's most-solid foundations are shaking.

Facing Our Finitude and Our Fallenness

There is no reason to assume that one side of a political or theological spectrum has all the truth. Blaise Pascal (1623–62), in his seventeenth-century reflections known as the *Pensées*, reflects deeply on the limitations of our intellectual capacity even amid humanity's great potential.[16] Christians, of all people, should know that humans are both finite and fallen.

As finite beings, our capacities limit our abilities to grasp the full reality of any situation—even if we want to do that. Sometimes this limitation is one of intellectual capacity. More often, we are limited by our context or perspective. Perhaps we have been steeped in a particular perspective in our family upbringing without even realizing it. It takes time to see that. That is part of what coming to college is for—to be freed from unhelpful and overly narrow views of the world. At any point in our life, no matter how hard we try, we simply cannot see everything from every angle all at once. Or perhaps it is a limitation of understanding. There may be specialized information that is required to make sense of a situation. That takes some time to sort out and to find ways of compensating for our own limitations.

For all these reasons and more, we need the larger human community for a complete picture of any reality. We need the benefit of those who are looking at a situation from different angles, who bring insights from different personal histories or from the understanding that comes from specialized training. This is why we need multiple witnesses in a courtroom to describe what happened in an accident. It is why we all resonate with the familiar tale of the five blind men describing an elephant. Each assumes the entire elephant is like the part that he felt. Just as in this story, it is possible that each person is speaking truth in that each has truly described part of the elephant. But no one has the full truth about the elephant until the five realities are combined.

Hosts in the courageous middle call for a convening in which multiple perspectives can be shared. They dare to step out and create safe and attractive spaces of hospitality where everyone's dignity can be preserved, even while being introduced to new information. No one has to be entirely wrong in what she or he believes in order to accept a larger or more complex picture of the situation. There is enough dignity to go around and enough time to come to see a more complete picture of the truth—not so that our convictions are diluted or weakened but so that our convictions are attached to deeper and more complete visions of whatever issue is in question.

16. See, for example, Blaise Pascal, *Pensées* 15.87–95, trans. A. J. Krailsheimer (New York: Penguin, 1966).

As Christians, we also affirm that human beings are not simply finite—we are fallen. That is, it is not merely that we have the limitations of capacity and experience. Because of original sin—however we understand this doctrine in our particular branch of the Christian tradition—we are not all that we are capable of being and not all that God intended us to be when we were created. There is something in us that is "twisted" or "bent." We do not even always *want* the truth. We have our own reasons for not *loving* the truth. This bentness can take many forms.

Sometimes we are afraid to find out something that does not fit our view of the world. It is just too hard to rethink one's entire picture of the world. I have already shared with you the conversation I had with my grandfather when I was preparing to go to graduate school. He was concerned about my confrontation with information or perspectives that would shake my faith. His encouragement was not what you might expect. He smiled and said, "You have to come to the point where you can truly say that if Christianity is not true, you want to be the first to know. Only then are you really free to pursue the truth with all your heart." The advice was both disconcerting and liberating.

Sometimes it is a matter of pride or pride's close relative insecurity. We just don't want to be *shown* to be wrong. Sometimes there can be personal animosity; we just don't want a *particular* person to be right and us to be in the wrong.

Calling people to confront their fallenness can take even more courage than calling people to confront their finitude. We do all we can to hide from others and even from ourselves that our hearts and our attitudes might not be in the right place. The Scriptures speak of our resistance to coming to the "light." We do not want to face the fact that we might be afraid or proud or just wanting to be right more than we want the truth.

Ambassadors of the middle must be creative as well as courageous in knowing how to helpfully, winsomely, and compellingly invite individuals from both sides of any spectrum of opinion to confront their limitations of capacity and their bent hearts and to listen to each other and to learn from each other.

As hard as it is to step out and remind fellow human beings of inconvenient truths that they may have never known or truly forgotten or just do not want to remember, there is another kind of courage that it takes to be in the middle.

The Courage of Facing the Unknown

This second kind of courage is more like the courage of the explorer or pioneer. It is about inviting people into new territory. It takes courage to affirm that, at certain moments, the truth may be more complex than anything we have yet encountered. It takes courage to invite people into territory where they have not been before. Given the several ways in which God teaches us—through the Scriptures, through science, through our reason—why would we be surprised when we encounter truths that are too large for our current categories? We are told in the Gospel of John that there are truths we are not yet ready for. Jesus explains that part of the gift of the Holy Spirit is that he will guide us "into all the truth" (John 16:13).

We might think of the notion of being guided into more truth as only a spiritual reality. But this also happens in the natural sciences. Even many of us who are not physicists have heard that sometimes light behaves like waves and sometimes like particles. What a dilemma. How frustrating to discover that light is not as simple as we once thought. What do we do with that?

As human beings in general and certainly as Christians who claim to desire and seek the truth, we do not like to confront complexity that we cannot resolve. We do not have strong models in the Christian tradition for living with such ambiguity. We know what it means to be faithful in the context of clarity. We are less sure what it means to be faithful in the context of ambiguity.[17]

This uncertainty about how to be faithful Christians when faced with tensions that we cannot resolve—or mysteries that defy easy resolution or questions that we cannot answer—may be especially pertinent to the evangelical tradition, which has been known for its clarity, its simplicity, and its accessibility. But the tendency to run from complexity and ambiguity is not unique to evangelicalism. This pattern of purchasing clarity and decisiveness, rather than living with complexity and ambiguity, has a long and tragic tradition in church history. It is so much easier, especially when there are issues of power at stake, to assert clarity than to live with ambiguity. It is easier to be reductionistic or to ignore what we do not understand than it is to live with intellectual tension or to "wait" on the complexity. We find it hard to believe that if we cannot find a resolution now, there might yet someday be a resolution. It just seems too scary and unsettling to live in the tension.

Admittedly, this difficulty of living with complexity and ambiguity is not merely theoretical; it is also practical, especially for organizations. Policies and protocols do not lend themselves easily to making room for particulars

17. I must acknowledge at this point the contribution of Robert Wennberg, longtime colleague and professor of philosophy at Westmont College, who first pointed me to the special challenge for Christian believers of witnessing in the context of complexity and ambiguity. We noticed that students often found themselves feeling less confident about their Christian witness once they realized that they did not have all the "answers." He explored this notion in the context of Christian apologetics. See Robert N. Wennberg, *Faith at the Edge: A Book for Doubters* (Grand Rapids: Eerdmans, 2009).

or exceptions. But this is all the more why we emphasize the need for courage and imagination. The church's inability or unwillingness to make room for complexity and ambiguity has been costly for the church's intellectual and moral authority in the modern period.

The Tragedy of Opting for Reductionism

This settling for reductionist clarity rather than making room for complexity and ambiguity is most pronounced in the Western tradition in the developing relationship between the church and science. We think first of the Galileo controversy in the seventeenth century. What is remembered in the Western tradition is that the Roman Catholic Church, to protect itself, chose to silence and even punish Galileo for the evidence he found that challenged long-received truths about the natural world. In short, the story goes, the church chose religion rather than science because it had the power to do so. Hardly anyone today knows that Galileo himself was a person of deep faith who argued that God had spoken in two ways—through the Word and through the world—and that there could be no contradiction between the two. God used words to speak in the Scriptures and the language of mathematics in telling us about the natural world. Few people stop to note or to try to understand the sense of vulnerability that the Roman Catholic Church felt in the early seventeenth century as it faced both the challenges of the Protestant Reformation in Europe and the challenges of Islam on its eastern borders. It's not that feeling vulnerable should justify any silencing of complexity in the truth, but knowing the context does modify the notion of an all-powerful institution just shutting down science for its own purposes. Hardly anyone has stopped to delve into the complex story of the theological and philosophical subtleties involved or the church's painstaking negotiations with Galileo to try to come to some resolution.[18]

In the end, it was just too complicated for the church to live with the complexity and ambiguity of Galileo's research, as it seemed to challenge the church's longstanding authority. Even when we seek to understand the perspective of church authorities and their own sense of vulnerability at the time, this does not change at all the tragic legacy of this situation for the entire modern world. What has come down to us over the past several centuries is the cultural memory that the church and science were at odds—that somehow religion is the enemy of science—and perhaps worst of all, that the church would guard its power rather than yield to truth.

18. For a rich and full account of the historical circumstances of the Galileo controversy, see Owen Gingerich, *God's Universe* (Cambridge, MA; Belknap, 2006).

It rarely helps to remind people today that many scientists of the seventeenth century outside the Italian states practiced science without any perceived conflict with their own personal faith or the religion of the authorities. The story of Robert Boyle and Isaac Newton in seventeenth-century England is quite different from the story of Galileo in Rome.

The trouble between science and religion emerges in nineteenth-century England first in the context of scientific study in geology and biology. Even before Darwin's proposal in *Origin of Species* in 1859 of a mechanism such as natural selection to account for evolution, there was a growing uneasiness about what geology was suggesting about the age of the earth.[19]

This unease became etched in the public's mind after the June 1860 debate in Oxford about evolution between the bishop of Oxford, Samuel Wilberforce, and Thomas Huxley, a biologist who helped popularize Darwin's ideas. The event, occasioned by the opening of Oxford's Museum of Natural History, was attended by a crowd of approximately five hundred. The debate seemed to pit the bishop's clever rhetorical skills against the scientist's more compelling empirical claims. So while Wilberforce may have made the crowd laugh when he questioned Huxley about which side of his family had descended from apes (thus winning the battle of wits), Huxley's sharp retort about Wilberforce's choice to use rhetoric to gain an edge in a debate about science clearly won the longer cultural war.

The popular sense that science and religion were at odds in the Anglo-American world became even more exaggerated at the 1925 Scopes Trial in Dayton, Tennessee, when a high school teacher was put on trial for teaching evolution. The national profiles of the lawyers in the case, William Jennings Bryant for the prosecution and Clarence Darrow for the defense, made the trial national theater. The actual outcome of the trial, in which the defendant was declared guilty, though the verdict was eventually overturned on a technicality, was less important than the public perception that, rhetorically, science had won over religion. The trial, coming as it did amid the fundamentalist-modernist discussions within the world of academic theology about the nature of biblical authority, brought the concerns of scriptural credibility to the public square. The American public took as the lesson of the Scopes Trial that one must choose between the authority of science and the claims of religion—at least the traditional revealed variety of religion grounded in the biblical text. This is still the orthodoxy of most science classrooms in our public schools and universities.

19. See, for example, Robert Chambers, *Vestiges of the Natural History of Creation* (1844). Layers and layers of sedimentary rock did not seem to fit well with the customary Victorian dating of creation to 4004 BCE. (This was the date assigned in the seventeenth century to the Genesis account of creation by James Ussher, archbishop of Armagh and primate of All Ireland.)

This concern over the nature of biblical authority itself gradually became hardened into binary categories around the word *inerrancy* in the late nineteenth and twentieth centuries. College students today have mostly been spared the flaming debates that were part of everyday dialogue on Christian campuses in the 1970s when I was in college. Mostly, I am glad for that—though everyone should have a theology of biblical authority that answers such questions as Why do I give the Bible authority in my life? What kinds of questions does the Bible seek to answer? How do I think about the different kinds of literature within the Bible as a whole? How do I allow the Bible to interact with other kinds of authority—for example, reason or the findings of science? How does the Holy Spirit speak to me through the Scriptures? Hopefully, these are questions that you will encounter soon if you have not already.

The more usual language for speaking about the authority of Scripture prior to the twentieth century had been that of the term *inspiration*[20] or of Scripture's providing "all things necessary to salvation," as in the Anglican or Methodist tradition. Once challenged by the German higher critics, those who wanted to defend biblical authority became more and more associated with the language of *inerrancy*, which came to mean in the popular mind "without error." This new language seemed to be the strongest way to defend the traditional Protestant vision of scriptural authority against those in the modernist tradition who sought to bring to the Scriptures critical questions posed by a study of history or science, as well as those who, in the face of these questions, chose more and more to focus instead on the ethical teachings of Jesus. This pitting of biblical authority against the social gospel formed the categories of much of the controversy within early and mid-twentieth-century Protestant Christianity in America, at least in the culturally influential northeastern part of the country. It came to the fore again in the 1970s, as I mentioned earlier, with the publication of Harold Lindsell's *Battle for the Bible*.[21]

Even the effort to clarify the meaning of *inerrancy* in the 1978 Chicago Statement on Biblical Inerrancy as authoritative "in all matters upon which it touches" (point 2 under "A Short Statement") did not change popular perception of what the word meant. (The council that produced the statement consisted of approximately three hundred evangelical leaders who sought to clarify what was meant by the term.) The notion remains in the minds of countless conservative Christians today that being true to biblical authority means that one takes the words of Scripture at "face value," without seeking

---

20. See, for example, Archibald Hodge and Benjamin Warfield, "Inspiration," *The Presbyterian Review* 6 (April 1881): 225–60.

21. Harold Lindsell, *The Battle for the Bible* (Grand Rapids: Zondervan, 1977).

to "complicate" the words with the insights of history or theology or even the original languages.

In the face of the simplicity of these binary categories—faith versus science, science versus religion, social gospel versus biblical inerrancy—it simply became too difficult to make room for the careful discussion of the appropriate relations of the biblical text, human reason, the findings of science, and even the traditions of the church over time in coming to understand how God speaks authoritatively and compellingly into the realm of human experience. Thus, we have in the twentieth century, in many quarters of American Christianity, a polarizing of the findings of science and biblical authority that would shock such heroes of the Protestant tradition as Augustine, Martin Luther, John Calvin, and John Wesley.

This failure to make room for appreciating the complexity of how God has spoken to us over the centuries and, in particular, for discerning how God's eternal Word in Scripture is to be appropriately interpreted and contextualized for the new moral and ethical challenges of each succeeding generation has only made the reductionistic approach to biblical authority more costly and painful for the church's credibility over the decades. After all, one does not find explicit references in any concordance to such contemporary ethical challenges as biomedical engineering, artificial intelligence, space exploration, or environmental sustainability. We do not find prooftexts for how to bring healing to deeply divisive race issues, much less the current discussions swirling around the framework of critical race theory. We do not find developed outlines on how to embody fully the truth and grace of the gospel in walking with members of the LGBTQ+ communities on our campuses, in our churches, or in society. We wish that Jesus had faced firsthand some of the situations we face today so that we would have more explicit guidance as we seek to follow our Lord in these times. Nor can one simply ask Siri or Alexa about a biblical theology that is adequate for addressing the longstanding concerns of justice that haunt race, gender, and class relations within each individual society and that lurk in the background of every aspect of international relations. We know in our inner beings, as Christian believers in the contemporary world, that documents such as the American Constitution and the United Nations' Universal Declaration of Human Rights do not have sufficient authority to provide compelling and unifying guidance for the world's challenges. But we also know that we are not practiced in the skills of helping Christian communities draw on their theological and moral resources to provide imaginative, constructive, and winsomely compelling guidance even for their own communities, let alone for the larger civic culture. Amid the vexing moral and ethical choices of our time, the Christian community's voice all too often seems either devastatingly simplistic or too vague to be of any help at all.

In a world of binary categories—objective/subjective, public facts/private value, faith/science, church/state, and a host of others—it takes courage to invite parties to reconsider the categories, to delve more deeply into the history prior to the emergence of the modern faith in science, to study the longstanding efforts throughout church history to understand the appropriate balance of faith and reason in our efforts to know God and to understand God's voice in the world, to incarnate anew the truth and grace of the gospel in our own time. It especially takes courage in a moment like ours when traditional Christianity already seems to be under siege in the culture. It will no doubt mean being criticized by both sides, and it will certainly be a long and painstaking task. It requires patience on the part of the individuals in leadership, but also patience and support from those who are funding the organizations with the gravitas to host these complex conversations.

Glimpsing the Courage to Confront Complexity

We saw something of this courage—though from the side of science—when in 2010, the American Association for the Advancement of Science convened a gathering of scientists, sociologists, journalists, and evangelical leaders to discuss how to reduce the tensions between science and America's evangelical Christians. (I happened to be there as a representative of the board of the National Association of Evangelicals.) While no one questioned the assumptions that had precipitated the gathering, nor the desirability of addressing the presumed tensions, it became evident immediately how difficult such a task would be. For example, it seems that these tensions are unevenly distributed across the world of conservative Christianity (e.g., one of the African American church leaders there suggested that the issue is more for the white church than the African American church). It also became clear that the tensions are uneven as they relate to various aspects of science (e.g., it is not so much chemistry that raises concerns as it is biology—and in that area, it is primarily the questions of origins). The group concluded that it was, in the end, not so much science itself but *scientism*, or the faith in the power of science, that was the object of concern for evangelical Christians. While the day provided stimulating dialogue and much agreement among the participants, it was evident that any real progress in changing the popular mind about the tension between religion and science would be long and painstaking. No one knew exactly how to get it out of the convening space and into the larger culture. That would take too long—and frankly, it was not those on the side of science, who had hosted the convening, who would have the most to gain from carrying the discussion further.

This embracing of humility and making time for such rethinking is the work of those who dare to sign up to be ambassadors of the courageous middle. It is hard work. It is creative work. It is work that the church is not well practiced in. It is work that the church or religious individuals could avoid in a time when religion still held some kind of sway in the culture. It would have been better if we had started on this work earlier. But it is too late to lament the past. This is the urgent call to learn what it means to be faithful while also facing, with ruthless honesty, the tensions, complexities, and ambiguities of our world. This is the invitation that is before us.

We have only the opportunities ahead of us in the present. It is the purpose of this book to inspire a great company of individuals in our society, especially those who are just now entering college and university, to dare to step out into the middle of our polarized society—motivated by the gospel of Jesus Christ and empowered by the Holy Spirit to choose to be hosts of middle space, turning this space from a place of timidity, passivity, and blandness to a space of redemptive and radically imaginative possibility. By calling our communities beyond polarization, we are inviting them into new territory where our collective energies can be mobilized to consider new, alternative responses to the challenges that divide us, informed by the wisdom, knowledge, and convictions of those on both sides who want to see clearly and to be shaped by the truth. We are inviting them to dare to trust those who think differently on certain issues to explore what they share—rather than to focus entirely on where they differ—to consider where they might be able to collaborate for the common good, to move our churches and our societies beyond fear to hope.

Questions for Discussion

1. Can you relate to Margaret's story? Have you ever felt that you did not fit in? In what setting did you most feel this? How did you handle the situation?

2. Was there ever a time in school when, as a person of faith, you chose to travel incognito because you were concerned that your beliefs would not be respected?

3. How did your Christian faith figure in your own choice of a college or university? If you chose to attend a Christian college, can you articulate

why you made that choice? Was it more for social, personal, intellectual reasons, or was it for spiritual reasons?

4. Have you encountered an apparent conflict between the authority of the Scriptures and the authority of science? If so, how have you sought to work that through? Do you have a theology of scriptural authority that you can articulate?

5. How do you think about developing a biblical view or theology of various topics in your own life about which the Scriptures do not give explicit guidance (artificial intelligence, video gaming, environmental stewardship, etc.)?

6. Have you ever experienced personally a situation in which you believed that well-meaning people were opting for a reductionist approach rather than dealing with presenting complexity?

7. Can you think of a situation in which your own finitude, fallenness, or fear of the unknown limited your ability to see what needed to be seen? How was this addressed? Or are you still addressing this?

8. Which of the risks of signing up to be a host of middle space most resonates with you? Can you think of others that are not mentioned in this chapter?

9. Have you personally experienced a community deliberately refocusing its attention from where its members differed to what they shared?

3

The Middle Spaces
of the Scriptures

*The Invitation to a Biblical
and Theological Tradition*

For sixteen years, from 1984 until 2000, I co-led a travel study program during our institution's May term called Art and Ideas of the Western Tradition. We focused on eight of Europe's key cities, from Prague to London, inviting students to explore, reflect on, and integrate the historical, aesthetic, philosophical, and religious aspects of the European cultural heritage. It was a different way of being invited into an understanding of the Western heritage and, for most students, a preferable way of fulfilling their general education requirement in civilization. While teaching and learning well in a travel context present challenges for both faculty and students, one of the primary benefits, from my perspective, was the privilege of seeing many of the world's great artworks in person.

I still remember the breathtaking impact of walking into one of the rooms at the Gallerie dell'Accademia in Venice and seeing for the first time Paolo Veronese's 1573 painting *The Feast in the House of Levi*. It is purportedly one of the largest paintings done in the sixteenth century—measuring more than eighteen feet in height and more than forty-two feet in length. Besides the impact of its size alone, it is done in the exaggerated style of the postbaroque mannerists and designed to evoke an emotional response from its audience. As a historian, I am not equipped professionally to comment on its aesthetic value. What intrigued me from the beginning was the way that Jesus is portrayed. I recognized immediately that it was a variation on the familiar biblical theme of the Last Supper. But it was not at all like the much more familiar *Last Supper* by Leonardo da Vinci. The only clue to the identity of Jesus to those unacquainted with the Gospel narratives would be the ever-so-slight light that surrounds the head of Jesus. And, yes, Jesus is sitting at the table with a group of men, suggesting the twelve disciples. But they are not at all the central figures in the scene, nor are they portrayed as being by themselves, having a quiet, reverential Passover meal, as we usually think of them in the traditional telling of the story. The host of the feast dominates the painting at first glance, by size and placement, and is joined by a motley cast of characters quite anachronistic to a first-century setting—including African servants and German soldiers—not to mention a variety of animals. At the very least, it expands our imagination of the Last Supper that we saw portrayed in Sunday school.

Today's viewers are not the first to be surprised. Despite the current title, the painting had, in fact, been commissioned as a "Last Supper" and was intended to be hung in a Dominican friary in the Basilica dei Santi Giovanni e Paolo in Venice, to replace an earlier Titian painting of the same subject that had been destroyed by fire in 1571. Given its unconventional approach to such a sacred topic, it came to the attention of the papacy in the context of the post-Protestant Reformation days, when the church was seeking to regain its control of orthodoxy. We should not be shocked that the painting was investigated by the Holy Tribunal in Rome associated with the Inquisition.[1] To accommodate the concerns of the Inquisition, Veronese chose to change the name of the painting rather than modify the content of the painting itself. Clearly, the biblical supper at the house at Levi allows for a larger set of characters and a more raucous portrayal of feasting—and it is less central to the more heavily guarded narrative of our Lord's last days.

I can certainly understand the concerns of Veronese's contemporaries, especially in the context of the multiple challenges in the late sixteenth century to the Vatican's political and religious authority—threats from both geographical directions, Protestants in central and western Europe and Muslims in the Balkans. The church at Rome was seeking desperately to preserve its

---

1. See Edward Grasman, "On Closer Inspection—The Interrogation of Paolo Veronese," *Artibus et Historiae* 30, no. 59 (2009): 125–34; see also William Fleming, *Arts and Ideas*, 9th ed. (Belmont, CA: Wadsworth, 1994), 354, 356–57.

powerful authority over Christendom in all its aspects—cultural as well as ecclesiological. But from a theological and devotional standpoint in the late twentieth century, I found the painting intriguingly provocative. Here was Jesus being portrayed in this particular context doing precisely what Jesus did throughout his earthly pilgrimage. Whether talking with the woman at the well in Samaria, or teaching on the temple steps, or responding to the inquiry of the rich young ruler, or meeting with Nicodemus under cover of darkness, or pronouncing healing and wholeness on the man let down through the ceiling by his hope-filled friends, Jesus was always challenging the comfortable assumptions and enlarging the customary categories of his contemporaries. By his very presence, his questions, his comments, and his invitations, he demonstrated a way of being in the world that called his audience beyond the accepted cultural understanding of what was considered good and bad, right and wrong. Jesus was not at all relativistic. Rather, he called people to a deeper and larger understanding of the categories of truth and goodness and beauty, which accommodated more of the fallen world's complexity and complications. Jesus knew that our world—and each person and situation in that world—is marked both by the impact of God's good activity in creation and the twistedness and bentness that came into the world through the fall.

Furthermore, Veronese's painting reminded me powerfully that the most truly significant elements of our lives as individuals and as communities often happen in the context of confusing circumstances that clutter and obscure our understanding of what will ultimately prove to be important. Our task, like our Lord's in the painting, is to seek in each moment to be about our Father's work, confident that whatever we see around us, the Father is in charge and will accomplish the purposes of his kingdom.

This painting symbolizes for me the biblical and theological invitation to a life that boldly and graciously challenges simplistic—usually binary—categories; that opens up the imagination to creative, redemptive possibilities that have not yet been considered; that actively inspires all those around us to bring themselves fully, in all their diversity and individuality, to the table of our life together; and finally, that purposefully hosts that conversation for the good of the church and our world.

Middle Space and the Biblical Text

No one in either the Old or the New Testament had ever heard of "red" or "blue" states, the Republican or Democratic Parties, free speech or cancel culture, or Fox News, CNN, or MSNBC, for that matter. We cannot find mention in our concordances of *diversity* or *inclusion* or *the right to carry* or *religious liberty* or any of the other terms that we treasure from the Bill of Rights in the American Constitution. We look in vain for references to theocracy or democracy or pluralism or civil society or international law.

Nor do we find strict rules for balancing our loyalty and adherence to the multiple authorities that exercise claims on our daily lives—the government, the Scriptures, science, professional organizations, and family traditions, not to mention the various individuals who claim to speak on behalf of these multiple authorities. This confusion of allegiance is only made more difficult in the context of modern liberal democracies, whose legitimacy derives from the support of their citizens.[2] As Christians seeking to honor the values of God's kingdom, who find themselves also as citizens of particular earthly states, how should we think about our responsibilities to both our eternal and temporal communities? Do we seek to shape our earthly state and society by the same set of values as the values of God's kingdom? Or is there one set of principles we ought to support for society, which includes a plurality of value systems, and another set of principles we ought to support for the church? Figuring out what Jesus meant by "giv[ing] . . . to the emperor the things that are the emperor's, and to God the things that are God's" was easier when we were not responsible for speaking both for "the emperor" and for God (Matt. 22:21).

For those in the Christian tradition who have committed themselves to the convictions that the Scriptures of the Old and New Testaments are true, that they are God's very Word, and that our lives ought to be shaped in accordance with their teachings, living fully consistently with these convictions in the context of this world has never been easy. (Many of these same points would also apply to those in the Jewish and Islamic traditions, as they reckon with the authority of their sacred texts in the context of contemporary culture.) Whether one is committed to following each word of the Scripture just as it appears on the page, or whether one prefers a more complex understanding of interpretation that involves one's reason, one's experiences, and the authority of church tradition in some form or another, there have always been complications, if one is absolutely honest. There are complexities of translation, of apparent tensions within the Scriptures themselves, of how to understand the nature of the truth being communicated through the different genres of the biblical text (e.g., some of it is poetry, some history, some apocalyptic

---

2. Note that by *liberal democracy*, we mean only that form of government that seeks to be guided by the twin—and sometimes competing—values of individual liberty and the majority voice of the entire community. The word *liberal* is used in the historic sense of protecting individual liberty—not as it is used today to signal either a particular political party or a progressive worldview.

visions). And, of course, there are challenges of context. No matter how loyal we want to be to scriptural authority, the world—or worlds—into which the various biblical texts were first given was profoundly different from our own.

One of the challenges of the first several centuries of the Christian church was determining which scriptural texts would be considered authoritative. While there was a general stability to the canon by the fourth century, this discussion has, to some extent, gone on formally and informally ever since. Even today, there are Apocryphal books that appear in Roman Catholic versions of the Bible but not in Protestant versions. Interestingly, the King James Version of 1611—though designed to provide uniformity of biblical authority in a non–Roman Catholic country and considered the standard English translation of the Scriptures for centuries—did originally include the entire Apocrypha. Perhaps we should not be surprised, given King James's continued private loyalty to the traditions of the Catholic Church, even as the official defender of the national English church.[3]

Apart from the separation between the strictly canonical books and the Apocryphal books, there has been no formal rank ordering of the various genres of Scriptures as to their relative authority. Such a separation has emerged within each branch of the Jewish and Christian traditions and informally within each local church and even within each family as it is determined which parts of the biblical text seem most relevant to our daily lives. Do we celebrate the seventh day of the week or the first day as the Sabbath? Which of the dietary and dress codes of Leviticus should guide us in the twenty-first century? What do we do with the polygamy of the Old Testament patriarchs? Do we allow women to speak in the church—or perhaps even to be given leadership? And if so, on what biblical grounds?

As much as we might wish, neither has there been any formally serialized canonical update provided throughout the centuries. No matter how much we want to be loyal to the Scriptures alone (which, of course, has been one of the core commitments of the Protestant tradition since Martin Luther) or to lend to our convictions the legitimacy of the Bible, the appropriation of the words of Scripture for our lives, whether we do it well or badly, will involve interpretation. Sometimes this will happen intentionally—and even then, it can be done either with great care or unhelpfully casually—but sometimes it occurs quite unintentionally through honest mistakes, lack of relevant knowledge, or the blindness of prejudice. But interpretation will happen. It is the

---

3. The discussion is reflected formally in the various doctrines of Scripture. See, for example, article VI in the "Articles of Religion" in the Anglican tradition or in the multiple articles or statements of faith that characterize most denominations and institutions in the Christian tradition.

nature of the situation. We cannot avoid it. Scripture, except in the cases of the Ten Commandments or the Levitical codes, does not for the most part teach us in the form of rules, mathematical equations, logical syllogisms, or formulas of any sort. We cannot look up our questions like many of us used to use a telephone book or a recipe file—or as we now might ask Siri or Alexa, our tireless electronic research assistants.

In short, no matter how much we claim to believe in the absolute authority of the Scriptures, and no matter how much we want to align our lives according to the very words of the text, the nature of the source does not lend itself to the ways that we as humans have so often wanted to make use of it. Most often with the best of intent, we—especially in the Protestant tradition—want to develop systematic theologies, to agree on globally applicable church doctrines and practices, to defend certain understandings of right and wrong, to write policy statements, to create organizational structures, to write behavioral handbooks, to establish boundaries for family behavior patterns that carry the full weight and legitimacy of biblical authority.

Most certainly, we can find parts of the Scripture that speak to any questions we ask or present to the Scripture for guidance. In fact, we can even find most anything we want to find in the Scriptures somewhere. We call that "prooftexting." The challenge is that so much of the Old and New Testaments does not provide its guidance and wisdom in the legalistic, formulaic, organizational-policy ways that we want to use it. We usually want to use it, in some way or another and often quite understandably, to support our efforts to tame the world, to set protective boundaries around an arena of order, to guard against the multitude of threatening forces that would disrupt our safety, to defend a position that we believe is right, or otherwise to wield control of some sort or another. Most of this use is not bad. It is simply limited. The full richness of the Scripture is always bursting our efforts to contain its wisdom, its knowledge, and its truth. The more we know of the Old and New Testaments, the more we sense the magnitude of their vision for the redemption of the whole created order, the depth of complexity in its wisdom, the beauty and freedom that God is yearning to offer us as human beings created in his image. This vision is just beyond our capacity to imagine and certainly to incarnate in the context of our lives, our families, our organizations, and our communities.[4] We might prefer that God had spoken to us only through a book of laws and rules or perhaps a collection of

---

4. For a particularly rich discussion of the complexity of the biblical text, see Walter Brueggemann, *Theology of the Old Testament: Testimony, Dispute, Advocacy* (Minneapolis: Fortress, 1997). While Brueggemann's study is limited to the Old Testament, the book offers insights for our working with the entire canon of Scripture. For a more popular treatment of similar issues

mathematical principles or chemical equations or a set of logical syllogisms. We could have managed that. We would know how to operate and how to ensure that we are on God's side and, more critically, that God is on our side. Instead, God has invited us into a story. We have the general outlines of the plot and a range of sources to draw upon for guidance, but we are expected to be active partners in the unfolding of the particular details of the story. It is, frankly, much more than we have bargained for. We want a world that is predictable, that we can manage, a world in which the good and bad are clear and immediately recognizable, where right and wrong are easily discernable. We would have preferred a morality play or a melodrama in which the heroes wear white and the music always signals ominously that the villain is on the premises. Instead, we find ourselves amid a spy novel in which the fate of the world is at stake, in which we are asked to save the world for all that is good and true and right, and in which we find it difficult sometimes to know for certain who our enemies and who our friends are.

Fortunately, the Scriptures that God has given us are designed exactly for the complexities of this life-and-death, ultimate adventure in which we find ourselves and in which we are being invited to be on the front lines. While we may be tempted to seek a less visible position further back in the conflict or to join up with those who confidently stake out a position on some particular part of the territory based on what is absolutely clear to them, someone must have the courage to give leadership to the entire effort. Someone must engage boldly but humbly with the complexities and ambiguities of a world that at every turn manifests signs of both the creation and the fall, that at every turn shows hints not only of the richness and extravagant diversity of God's kingdom but also of the impact of fearful small-mindedness, selfishness, and willful blindness to the beauty all around. Someone must have the courage to submit to the vulnerability of being criticized and misunderstood on all sides, in order that, out of the complexity and confusion, a deeper clarity might emerge. That is the work of the third way. That is the work of the courageous middle.

Glimpses of a Third Way in the Scriptures as a Whole: The Narrative Form

We have suggested that God's very form of addressing us in the Scriptures of the Old and New Testaments provides a theological framework for

---

of biblical interpretation, see Peter Enns, *The Sin of Certainty: Why God Desires Our Trust More Than Our "Correct" Beliefs* (San Francisco: HarperOne, 2016).

understanding the work of leading people beyond unhelpful polarization. The overall message of the Scriptures comes to us in a narrative form, rather than primarily in the form of rules or formulas or abstract logical propositions.[5]

In brief, the Scriptures present us with a narrative of a God who created a world of order and beauty out of nothing by the sheer power of his word. That same God created human beings for loving relationship with him and with each other, inviting them to partner with him in caring for the world. It is the story of a God who relentlessly pursues this relationship no matter how human beings respond to him—always seeking to bring good out of whatever happens to them, always ready to forgive them for turning their backs on him, and always seeking to call them back to the plans and purposes that he has for them. This continued pursuit results finally in God himself taking on human form and coming to live among us, submitting himself to the terms of the created order, and being killed at the hands of his own creatures.[6] The story does not end there, much to everyone's shocking surprise. This God in human form, whom we know as Jesus of Nazareth, rose again from the dead in bodily form, as a sign of what he is planning for all of his children. We are told that this same Jesus will return to earth someday, not this time in the obscurity and vulnerability of a baby in a manger but in power and majesty to reign over the entire creation—renewed by God's continued redemptive improvisation—for eternity. There is much that is mysterious in the narrative. We have only glimpses of what it all means, but as Blaise Pascal, the brilliant seventeenth-century science apologist, reminds us in his "thoughts," "there is enough light for those who desire only to see."[7]

I am not at all suggesting that the narrative is void of direction in how God wants human beings to live. It is not. In Exodus 20, we have one of the ancient world's early codes of behavior in the form of the Ten Commandments. These ten statements provide clear foundational principles for the way that human beings are to relate to each other in families and in community and how they are to relate to the God who gave these principles. There is to be respect and honoring of one's parents; there is to be no killing, no telling lies about each other, no violating of sexual integrity, no stealing, and no yearning for what belongs to someone else. God, the Creator and Sustainer of all that is, is to be revered above all other gods, is not to be confused with anything in creation

5. If you are not familiar with this overall narrative, you might want to read James Bryan Smith, *The Magnificent Story: Uncovering a Gospel of Beauty, Goodness, and Truth* (Downers Grove, IL: IVP Books, 2017).

6. For a full exploration of the cosmic meaning of this final dying, see Fleming Rutledge, *Crucifixion: Understanding the Death of Jesus Christ* (Grand Rapids: Eerdmans, 2017).

7. Blaise Pascal, *Pensées*, trans. A. J. Krailsheimer (New York: Penguin, 1966), 80.

itself, and is to be remembered as God by setting aside one day each week for rest, restoration, and renewal in proper relationship with that God. There are other specific and, indeed, absolutist rather than relativist guidelines for behavior scattered throughout the Old and New Testaments. Often these guidelines are given in specific contexts. The most obvious example would be the exquisitely precise dietary and clothing-related regulations of the book of Leviticus, which provided a framework for a people on pilgrimage through the desert. It is a matter of debate both in the Jewish and Christian traditions how much of this framework was intended for all time.[8] One of the strongest summaries of the law comes from the mouth of the Lord Jesus himself in the context of the New Testament. When one of the Pharisees comes to Jesus asking which of the commandments is the greatest, the narrative provides the additional interpretative detail that the question is meant "to test him" (Matt. 22:35). Jesus responds with great clarity: "You shall love the Lord your God with all your heart, and with all your soul, and with all your mind. This is the greatest and first commandment. And a second is like it: 'You shall love your neighbor as yourself.' On these two commandments hang all the law and the prophets" (vv. 37–40). Interestingly, Jesus chooses to answer not from the Ten Commandments as recorded in Exodus 20, nor even from the reaffirmation of these commandments in Deuteronomy 5 as the children of Israel were about to enter the promised land. Rather, he quotes from the summary commandment, in Deuteronomy 6:4–5, that has become known as the Shema and taken to be the essence of the Jewish tradition to this day. Nevertheless, when he chooses the summary version of the commandments, there is no hint of relativism or ambiguity.

It is quite understandable that some who want to honor God would choose to shape their lives and the lives of their communities in an effort to obey and to defend the absolute inviolability of one or another of these absolutist commandments. The best example of this in our time is the pro-life movement's effort to ground its absolute ban against the taking of the life of the unborn on the commandment not to kill. It is also understandable, then, that those who see this command in tension with other teaching in the Scriptures—or for whatever other reasons do not believe this absolute prohibition is the best way to organize a society—would then move to a polar-opposite position. The nature of the case is that to give any leeway on the one side or the other is seemingly to abandon the absolute nature of God's commandment. God

8. For example, whether one abides by these dietary restrictions determines which branch of the Jewish tradition one affiliates with. The Seventh-day Adventist denomination, within the Christian tradition, is stricter than most other Christians in honoring many of these guidelines up to the present.

says, "Do not kill." God does not say, "Sometimes do not kill," or "When it is convenient, do not kill." God says, "Do not kill." So it is not a mystery that there is polarization around this and a host of other issues in our culture—and at most times in church history. Nor is it a surprise that this commitment to one pole or another is often grounded in the Scriptures. One cannot *sort* of obey an absolutist commandment, nor can one form a legal framework for an organization of any kind with policies that sometimes apply. A polarized world does not need to be explained. It is, in fact, the default in a world that seeks to create clear lines between what is "right" and "wrong" and between what is "good" and what is "evil."

Nor am I suggesting that the Scriptures are without many examples that suggest the appropriateness of binary thinking. We can start in the Garden of Eden.[9] The prohibition not to eat of the tree of knowledge of good and evil is absolute. The terms are clear. Adam and Eve are instructed to honor that prohibition under all circumstances. There are no exemptions. A bit later in the canon, there is the resounding invitation delivered by Joshua in Joshua 24:15 to the children of Israel as he is about to die: "Choose this day whom you will serve"—either the gods that surround you on every side in the land or the God who brought you out of Egypt. You cannot have it both ways.[10] This call to hard choices is also found in the New Testament. In the Gospel of Matthew, we are told in no uncertain terms by the Lord Jesus that we cannot serve two masters; either you serve God or you serve wealth (6:24). It is impossible to be utterly devoted to two patterns of living. Later in the same Gospel, we are told the parable of the sheep and the goats (25:31–46), calling us to imagine a picture of the end of the world, when all nations will be judged to be either "sheep" or "goats" depending on how they treated those among them who were considered "the least of these who are members of [the King's] family" (v. 40). There are no two ways about it—no hybrids in the parable. Either you are invited as a sheep to "inherit the kingdom" or you are banished to "eternal fire prepared for the devil and his angels" (vv. 34, 41). There are those on the right hand and those on the left hand. No middle way. There are clarion calls in the Scripture to shape our lives in one way rather than another, and we must be attentive to these calls if we would be faithful members of God's family. There are times when we must choose one side or another. It is understandable why the notion of a third way or any alternative to a moral or spiritual world of "black" and "white" seems inimical to many in the Christian tradition.

9. See the account of the fall in Gen. 2:15 through chap. 3.
10. For a fuller description of the context for this invitation, see Josh. 23 and 24.

What I am suggesting is that woven throughout the Scripture, alongside the absolutist commands and often inextricably mixed with the portrayals of black-and-white clarity, is a picture of a third way—no less grounded in conviction or commitment to God's kingdom rule but more complicated and less able to be defended by a particular passage of Scripture. The necessity of this alternative pathway is occasioned by one of the very first narratives in the Bible—the "fall." Next to the cosmic significance of creation itself, the implications of the fall have served to shape the terms of our world perhaps more significantly than anything else. There is much that we do not understand practically about what happened when the first man and woman chose not to honor the one prohibition God had given them. What we do understand, theologically at least, is that every person, every situation, every relationship, every aspect of the created order was forever changed—and not for the better. There is a pervasive twistedness, a bentness, that has marked all that God has created and intended from that point on. C. S. Lewis speaks of it in terms of "infection,"[11] an image that has taken on powerful new meaning for us since the beginning of the COVID-19 pandemic. There was no preventive vaccination available for the impact of the fall.

The practical impact of this cosmic event is that every person and situation exhibit the marks of both the creation and the fall. The promise and beauty of God's creation is still there. But so is the bentness of the fall. The impact of the creation and the fall are inextricably intertwined in such a way that no one can be said to be all "good" or all "evil"; no one can be said to be totally in the "right," but no one is totally in the "wrong" either. As we deal with each other, we must remember that we are dealing with someone who bears the image of the eternal Trinity. We must also remember that this image is marred. We must reckon with both realities in every moment of our earthly pilgrimage.[12]

This reality is especially critical as we seek to move beyond any kind of polarization or binary understanding. Each person is worthy of our respect. Each person has the potential for being a bearer of truth, beauty, and goodness. No person—no matter their appearance to the contrary—is free from the impact of the fall. No matter the goodness of intent, there will be a gap between that intent and the execution. On the other hand and most significantly, no person or situation is beyond the reach of God's redemptive improvisation. God is at work in each person and situation, seeking to bring about truth,

11. See C. S. Lewis, *Mere Christianity* (New York: HarperCollins), 172–77.
12. One of the most powerful essays on the implications of this complex reality is C. S. Lewis's "The Weight of Glory," from the collection of essays by that name. C. S. Lewis, "The Weight of Glory," in *The Weight of Glory* (New York: HarperCollins, 2001), 25–46.

beauty, and goodness, and he invites us to be active partners in this project of cosmic restoration. So whatever appears to be the case, in each example of adversarial polarization, there is truth to be gleaned from each side. There is wisdom and insight to be wrested from everyone along the spectrum of polarization. And there is a path forward to be forged creatively that reflects the impact of having dealt respectfully with all that one has learned. It is not simply the averaging out of all perspectives, nor a bland compromise, nor a submission to one or two of the most powerful voices. It is an entirely new vision, animated by the holy imagination of the person who has dared to follow God into the fray of his fallen creation.

The nature of God's written revelation to us also calls for an engagement with the text that goes beyond passive reception or an approach that reads any one passage apart from the context of the entire biblical framework. No matter how well-intended those who base a position on just one of the biblical themes or commands are, there is a need for other voices to help set those voices in the context of the whole of God's written revelation. The Scriptures, at first glance, do not always seem to speak with one voice. The complexity of God's written revelation matches the complexity of the created but fallen world in which it has been given. Most obviously, as we have already mentioned, it is composed of a range of genres. Poetic truth (reflected in the Psalms, Proverbs, and the Song of Solomon—those parts of the Scripture known as the Wisdom literature) requires a different hermeneutic than truth mediated through historical texts (e.g., 1 and 2 Kings, 1 and 2 Chronicles), and both are different from the nature of truth mediated through prophecy (e.g., Isaiah, Jeremiah, Hosea, Amos) or apocalyptic texts (e.g., Daniel, Revelation). God's written revelation was composed over a period of centuries—no matter which view one takes on the authorship of particular portions of Scripture— and it emerged from radically different cultural contexts. Furthermore, the teachings of biblical revelation, taken as a whole, embody within it tensions, to say the least. Some might even say absolute contradictions. How do we find a theological unity that combines the biblical prohibition of killing with the myriad accounts of slaughter by God's people, carried out in God's name and apparently receiving divine approval? And that is even before adding in Jesus's blessing of peacemakers in the Beatitudes (see Matt. 5:9). So we have those who frame a theology of just war and those who frame a theology of pacifism, both claiming to honor the Scriptures.[13] Someone needs to come along and seek to reckon what each side has seen and lead God's people

---

13. See, for example, Roland H. Bainton, *Christian Attitudes toward War and Peace: A Historical Survey and Critical Re-evaluation* (1960; repr., Eugene, OR: Wipf & Stock, 2008).

beyond the legitimacy of each position to a vision that honors both what each has seen clearly and how each is incomplete.

How do we come to see the God of the Bible as a unity when so often the God of Old Testament justice does not seem remotely like the God of New Testament love?[14] How do we reconcile the biblical passages that suggest that God hears and answers even our most seemingly impossible prayers (e.g., Matt. 17:20) with what appears to be clear and pervasive evidence to the contrary, even within the Scriptures themselves (see, e.g., Saint Paul's discussion of the "thorn in the flesh" in 2 Cor. 12)? Perhaps most troubling of all for those through the ages who have wanted to believe, how do we understand a God who is supposedly all powerful and all seeing and all love, but who risked a creation that would make possible the magnitude of suffering that we see in our world, especially the suffering of innocent children, and then apparently put a stamp of approval on perpetuating that suffering for eternity? The human effort to make sense of a God like that, mercifully, begins within the biblical text itself, in the book of Job. The permission to wrestle honestly with perplexity and even apparently to bring this wrestling to God directly is granted liberally, not only in the book of Job but throughout the Psalms. Yes, the biblical revelation is a book of questions—as much as it is a book of answers. It includes in its pages a place for mystery, the aspects of our existence that await further understanding from God. In the comprehensiveness and complexity of the overall revelation, the Bible illumines the full range of our experiences in this earthy pilgrimage. It certainly provides fodder for those who see their calling as crusaders for some aspect of the truth of the Scripture. But it also permits—indeed, compellingly invites—those who would have the courage to work actively among all the crusaders to help them see each other and to move forward under a more complete banner of God's entire revelation.

Finally, the biblical revelation, as a whole, recognizes that truth must be mediated into concrete situations before it can do its proper liberating work (see John 8:32). One can have the most eloquent and internally coherent systematic theology—of any scope—and if it is simply viewed in the abstract, it becomes a weapon of power and control and not of redemptive transformation. Furthermore, the more fully coherent and compelling such a theology would be in speaking to one period of history, the less relevant it might be to others. Part of the genius of God's written revelation, part of what would seem to count for its trustworthiness, is that it does not purport to speak in eternal terms of logically consistent abstraction. Rather—and somewhat paradoxically,

---

14. Once again, I reference here Walter Brueggemann's expansive exploration of these issues in his *Theology of the Old Testament*.

to be sure—its universal appeal over the centuries and around the world is grounded in its particularity—indeed, in its diversity of particularity. The biblical revelation is universal, precisely because all persons, no matter what century or what continent of the globe they are in, can see themselves in the convicting mirror of its message. God's Word speaks to us not primarily by telling but by showing. It teaches us by showing God's interaction with real individuals amid their concrete and often very complicated circumstances. It is to examples of these individual encounters that we now turn.

Examples of Biblical Characters Called to Lead from Middle Space

Yes, Scripture does provide guidance for those who want to ground their communities in its clear teachings. Such communities have sought to embody in their particular times and places the black-and-white teachings of either the Old or New Testaments, as given to the children of Israel as they were being formed as a people on their way to the promised land or as given by our Lord Jesus Christ to the community of his followers, who were being formed as a new Israel in the first century. We see examples of this approach in John Calvin's sixteenth-century Geneva or in the various community "rules" of the orders of the church under Rome, beginning with Saint Benedict and continuing with the Franciscans, the Dominicans, the Augustinians, the Jesuits, and the host of others who sought to show the world what a tangible embodiment of God's people might look like.

The Scriptures also provide a mandate for those who feel called to live out a faith-filled discipleship as active agents of stewarding what is mysterious and perplexing in the Scriptures, in the context of the complexities of this created yet fallen world. They are confident of God's truth, but they are also humbly and fully aware that as fallen, finite creatures, they must recognize their own inadequacy to access that truth fully. They know that because of the fall, good and evil, right and wrong, will be inextricably intertwined in each situation and in each person, including in their own person. They know that being a person of the truth is more than having cognitive "head" knowledge. Being of the truth requires a wisdom—a practical understanding—of how to apply this knowledge productively in the context of real and often extremely complicated circumstances. They are so clear on who they are as God's children that they will venture boldly into spaces of ambiguity and complexity to be active agents of making the truth of God's power and presence more fully and comprehensively visible. They are culturally and often linguistically bilingual, able to interpret and translate for others who are monolingual and, thus, to cultivate and nourish a common community beyond the differences. Finally, they know that they are not in charge of the world—they are not called to be heroes on the models of the gods of Greek and Roman legend. They are called to be faithful servants of the God of all creation, who will accomplish his purposes for the cosmos and has invited us to be creative partners in that redemptive enterprise.

We will explore briefly five biblical examples of such characters: Joseph, Moses, Daniel, Esther, and Paul. Four of these come from the Old Testament, one from the New. While there are differences in their stories, there are also compelling commonalities. All are young. All are called and prepared to understand who they are as God's children and to embody that identity through faithful practices. All are offered opportunities to expand their knowledge and understanding of the world beyond the knowledge of their particular community's tradition. All find themselves living out their lives in cross-cultural contexts that do not understand or support their identity as children of God. All are recognized—even in these contexts, in which they are not fully at home—for their skills, wisdom, and capacity to render service to the cultures in which they find themselves and invited into leadership positions. In the context of these leadership positions, all proactively, creatively, and imaginatively magnify opportunities for God to be magnified and to be at work in those spaces. Finally, all see a way forward in the midst of their circumstances, a way that draws on the multiple resources available to them, but one that has not been imagined by others. It is not a bland compromise or a messy patching together; it is a new thing altogether. Furthermore, the way forward benefits not just them or those like them, but the entire community in which they find themselves.

In their stories, we find validation and inspiration for the work of middle space that we are called to do in our contemporary circumstances, in which God's people find themselves in various contexts of "exile," where they do not feel entirely at home.[15]

Joseph

We meet Joseph in the book of Genesis. He is the eleventh son of Jacob, the third of the Old Testament patriarchs, and the first son of Jacob's favorite

---

15. This metaphor of exile has been developed explicitly in such works as Walter Earl Fluker, *The Ground Has Shifted: The Future of the Black Church in Post-racial America* (New York: New York University Press, 2016), which explores its value for understanding the current context of the Black church. A similar work is Mark R. Schwehn, *Exiles from Eden: Religion and the Academic Vocation in America* (Oxford: Oxford University Press, 2005). The metaphor has implicit application to most of the contexts in our world today where Christians are seeking to live out their callings.

wife, Rachel.[16] We are told that Joseph is Jacob's favorite son—he has made Joseph a special robe as a mark of that special relationship. Joseph also has dreams suggesting that, though he is at the time the youngest of Jacob's sons, he will someday stand out above all his older brothers. Furthermore, he has no qualms about sharing these dreams, much to the annoyance of his brothers. At some point, they have had enough. On one occasion, Jacob sends Joseph to locate his brothers, who are tending the family flocks away from home, and to bring him back news of their well-being. The brothers see their opportunity for revenge. Separated from their father's special protection, Joseph is an easy target. They think of killing him but opt instead, upon the oldest brother's advice, to throw him in a pit. Finally, seeing the chance both to get rid of him and to profit in doing so, they sell him to a band of traders on their way to Egypt. In the language of today, Joseph is the victim of human trafficking. In Egypt, Joseph experiences a series of injustices that could well have disillusioned him and left him angry and bitter. First, he is sold to Potiphar, one of Pharaoh's guards, who sees very soon that Joseph is a man of integrity and gifted in management. He is put in charge of Potiphar's household. All is going well until Potiphar's wife decides to seduce him. When Joseph refuses to accede to her plans, she tricks him and makes it appear as if Joseph has attacked her. Potiphar takes his wife's word and sends Joseph to prison. Joseph's leadership skills quickly become evident to the master jailer, who puts Joseph in charge of all the prisoners, so much so that we are told that the chief jailer doesn't worry at all about anything in Joseph's care (Gen. 39:23).[17]

It turns out that the very gift of interpreting dreams that had been Joseph's nemesis within his family becomes ultimately the avenue to his freedom. He first interprets successfully the dreams of two of his fellow prisoners. Though the cupbearer is restored to his former role in Pharaoh's house, as Joseph predicts, he forgets Joseph's request to bring his case to Pharaoh's attention—at least for a long time. It is not until Pharaoh himself has troubled dreams and can find no one among the Egyptians to interpret these dreams that the cupbearer remembers. Pharaoh summons Joseph immediately. Here at least is a new possibility in his moment of panic and desperation to understand the

16. For the entire biblical account, see Gen. 37–50.

17. Interestingly, we are also told explicitly that in these two places of confinement, where Joseph is the victim of injustice, God is with him. Where we might expect God's presence to result in the freeing of Joseph and the correction of injustice, we read instead that God gives him favor with those under whose authority he finds himself. At least in Joseph's life, God's steadfast love manifests itself in such a way that Joseph is sustained within a context of injustice rather than freed from it. This is not the evidence of God's presence that Joseph would have chosen, nor would we.

meaning of his puzzling dreams. After being cleaned up, Joseph is ushered into Pharaoh's presence and told of the dreams. Joseph testifies that it is not really him but God who provides the interpretation. Whether Pharaoh notices this or not, we are not told. What catches his attention is the interpretations of the two dreams, which turn out to be the same. Seven years of plenty are coming to his land, to be followed by seven years of severe famine. He is being given an opportunity to plan for the famine during the years of plenty. Joseph offers not only an interpretation of the dreams but also a strategic plan to act on the information delivered to Pharaoh. While Joseph does not volunteer for the task of leading the execution of the plan, Pharaoh decides that he is the person to do it. His managerial skills, honed in Potiphar's household and in prison, are now to be tested at an entirely new level. He is placed over the entire project of preparing for the expected famine and put in a position of leadership within Egypt, second only to Pharaoh himself—and all this by the time he is thirty years old (Gen. 41:46).

From here, the story gets even more complicated. The famine turns out to reach well beyond Egypt. Back in Joseph's homeland, Jacob hears that there is grain to be had in Egypt. He sends the oldest ten of his sons, keeping back Joseph's younger brother, Benjamin, to Egypt to buy grain. Joseph recognizes his brothers immediately, though they do not recognize him—understandably, given the circumstances under which they had last seen him. Joseph plots a series of events that eventually results in Jacob sending even Benjamin— Joseph's younger brother and son of his own mother, Rachel—down to Egypt, despite his father's profound reluctance to do so. When he is satisfied that his brothers have appropriately come to terms with their earlier behavior that had caused great pain for him (but even more significantly in that culture, for his father), Joseph chooses to do one of the world's first recorded and perhaps still most fantastic "reveals." He orders a great feast, invites his brothers, and tells them who he is. He then invites them to bring their entire extended family, including his father Jacob, to Egypt and arranges with Pharaoh for them to have land in nearby Goshen, where they will be free to engage in their work of shepherding—an occupation much looked down upon by the Egyptians. And thus, the children of Israel land in Egypt of their own free will, a place where they will remain for several hundred years and in which they will eventually become abject slaves of the Egyptians.

There is much in Joseph's story of value even to God's people today. The mysterious line in Genesis 45:5–8, where Joseph credits God, not his brothers, as ultimately responsible for his being trafficked into Egypt, has been a source of both comfort and dismay to God's children throughout the centuries. Of course, we are glad to know that God is in charge. But if God is in charge, can't he get his redemptive work done some other way? Certainly, we are open to being God's partners, but we would prefer to choose our particular roles. Then, in the final moving scene in Genesis, we see Joseph tearfully forgiving his brothers, also in tears, fearful that now that their father is dead, Joseph will finally have his revenge on them. Joseph instead sets an example for all who have ever been tempted to lord their power over those who are at their mercy. He essentially explains to them, "Whatever it looks like to you, you are not in my hands. You are in God's hands. God is in charge, not me. And whatever evil you might have intended when you sold me to those traders so many years ago, God intended it for good."

For our purposes, however, we want to notice in particular those features of the story that allow Joseph to point the way forward for a human community caught in circumstances for which no one else had a solution. It is a solution that draws on elements gleaned from his experience within two otherwise mutually exclusive and even antagonistic communities. No one within either community could, by him- or herself, arrive at the solution. It is a new thing, conceived out of the imagination of someone with the courage to be fully himself and fully at the disposal of God's purposes for his life, even amid complex circumstances in which no formulaic or abstract set of black-and-white principles could have prepared him. Joseph's leadership rests on such seemingly disparate tools as his ability to interpret dreams—not in the fashion of the Egyptian magicians but in the tradition of his fathers—and his well-honed management skills developed mostly in Egypt. He treats everyone he encounters with respect and dignity—whether those in prison or those in Pharaoh's household. He knows the language and customs of his homeland as well as the language and customs of Egypt. He is bilingual and bicultural. Consequently, he knows how to mobilize those under his command in Egypt to orchestrate the several acts of the puzzling power drama that results in the final redemption of his family and the well-being of the entire multicultural community under his authority. He is willing to be misunderstood by both communities for the sake of what he understands as his calling to bring a new and previously unimagined good into being. Who could possibly have anticipated a Hebrew slave becoming second-in-command in Pharaoh's Egypt? Throughout all of this, he does not rely on his own ingenuity alone. He puts his trust in God, even when he does not understand what God could possibly be doing.

Moses

What starts out as a tale of redemption and freedom under Joseph turns progressively ugly for the children of Israel. Joseph, who in the book of

Genesis refuses the offer of his brothers to be his slaves, passes away (Gen. 50:18–21). A new pharaoh, who doesn't know Joseph, comes into power (Exod. 1:8). The children of Israel have, in fact, become a perceived threat to the Egyptian people, among whom they find themselves. At the command of the new pharaoh, they are intentionally turned into the slaves of the Egyptians, a bondage that becomes ever more inhumane as time goes on. It even comes to the point where the Egyptians order midwives to kill all male babies as they are born. One Hebrew family seeks to save their newborn boy by hiding him in the reeds on the edge of the river. When he is discovered by Pharaoh's daughter, she brings him to the palace and raises him as her own son (Exod. 2:10).

Moses, a Hebrew child, grows up then amid the splendor of the royal palace, even as his own people continue in slavery. When, as a young man, he sees an Egyptian beating one of his own people, he kills the Egyptian in the heat of anger. When Pharaoh discovers what has happened, he seeks to kill Moses, who flees immediately to the land of Midian. In this new homeland, Moses marries and settles down as a shepherd—that is, until one day God calls to him out of a burning bush and asks him to return to Egypt to deliver his people. After a great deal of negotiation (Exod. 3–4), Moses returns—reluctantly, to say the least—along with his brother Aaron as spokesman, to tell the new ruling pharaoh to let the Hebrew children have the freedom to worship their God in the nearby wilderness. Pharaoh, instead of granting the request, takes this as a sign that the Hebrew slaves have entirely too much time on their hands and orders that their work be made even harder by having to collect the straw to make their same quota of bricks.

Rather than appreciating Moses's effort to obtain them more freedom, the Hebrew slaves blame Moses for making their slavery even more onerous. God continues to call Moses (and now his brother Aaron as well) to keep asking. The drama continues, settling into a pattern of Pharaoh initially agreeing, then backing out, only to be followed by a series of intensifying signs of divine judgment on the people of Egypt (see Exod. 6–12). At the end of a series of plagues—including frogs, locusts, flies, and polluted water, to mention a few—God warns Moses of the final plague. God will be coming through Egypt to take the life of every firstborn member of each family and herd of livestock. In order to preserve the children of Israel, Moses is instructed to post on the door of each of their homes a sign made with the blood of a sacrificed lamb. This will alert God to pass over their homes, while inflicting death on the firstborn of the Egyptians and their other slaves and livestock.

Not surprisingly, Pharaoh, after witnessing this wave of death throughout his kingdom, including his own household, has had enough. He gives the

Hebrews permission to leave. Moses has prepared them for a swift departure. They flee in the direction of the Red Sea, only to be followed by Egyptian chariots after Pharaoh once again changes his mind. God continues to act on behalf of his people, parting the Red Sea so that they can cross on dry ground and then drowning the pursuing Egyptians once the children of Israel have crossed over safely. The ongoing story of their journey through the desert on the way to the promised land of Canaan is recorded in the rest of the book of Exodus. It is a long and wandering journey in the wilderness, punctuated by repeated accounts of the weary children of Israel complaining to Moses that it really would be better if they had never left Egypt, only to be followed by some responding new sign of God's faithful provision for their needs.[18] It is during this wilderness season that God delivers the Ten Commandments to the people, provides them with precise instructions for the building of a tabernacle of worship, and lays out for them patterns that will guide their life together as a society as well as their relationship with their God. The story of their deliverance from Egypt, the exodus, becomes not only their defining story of identity as a people (for centuries) but also the foundation upon which their relationship with their God is to be built. This is the God who has brought them out of slavery and has invited them to be a new people—indeed, a special people, shaped by their own powerful and peculiar story of deliverance and invited to become agents of generosity and freedom in the lives of others around them.

While the exodus story has a particular meaning for those in the Jewish tradition, it is also the story of the spiritual journey of each of God's children—no matter their time or place. Israel's repeated failures to trust, its engagement in active rebellion, and the persistent reminders of God's character, mercy, and provision all have parallels in our own stories. Once again, God's Word is universally powerful because it emerges out of the concrete stories of particular circumstances.

Despite the larger potential application of the exodus for all of our stories of discipleship, and despite its value for aspiring leaders as they learn from Moses's dealing with the children of Israel, we are concerned here with Moses's special preparation to lead his people forward out of the paralyzing, polarizing relationship with the people of Egypt. Through no fault or apparent choosing of his own, Moses finds himself in uncomfortable middle space. He knows that he cannot fit all of who he is within either of the poles of identity

---

18. While we are not wandering in the desert, we can recognize the familiar human tendency to prefer known suffering, no matter how egregious, to the promise of a potential but unknown and uncertain future relief.

he sees before him. He cannot feel fully at home within Pharaoh's palace. Nor is his experience at all fully congruent with that of his family of birth. And yet it is these very burdens of the painful "inbetweenness" that God turns into gifts to prepare Moses for his unprecedented opportunity to help God's people imagine a new life for themselves. They have known themselves only in relation to their slavery. God invites Moses to help them renew their identity as the chosen people of the God of their fathers, Abraham, Isaac, and Jacob. None of his experiences in the middle space is wasted. He has acquired the capacity to speak multiple languages and an understanding of the customs of both the Egyptians and the Hebrews, thus enabling him to be an effective translator between the relevant antagonistic parties. He has also had an entrée into the court of Pharaoh that would not have been readily available to any of his fellow Hebrew brothers and sisters. While his "middling" identity would make those on both poles at times suspicious of his trustworthiness, he earns sufficient credibility to "host" the ensuing drama that results eventually in a resolution that no one could possibly have imagined. Who could possibly have planned for a path through a body of water—and the subsequent weaponization of this very water to destroy the Egyptians?[19]

Daniel

Several centuries later, long after the conquest of the promised land, after the period of the Judges and the glory days of the Israelite kingdom of David and Solomon, God's people once again find themselves at the mercy of a foreign power. The northern part of the kingdom had been conquered in the eighth century BCE by the Assyrians. The Southern Kingdom, known as Judah, had continued to survive for over a century on its own. Finally, in 586 BCE, the Babylonians, a people located in roughly the current area of Iraq, had invaded Jerusalem, destroyed the Solomonic temple, and carried away the majority of the people—the ones healthy enough to travel—to their homeland of Babylon. Among these prisoners of war were a young child of God's chosen people and three of his friends. Daniel and his fellow captives soon came to the attention of the Babylonian king for their noble lineage, their physical health, and their apparently wide-ranging knowledge of the world as potential ideal servants in the king's palace. They were to be given a special diet and put through a three-year training program in the languages and culture of their new homeland, at the end of which they were to be given an assignment in the king's court.

---

19. For a full recounting of the exodus journey after leaving Egypt, see Exod. 14–40.

Once again, one of God's children finds himself involuntarily in a place where he does not fit fully into any of the available spaces. Daniel finds himself given the best that the kingdom of Babylon can offer. And while he is successful in the assignments given to him, he knows that he does not, nor will he ever, feel at home in Babylon. In fact, he determines intentionally to commit to the habits of diet and religious devotion of his native land, so that even in this strange place of exile, he will remember his core identity. As the story unfolds, Daniel is caught in several dilemmas, always with life-and-death stakes, between his dual but ultimately mutually exclusive loyalties. Despite every effort to fulfill his obligations as an increasingly trusted servant to several successive leaders of his new home, he cannot ultimately do anything that conflicts with his most fundamental and defining loyalty as a child of the God of Israel. In each case, however, it is his very commitment to occupy this middle space with integrity, without making himself smaller to make things easier for himself or for anyone else, that enables him to move beyond the apparently paralyzing dilemmas of his circumstances to a new place of productive service to those around him. Daniel's bold decision to offer to interpret the king's dreams, thus saving the lives of the Babylonian "wise men," and then even more dramatically not to cease praying at his regular time to his own God—in both cases in full awareness of the potentially dire consequences—earns him the respect in the first instance of the Babylonian king, Nebuchadnezzar, and in the second instance of King Darius, the king of the Medes whose kingdom succeeds in conquering the Babylonians. In each case, Daniel's courageous commitment to the complexity of his loyalties, both as a civil servant in his home of captivity and as a servant of the God of his birthplace, earns him new and added responsibilities and respect for his God. His faithful navigation of this space—empowered, as in the earlier narratives, by his bilingual and bicultural training and his own dogged commitment to faithful obedience to God's calling—enables him to imagine alternatives pointing a way beyond the mutually exclusive options that circumstances have created for him. In Daniel's case, they enable him to continue using this complexity of gifts to be a credible and powerful witness to the God of his people, even as he continues to bring his outstanding gifts to the service of his community of captivity.[20]

Esther

Just over a century after Daniel had found himself a prisoner of war in the kingdom of the Babylonians, another member of God's chosen people, Esther,

20. See the entire story in the book of Daniel.

finds herself an orphan amid the equally foreign but even more powerful kingdom of the Medes and Persians. Her uncle Mordecai, who had adopted her
as his own daughter, is a descendant of one of the southern tribes of Judah
that had been carried away to Babylon decades earlier, along with Daniel
and his friends. The options for young women at the time, especially when
they are orphans and presumably without an established lineage or dowry,
are limited. When her uncle hears of the king's open competition for a new
wife, he suggests to Esther that she enter, giving her careful instructions not to
reveal her ethnic identity in the course of the contest. Esther quickly becomes
a favorite of the supervisor of the king's harem, who provides all manner
of special beauty treatments to her so that she would be in the best possible
position to receive the king's favor. It works. When her invitation comes to
go to the king, she is chosen to be the new queen. We are told that "the king
loved Esther more than all the other women" (Esther 2:17).

Despite her chosen status as the new queen, Esther remains under a strict
set of rules that govern her access to the king. She continues to keep her family
identity private. Even while she submits to the close supervision of those in
charge of the royal harem, Esther also gives appropriate respect and obedience to her adoptive father, "just as when she was brought up by him" (Esther
2:20). Mordecai keeps watch over her well-being as best he can from outside
the palace. Esther is a woman of two worlds—seeking to be faithful to the
conflicting expectations of women in general and of herself in particular in
these two entirely different cultural frameworks.

We might never have heard of Esther if the story had stopped here. It
does not. The king's chief administrator, who has already commanded the
enforced loyalty of the king's officials and servants, becomes annoyed that
Mordecai, loyal to his Jewish tradition, doesn't bow down to him as everyone
else seems all too ready to do. Rather than simply punish Mordecai, Haman
dreams up a plot to kill all the Jews throughout the land, assuming that they,
too, might prove a threat to the supreme authority of the Persian leadership.
Convinced of Haman's argument, the king orders that the plan to execute
the entire Jewish population go forward. This first recorded, systematic effort
at "ethnic cleansing" might well have succeeded without what happens next.

Word of the order quickly spreads throughout the Jewish community in
the 127 provinces of the kingdom, causing understandable panic, fear, and
helplessness. It comes to Mordecai as well, sitting outside the royal palace,
who makes a point of signaling his grief in such a way that Queen Esther
sends word to find out what is troubling her beloved guardian. In his reply,
Mordecai includes a plea that the queen use her royal status to implore the
king to change his mind. Of course, Esther knows only too well the rules of

the palace. She is only supposed to go to the king when he invites her. To take that initiative on her own would open her to the possibility of immediate death, unless the king held out the golden scepter indicating that he was granting an audience to the uninvited guest. In back-and-forth dialogue with Mordecai—through third-party messengers, of course—Esther realizes that this might be the very moment for which she had been created. After all, what would her life be worth if all of her people were killed—even if she were spared within the palace—knowing that her voice might have saved her people? After soliciting a commitment from Mordecai to engage the Jewish community in prayer and fasting on her behalf, she agrees to risk her life and visit the king.

The king, much to Esther's relief, is immediately drawn to offer her an audience and to offer her whatever she might possibly request—"even to the half of my kingdom" (Esther 5:3). We will never know what would have happened if Esther had chosen on that first visit to ask for mercy for her people. We can only imagine the king's confusion as she attempts to make her case and her own personal reasons for taking up this risky adventure to bring the situation to the king's attention. Instead, she makes the simple and quite disarming request that the king and Haman be her guests at a banquet—a quiet event apparently just for the three of them. At the banquet, she again chooses to keep the king in suspense, asking that he and Haman come to a second banquet, at which she will finally provide the deeper reason for the requested meeting, information that the king is by now evidently quite curious about.

Unbeknownst to Haman, who is quite delighted at how his own plans are proceeding, the king has a sleepless night between the first and second banquet. Upon being reminded in the course of the typically soporific reading of the royal chronicles of a plot on his life that had been uncovered by Mordecai in time to save his life, he asks what had been done to reward this person. Nothing apparently, at least according to the record. King Ahasuerus immediately goes about doing what he had always done when wanting one of his desires executed expeditiously. He consults with his chief administrator, Haman. Ironically and much to Haman's annoyance, he is charged to carry out for Mordecai the very elaborate plan that he had recommended to the king for someone the king might want to honor—assuming, of course, that the intended recipient would be Haman himself.

Even amid processing this humiliation at the hands of one of the very persons he has arranged to kill, he is hurried off to the palace to be the special guest at the second of Queen Esther's exclusive feasts. Haman's life goes downhill precipitously. At this second banquet, Queen Esther tells the king of a plot to kill her and her people. This unexpected revelation is followed by the even more shocking news that it is Haman, his trusted servant, who has planned this entire massacre.

Haman is summarily hanged on the very gallows he had prepared to punish Mordecai. The king removes his signet ring from Haman and gives it to Mordecai, who is promoted over the entire house of Haman. At the queen's request, the king revokes the order to execute the Jewish people. The story ends with a great celebration among the Jewish people throughout the kingdom—their descendants of whom continue to commemorate this extraordinary deliverance in their annual ritual of Purim.

Esther's story comes from a culture far removed from the twenty-first-century world of most women in the West. It is a reminder nevertheless that even today, throughout the world and even our own country, the structures that shape women's lives are often quite different from and more constrained than those shaping the choices of their male contemporaries. It is also a reminder that God calls both men and women to significant tasks that can make a difference, not only for their families but for their entire communities. Esther, like Joseph, Moses, and Daniel before her, finds herself in a place that she has not chosen, caught between the customs of her own people, in a place far from their homeland, and those of the people among whom she finds herself. She is an orphan and thus vulnerable in ways that would not be considered the norm. She does not have the means, on her own, to find a place of comfortable belonging either among her own ethnic community or among the peoples of the Persian Empire. And yet, once again, it is out of this uncomfortable middle space that God calls her, with the particular gifts that she brings, coming as they do from both her connections with the Jewish people through Mordecai and her connections within the palace as the queen of the Persian monarch. It is through prayer, through her tradition's vision of God's sovereignty as Lord of history, and through the multitude of resources available to her as the king's consort, as well as through her own creativity and courage, that she is able to be the imaginative agent of a path beyond the confining and paralyzing dilemmas created for her and her people by Haman. While God might have found another way to deliver his people, as Mordecai reminds Esther in 4:14, she is given the opportunity to be the agent of that seeming impossibility if only she has the courage to step out into that risky space.

Paul

Once again, in the first century AD, the Jewish people find themselves under the domination of a foreign power, this time in their own homeland. They occupy one of the remote provinces of the vast Roman Empire, ruled politically by vassals of Rome and occupied by the Roman military. As always, God has not left his people without ambassadors to represent them in the context of the pagan, pluralistic culture of the empire. We know one of them as Saint Paul. Saul of Tarsus had been raised in a devout Jewish family to become an expert in Jewish law, a Pharisee. He was also a citizen of Rome and, as such, could travel freely throughout the empire and engage in commerce. He also had the right to a trial before being imprisoned or beaten, along with the privilege of making a legal appeal to the emperor himself. As we see from the stories of his travels in the book of Acts in the New Testament, this man was comfortable in whatever cultural setting he found himself—as much so in the Athenian marketplace, debating with the Epicureans and Stoics (Acts 17:18), as meeting with Jewish religious communities in local synagogues throughout the empire.

No doubt Saul of Tarsus could have lived a rich and interesting life as an interpreter of Jewish ethnicity and culture within the pluralistic context of the first-century Roman Empire. But God had an even bigger calling in mind for this most zealous of his children. One day, as we are told in Acts 9, as Saul was on his way to Damascus with authorization from the high priest to bring in any of his Jewish compatriots who were known to be followers of the newly proclaimed Messiah, Jesus of Nazareth, he is confronted with a bright light so powerful that it brings him to his knees. Out of the light comes a voice claiming to be Jesus himself. God is inviting Saul of Tarsus, precisely because of his stellar credentials as both a Jewish leader and a citizen of Rome, to use these gifts no longer to persecute the followers of Jesus but to become a designated instrument to bring his name beyond the bounds of the Jewish community to the entire world (Acts 9:15). Saul, soon to be renamed Paul, is to be the ambassador, the cross-cultural translator to carry the good news of God's intended purpose in sending God's Son to earth to the entire world. Jesus of Nazareth is to be a Savior—the promised Messiah—not just for his own Jewish people but for the entire human race. Upon recovering from the initial shock of being redirected in his mission, Paul begins this new phase of his ambassadorial work, explaining to the surprised Jews in the synagogue of Damascus that, contrary to his earlier understanding, Jesus of Nazareth really is their longed-for Messiah.

Paul's usefulness as a host of uncomfortable middle space amid the pluralistic Roman Empire is made even more effective and multidimensional as a result of his conversion from being persecutor of the Jewish rabbi Jesus to being his disciple. His credibility as a witness to the good news comes, in part at least, from his earlier zeal in rooting out the new sect. The young

Pharisee who had once held the coats of those who stoned the first of the early church's martyrs (Acts 7:58) is now at risk for the same treatment at the hands of others from both the Jewish and Roman communities, albeit for difference reasons.

It is clear from reading about his activities in the book of Acts and from his letters, which provided the primary foundation for the theology of the early church, that Paul understood both the nature and the complexity of his new calling to work in middle space. Paul now had to embody within himself, with integrity, not only his identities as a child of the Jewish covenant and as a citizen of imperial Rome but his new identity as a disciple of Jesus Christ. Three cultures, three histories, multiple languages—all contained in one person. This was not a matter of averaging out or blending or softening the distinctions among these three ways of life. Nor was it the spineless, bland, and timid activity of minimizing his convictions and making himself as invisible as possible so as not to offend. Paul's was the creative, imaginative, proactive effort—every moment of every day—of taking all that he knew of the truth from his entire history and experience, all that he understood about each of the cultures in which he operated, and investing it in a vision for those around him of a way forward that drew from but transcended any of the smaller realities that they had experienced. His calling involved communicating with Jews and the complex ethnic mix of gentiles in the empire, in ways that they could receive, the good news of a God whose love for them could fulfill all of their deepest longings and their highest hopes for the good life of becoming fully human. We get hints of Paul's intentionality in this effort in Acts 17, as he interacts with the Hellenistic philosophers in Athens; in his negotiations at the council of Jerusalem, as he seeks to find a way forward to a unified vision of the church beyond the polarized perspectives of the Jewish and gentile followers of Jesus (Acts 15); in the passionate introduction of his letter to the church of Rome (see Rom. 1, esp. v. 16); and in his nuanced instructions to the church at Corinth on navigating various, apparently irreconcilable dilemmas as the early Christians sought to understand the implications of their newfound faith for their daily, traditional Jewish rituals and social ethics (see esp. 1 Cor. 5–8). He says it all when he explains in 1 Corinthians 9 that he has found freedom "under Christ's law" to "become all things to all people, that I might by all means save some" (vv. 21–22). These are not the words of someone who has abandoned his convictions. This is someone who has felt compelled by his particular calling to draw on all the gifts that God has provided him, through his history, training, and experience, to translate the power and mystery of God's large and liberating gospel—with integrity—into the more confined categories of meaning he saw among those all around him. His was the task of empowering them to imagine a way beyond the limitations of the various polarized options they saw around them—whether these be poles of an ethical dilemma or poles of a particular ethnically shaped way of life.

Summary of Our Five Examples of Hosts of Middle Space

We have explored briefly five of the individual stories of God's calling of individuals over a span of many centuries, of God's inviting each of them to partner in a very particular kind of work amid his created but fallen world. In each of the cases we have explored, God's people found themselves amid either circumstances intentionally adversarial to their flourishing or understandings of the world too small, reductionistic, or rigid to embody the full richness of the revelation God intended for them. None of these examples will be exactly parallel to the worlds in which twenty-first-century readers find themselves. They could not possibly be. But they do suggest a theological home in the Scriptures for a calling—of some of God's followers in every age—to the intentional, imaginative, and costly work of hosting middle space in such a way as to lead God's people to new understandings of what it means to be fully at home as God's people even in contexts that, in every way, feel like places of exile. Furthermore, in so doing, each of these examples has contributed in some way to the well-being of the larger community—and not just those who might stereotypically have viewed themselves as "chosen."

Jesus, the Ultimate Host of Middle Space

Finally, while exploring a biblical home for the work of hosting middle space, we turn to the most complete embodiment of the ministry of uncomfortable middle space—our Lord Jesus himself. From start to finish, our Lord modeled for us what it is to live intentionally and with integrity as a hospitable, convening host inviting redemption to emerge from all the middle spaces of the cosmos. We might think of the four Gospel narrators of the New Testament as inspired artists, each painting a vast mural portraying the events in the life of Jesus of Nazareth, from his birth in Bethlehem to the end of his earthly life in Jerusalem. Continuing with the metaphor, the various theological voices of the New Testament become the docents leading us through the art gallery, inviting us to see the full range of rich details in each of the murals and attempting, each in his own way, to explain how this Jesus of Nazareth is in fact the second person of the Trinity in human form. This Jesus *is* the Messiah, not only representing the fulfillment of all the hopes and longings of the Jewish people for their own future but bringing the reign of God's shalom to the entire order of creation.

In the rest of this chapter, we will only identify hints from the New Testament writers that point to a foundation in the life of our Lord for the calling to the ministry of middle space. Coming to a full understanding of what it means to follow our Lord in his creative and redemptive work in this world is the compelling preoccupation of a lifetime.

There are several passages in the New Testament that explicitly describe the work of our Lord in terms that we might understand as middle space. Let me explain. First and perhaps most obviously, we are told in the introduction to the Gospel of John that this Jesus is the eternal Word that had been present in Genesis 1 at creation and that he has come in human form; in seeing Jesus, we are seeing the very glory of God himself. We are told that in Jesus, we are seeing the embodiment of the truth and grace of God. God is not just sending truth through Jesus, as God sent the law through Moses. Jesus is embodying the truth in his very person. Yes, God had showed us his law through Moses; in Jesus, God is showing us his very heart (John 1:14–18). This must have been astounding news to both Jews and gentiles of the first century. It was unimaginable in terms of either Jewish or classical understandings of divinity.

This Jesus, born of a woman in a small town in Palestine, is described as bringing together, authentically and fully in his person, the eternal Word or Logos and the nature of a finite human creature—a notion that would be puzzling at best in either contemporary Jewish or Greek terms. In Jesus, God has come in human form to accomplish the restoration of all that God had intended in creation (Gen. 1–2), of the relationship between God and human beings that had been ruptured (not to mention the relationships between these human creatures), and of the beauty of the entire created order that had been twisted almost beyond recognition in the fall (Gen. 2–3). It is echoed again in John 14:6 when John records Jesus's statement "I am the way, and the truth, and the life." It is not "I will tell you the truth for this situation," or "I will give you the truth in this doctrinal statement." Rather, "I *am* the truth." The complexity and mystery of this new reality defied all efforts to capture it fully in statements of doctrine and fueled the multiple heresies that have always swirled around the orthodoxies of the church throughout the centuries.

Paul describes this imaginative work of middle space with the metaphor of a bridge—indeed, of a bridge of peace that connects the Jews as God's chosen people, through whom God has revealed his plan for all of creation, with the entirety of God's human family. In his life and work and most specifically in his death, Jesus is said to have "in his flesh . . . made both groups into one and . . . broken down the dividing wall, that is, the hostility between us," thereby bringing a new united human community into restored relationship with God (Eph. 2:14; see more broadly vv. 11–22).

Before John and Paul could put into theological language the meaning of the life and death of Jesus of Nazareth, there were witnesses who saw this puzzling embodiment of grace and truth at work in complicated middling spaces—in particular conversations and activities Jesus partook in while walking the roads of first-century Palestine. Time and again, especially through his questions, Jesus invited individuals and groups to see beyond the current limitations of their categories and what they could imagine to be possible in the world. Jesus rarely responded to questions on the terms in which they were asked. His answers invited his interlocutors into a larger and more complex understanding of the world. For some, this invitation was freeing. For others, it was merely aggravating, for it messed up the safety and comfort of their controlled understanding of what it meant to live properly and deserving of both divine and community approval in the world.

The Woman at the Well

In the Gospel of John, chapter 4, we find Jesus waiting by a well in the Samaritan village of Sychar, while his disciples are getting food for the group to eat for lunch. When one of the local women comes to draw water, Jesus asks her for a drink. The woman is understandably taken aback. A Jewish man has asked her, a Samaritan woman, for a drink. This was simply not done in that context. Jesus is not deterred. He goes on to say that if she knew with whom she was speaking and what God wants to give her, she would be asking him for "living water" (v. 10). She is even more surprised. "But how would you get water without a bucket?" she might have added; "I thought you just asked me for a drink." Jesus then reveals that he is speaking of a spiritual water that would nourish her inner thirst. And though the first appeal of this offer seems to be that the woman would not have the inconvenience of having to come to the well, she apparently begins to see that this water on offer is something other than what she has encountered before. When Jesus suggests that she get her husband, it becomes clear that she is not living a conventional life for a woman of that time. The woman first tries to change the subject to a theological discussion about the different views of where God should be worshiped—a key point of controversy between Jews and Samaritans. Jesus points a way beyond the poles to a new vision of God. "God is spirit," says Jesus (v. 24). He goes on to say that right worship is not a matter of getting our geography right; it is a matter of getting our heart right. About this time, the disciples return to find Jesus, to their shock, speaking with a woman. (Apparently, that was even more radical than that she was a Samaritan woman of questionable repute.) The woman, meanwhile, leaves to report on her unusual trip to the well.

In this brief story, Jesus moves into space that challenges the customary divides between men and women and between Jews and Samaritans. Furthermore, while honoring the legitimate importance of seeking to worship "rightly," he also points beyond the seemingly irreconcilable choices between the holy mountains to an entirely new vision of what right worship means. We don't know what conversations might have happened among the disciples about the situation; we only get a hint of what the woman reports to her social circles, along with its transformative impact. No one leaves the well that day without a larger sense of possibilities than when their day had begun.

The Healing of the Paralyzed Friend

One day, when Jesus was teaching apparently inside an overcrowded room, a group of men, who were anxious to get Jesus's attention so that he would heal their colleague, let their paralyzed friend down through the ceiling. It was a creative way to get to the front of the line. Clearly, the man wanted to be restored physically. Jesus instead spoke to his spiritual condition first. "Friend, your sins are forgiven" (Luke 5:20). This was not what anyone had expected. The ordinary folk were puzzled. "What does sin have to do with paralysis?" The Pharisees looking on were offended, perhaps even outraged. "Who does this person think he is? Only God can forgive sins." Once again, Jesus does not provide a full explanation to anyone's satisfaction. He does raise the question of the relationship between physical and spiritual wholeness—Are the two as opposite as we usually think? The man goes away quite satisfied at being able to walk. We are told that everyone else goes away shaking their heads, saying, "We have seen strange things today" (Luke 5:26).

Besides suggesting that true wholeness is not a matter of either the body or the spirit but rather of some state beyond one or the other, Jesus has troubled the categories of the teachers of the law. They know that healing a person is a good thing, but purporting to forgive sins is blasphemous. How are they to fit this person into one of their neat categories of judgment?[21]

Nicodemus

One of the Pharisees had enough curiosity about Jesus to want a private conversation. We are told in John 3 that Nicodemus, a Pharisee and a ruler

21. For a full account of this incident, see Luke 5:17–26.

of the Jews, sought out Jesus at night—under cover, as it were. He is pre-sented as someone who had some honest questions about this rabbi that he did not want to ask among his more skeptical colleagues in the light of day. Nicodemus had seen evidence that Jesus was good and from God but also knew that Jesus did not fit his understanding of what such a person should be like. Rather than ease the puzzlement, Jesus only makes the conversation more interesting. He challenges Nicodemus's understanding of what it means to come into God's kingdom. It is not about being good or working signs; it is about being born again. Nicodemus, like countless other curious inquirers over the centuries, has no idea what this could possibly mean. Clearly, the road to God's presence and God's pleasure was not at all what he had been trained to expect. It was a different kind of journey altogether.

We would like to know more about this conversation. The last we hear, Jesus is returning Nicodemus's puzzled question with one of his own. It is not necessarily an unkind one, but it does seem to have a provocative edge. "Are you a teacher of Israel, and yet you do not understand these things?" (v. 10). It could not possibly have been what Nicodemus expected. He leaves with more questions than when he arrived (see vv. 1–10 more broadly).

The Rich Young Ruler

In Luke 10, we are told of another teacher of the law seeking out Jesus, this time apparently with less honorable motives than Nicodemus's. He wants to "test" Jesus. So he puts a question to Jesus about how he might "inherit eternal life" (v. 25). Perhaps he had heard rumors among his colleagues of the strange notion of being "born again." This time, Jesus says something that fits quite well into the standard categories of the Pharisees. "What does the law say?" The lawyer, of course, is only too happy to display his knowledge, and he cites the traditional Jewish summary of the law from Deuteronomy about loving God and loving one's neighbor. Jesus affirms the answer. The lawyer, wanting to push things further, then asks, "And who is my neighbor?" (v. 29). Rather than carefully delineating for him what might count as a neighbor in the technical terms of the Jewish legal tradition, Jesus responds with a story. The lawyer is not prepared for this.

The story confuses everything. The supposed "good guys" (the priest and Levite), in keeping with their usual patterns, do not have room in their lives to be of help to someone in need. They certainly are not treating the man as they would want to be treated if they had found themselves in a similar situation. But, of course, perhaps they cannot even imagine themselves in that situation. Instead, it is the pariah, the outsider Samaritan, who turns out to be the neighbor—who treats the robbed and wounded man as he himself would want to be treated. We are told that he comes near the wounded man; feels pity for him, as for a fellow human being; and takes care of him. He even goes out of his way and finds a place for him to stay and pays the fee. Here is a picture of imaginative generosity that goes far beyond a formal legal requirement. The lawyer gets the point. Fulfilling the law is, in the end, not about completing a legal checklist. It is about seeing real need on one's path and having the desire and the will to meet that need. It is a new way of thinking—not part of the lawyer's curriculum up to that point.

The Questions of the Pharisees Sent to Trap Jesus

Throughout Jesus's earthly journey, he regularly encountered the religious leaders of his day. It makes sense that they were hanging around and paying attention. They wanted to know what to make of this person who seemed to care about the issues they cared about but not in the usual ways. His answers never fit into their categories. Furthermore, while claiming to honor the law, he called them to a much more expansive understanding of their obligations than even the most devout among them could imagine.[22] Toward the end of Luke's Gospel, we have a particularly pointed description of their interaction with Jesus.

We are told in Luke 20:20 that the religious leaders deliberately sent people to entrap Jesus, hoping to find a legitimate basis on which to take him into custody. They ask Jesus about paying taxes to Caesar, a particularly sensitive matter for Jews, since it seemed to put their loyalties to the emperor in tension with their loyalties to God. Shortly afterward, according to the text, some Sadducees frame a complicated question about the implications in the afterlife for a woman who had been betrothed to seven brothers successively. "To whom would she belong in the resurrection?" they ask. Since the Sadducees had questions about the nature of the resurrection itself, it is not entirely clear what they envision by this term. Mostly, they just want to see how Jesus answers. In both cases, Jesus refuses to fall into the trap of answering according to the confined categories anticipated by those who are asking. Instead, Jesus, while honoring the importance of the question, points beyond their frame of reference to a way of thinking that includes but expands their thinking. We are told that instead of forcing Jesus to respond on their terms,

---

22. See, for example, Matt. 5:17–48.

they recognize they have been taken beyond their depth. In both cases, there are no further questions!

Summary

We have only touched on a complete understanding of our Lord's work in middle space. We have seen enough, I trust, to alleviate the worries of any who fear that by bringing together those from various places on whatever spectrum of polarization we are encountering, we are therefore necessarily not "standing with Jesus." Yes, Jesus stands with all that is true. And we want to stand with Jesus in supporting in our time all that we believe is true. But our Lord regularly calls people beyond their current understanding of the truth and challenges their stereotypes of who is in and who is out. Furthermore, in the parable of the wheat and the tares (see Matt. 13:24–30), he explicitly discourages his followers from prematurely seeking to separate out the good guys from the bad. In this created but fallen world, sometimes the good and the bad are inextricably intertwined. We must leave this to God to sort out.

In seeking to be faithful to God's revelation in the Scriptures of the Old and New Testaments, it is certainly true that sometimes choosing to avoid any of the stark choices available on the poles can be an act of moral cowardice. Remaining in the middle can be a place of spiritual and ethical timidity or intellectual sloppiness. Furthermore, it can be a place utterly devoid of core convictions—where someone chooses simply to be blown about by the wind. (See James 1:6).

What we have sought to establish in this chapter is that in addition to those places in our moral and spiritual journeys that require clearly identifying with one side or another, there is a biblical and theological mandate—for *some* followers of God at least—to navigate the world with an eye toward noticing those places where the good and the right and the true are not so obvious. This way of life also requires conviction. It is the work of calling communities to imagine new possibilities that point beyond the all-too-often limited, binary, or polarized choices that fail to capture the complexities of this most strange and wondrous, created but fallen world.

While this is a risky way of life, as we shall see later—and one for which we do not have the kind of precise biblical guidance that we might wish for—we do have the promise that God has not left us alone in figuring it out. We can take great comfort in our Lord Jesus's promise in John 16:13 to send the Holy Spirit, the Spirit of truth, who will not only be our Advocate but also our Guide into all truth.[23] We dare proceed in our calling to work in middle space only in the confidence of that promise.

23. See the full context of the promise in John 15 and 16.

Questions for Discussion

1. What aspects of your own background have prepared you to be "bilingual" or "bicultural"? Where do you find yourself already doing the work of interpretation or translation between individuals or groups who do not understand each other?

2. What genres of the Scriptures speak most powerfully to you of God's overall narrative engagement with the world? The poetry? The history? The Gospels? The letters?

3. Identify a particular ethical or theological issue for which you would like clear guidance but which is not explicitly mentioned in the Scriptures. How would you go about exploring a biblical basis for thinking and behaving one way or another about this issue?

4. Think of a situation in your own journey in which you felt forced, either by your peers or by your church or your tradition, into choices that did not seem to capture the complexity of the goods at stake. What kinds of questions would you ask to help you imagine potential alternatives—alternatives that not only include what seems compelling in all the perspectives but also point beyond them?

4

Counting the Cost

A Risk Analysis of
Working in Middle Space

On a quiet Sunday afternoon during the fall semester of 2020, as I was squeezing in some Sabbath rest while also preparing mentally for the typical Monday morning onslaught in the president's office, I received notification from the chief student life officer that there was trouble brewing at the "Rock"—the large, artificial rock, sitting in a highly visible space in the center of campus, that had been established several years earlier by the student government as a context for the display of student opinion. All had gone well up to this point. The Rock had been used sometimes to convey words of celebration, sometimes words of protest. No one was obligated to "own" publicly what they painted on the Rock, nor was it assumed that others would agree with what had been written there. It was generally agreed that any message on it should be allowed to stay for at least twenty-four hours.

This was clearly a new moment. The Rock had been painted Friday evening with a rainbow flag by a group of students sympathetic to LGBTQ+ concerns. Overnight, under the cover of darkness, the Rock had been repainted with an American flag. The students who had painted the rainbow flag felt violated— and were planning to take matters into their own hands and respond in kind by painting over the American flag. I did not need the chief student life officer to tell me we had a problem. He went on to let me know that the first group of students not only was ready to move forward with the repainting but also wanted the administration to call the second group of students to account for the violation of free speech—or to consider the possibility of their taking the campus incident to the public.

The terms of the "problem picture" and its seeming insolubility were immediately and glaringly evident: two groups of students, each sincerely believing they were in the right and obviously so, each believing they deserved administrative support on campus, and each conscious of an audience well beyond the campus and accessible at the drop of a social media post—an audience that would be only too glad to support the righteousness of their cause.

Below the surface were other realities that further complicated the presenting problem. We did not know, at first, who was involved in the first group. We knew that both sides—and their supporters—would see this, at least initially, as an all-or-nothing situation. Either the college was for America or for the rights of the LGBTQ+ community. (Neither group would have seen, at least not at the moment, the profound irony of pitting these ideals against each other.) Both groups were, in some sense, testing the trustworthiness of the community they had chosen to join. Was it truly what it appeared to be? They were waiting for an answer represented by the response of the administration.

Over the course of the next few hours, we did discover who had painted the American flag over the rainbow one. These students, as is so often the case in such student life situations, had not seen—or at least claimed not to have seen—the potential implications of their action in the moment. It was a spur-of-the-moment reaction to something that had annoyed them. We initiated conversation with the first group, whose rainbow flag had precipitated the incident. They immediately clarified that they were not seeking to overturn the values of the college community but rather to affirm them through the expression of their opinion via one of the available avenues provided by our community. They understood the irony of the American flag being used to protest a controversial perspective within the community. They also quickly realized that repainting the rainbow would simply exacerbate the tension, rather than resolve anything. Instead, they offered to initiate a proactive celebration of the richness of our Christian liberal arts community by gathering the next day at the Rock and collectively repainting the rock with the many-colored handprints of all those who gathered. They proposed a litany that included Scripture and prayer, fully in accord with the community's typical practice of any celebrative occasion around which the community might gather. Their request was simple—or so it seemed to them. Would the administration generate the invitation to such an event—being appropriately explicit, of course, that the purpose of the gathering was to celebrate the community rather than a particular position on controversies within it?

It was clearly a judgment call. Saying yes could certainly be explained and even justified in terms of the longstanding values of the community. But with social media and the relative impact of visual impressions over words, it was not at all evident that we would have the opportunity to explain. Many would see this as the administration taking sides with the students who supported the rainbow flag rather than the American flag—and depending on their own views, would applaud or condemn the decision accordingly.

I chose to send the invitation—carefully worded, to be sure. But I sent it. I also chose to be at the event. I did decline the opportunity to speak as part of the program. That seemed a bridge too far.

The community gathered; a respectable gathering of students, staff, and faculty showed up—all properly socially distanced, of course. And the Rock was repainted with multicolored hands. It remained painted in that way the entire academic year.

Introduction

It was in the context of the "Rock incident," as it became known at the college, that I came to understand most personally the anatomy of the risk analysis for those working in middle space. The incident was arguably a microcosm of the potential perils and possibilities in all of those situations where individuals are venturing to do the convening, imaginative work of pointing a community beyond the paralysis of polarization. The costs of working in middle space seem both more obvious and immediate than the benefits; the opportunities to be achieved by this investment of time and energy are most often potential rather than actual and probably more ambiguous and long term. Furthermore, the costs seem to be driven primarily by fear, whereas the benefits appear driven by hope. Being more visceral and less cognitive than hope, fear seems to exercise a disproportionate level of influence, despite our best efforts at careful analysis. This asymmetry is not accidental or arbitrary. It seems to be in the very nature of the conditions of a polarized context.

Calculating the Costs

Risking the Loss of Objective or Absolute Truth

In a polarized situation of any sort, the very suggestion that there could be value in considering a position other than the one to which each side is completely devoted is met with immediate suspicion. This suspicion, whether or not it is articulated, operates at two levels. At one level, the suggestion to reconsider one's current position appears to be an attack on the possibility of absolute or objective truth about the topic in question. Thus, there is what philosophers might call an *ontological* objection.

At quite another level, such a suggestion appears to be an attack on the moral or intellectual capacity and commitment of the person holding a position about the topic in question. In other words, it appears to be questioning either a person's intent to seek and to hold to the truth or the person's ability or commitment to do the hard intellectual work of research and analysis to justify their conclusion. Thus, there is what philosophers would call an *epistemological* objection. No one wants to be accused of sloppy thinking or of not being sincerely, in fact, what they are purporting to be.[1]

Either of these concerns is understandable and indeed appropriate. There are good, defensible philosophical and practical reasons to want to avoid the proverbial slippery slope into relativism.[2] If nothing is truer or better or more right than anything else, then every human community is forced back on some version of the notion, asserted long ago by Thrasymachus in Plato's *Republic*, that "justice is nothing other than the advantage of the stronger."[3] Varieties of relativism have surfaced repeatedly over the centuries as a hypothetical philosophical position, even exercising a certain initial attractiveness for those resisting the tyrannical abuse of power by others in the

---

1. On this level, when a questioner raises questions about a group's position, it immediately raises the same concern in reverse. Has the questioner not done her homework—or does she have some underlying moral flaw that would lead her not to come to the same conclusions? For a group convinced of the truth of their position, there is simply no middle ground. If they have the truth, someone questioning their position must be holding to what is false, either because of some intellectual flaw or because of a moral flaw. Sometimes this questioning takes on a painfully personal aspect. I was recently asked how I could possibly care about someone and not take the same position on a particular ethical question.

2. See Mark Schwehn, "Academic Holiness," *Current*, September 27, 2022, https://currentpub .com/2022/09/27/academic-holiness.

3. For a brief introduction to the context of this discussion, see Eric Brown, "Plato's Ethics and Politics in *The Republic*," Stanford Encyclopedia of Philosophy (SEP), last revised September 12, 2017, https://plato.stanford.edu/entries/plato-ethics-politics. See also "Callicles" and "Thrasymachus" in the SEP.

name of religious or political absolutes[4] or individual or structural blindness derived from position or privilege.[5] Despite any initial appeal to relativism at the abstract level, it is difficult to sustain even at the philosophical level, for it is vulnerable to the charge of self-refutation (e.g., How can relativism itself be defended if nothing is truer than anything else?), and it has shown itself throughout history to be even more ineffective at the practical level. For example, if one wants to show that Nazism is truly wrong—and not just problematic for those who do not happen to like it—one has to be willing to defend the proposition that the values of Adolf Hitler and Mother Teresa really do not have intellectual parity.

It is important to resist the potential slide into relativism, and those working in middle space would do well to affirm this legitimate concern. What is required is to make a distinction between a belief in absolute truth (i.e., the ontological concern) and a belief that my current position—or that of my group—on a question fully embodies that truth (i.e., the epistemological concern).

There are also quite understandable reasons to resist the suggestion that in taking a particular position on the topic in question, either I or those who think like me have not done our homework. We tend to proportion the intensity of our conviction with our confidence that we are standing for some good of ultimate value. When the suggestion is made that a person committed to some good might consider modifying their position in one way or another or be open to other perspectives, or even to considering this good alongside other goods, it is difficult to imagine how one could do this without compromising one's conviction of the ultimate value of that good. After all, we take a position on the poles because we believe that some good or the other is absolutely true and that something of ultimate value is truly at stake. Not true under certain conditions. Not true 40 percent of the time. We go to the poles because we believe that something of value must be protected all the time, in every case.

By inviting those on the poles to consider the good to which they are committed alongside any other good, those working in middle space seem to be asking them to abandon their conviction of the truth or value of

4. For an example from the late nineteenth century that has influenced this discussion in the past century, see Friedrich Nietzsche, *Beyond Good and Evil: Prelude to a Philosophy of the Future*, trans. R. J. Hollingdale (New York: Penguin, 2003).

5. See, for example, Karl Marx and Friedrich Engels's *Communist Manifesto* (1848) and other works, as well as the application of Marx's analysis of economic structures to other areas of human activity, such as gender and ethnic relations. For a helpful twentieth-century edition of Marx's and Engels's thinking, see Robert C. Tucker, ed., *The Marx-Engels Reader*, 2nd ed. (New York: Norton, 1978).

that good. We do not have clear models of conviction or commitment that involve setting an ultimate good alongside other goods or advocating for that good under certain conditions. When something is true, it is hard to imagine making exceptions or naming appropriate exemptions. Furthermore, it is the clear conviction of the nonnegotiability of this good that makes advocacy effective and perhaps even possible. It is difficult to imagine posters or sound bites being framed in anything other than the strongest of terms. There is not room on the sign or enough letters in the tweet to allow for anything other than a few words. It is also difficult to advocate for legislation or executive or judicial action in anything other than absolute terms.

So there are reasons why those working in middle space will be attacked from both sides of the issues that have created the circumstances of polarization in human experience over the centuries. Their challenge is to reckon appropriately with the weight and legitimacy of these claims on both sides of the spectrum, even as they seek to invite all parties involved to imagine a path beyond polarization that is equally passionate in its conviction.

The available examples are everywhere throughout history. We will point here to a few of the more familiar to those in the Western tradition.

1. In the days of early Christianity, certain heresies related to the nature of Jesus and the nature of the Trinity emerged around apparently conflicting goods that needed to be protected at all costs—the divine nature of Jesus and the human nature of Jesus, the oneness of God and the multiple persons of God.

2. The debate over slavery in England's parliament in the eighteenth century pitted the supposedly ultimate good of private property against another equally ultimate value in the English constitution—namely, respect for the liberty of the individual person.

3. On the other side of the Atlantic, the debate over slavery in America was carried on in different but equally absolute terms: states' rights versus the rights of the individual.

4. During World War I, in the horrific days of 1915–16, when the unanticipated costs of the war at every level—human life, economic stability, political and social stability—were becoming apparent, it was the reluctance to call into question the value of the sacrifices that had already been borne (in the name of convictions to conflicting national loyalties) that worked against early efforts to have conversations about peacemaking. The very idea of meeting to discuss peace seemed to be

an unacceptable devaluing of the millions who had already suffered the cost of their clear convictions.

5. In twentieth-century Germany, German Christians were caught in the tension of whether to honor the apparently clear directives from Scripture in Romans 13 and honor the government or to honor the equally clear directives to love one's neighbor as oneself. For Dietrich Bonhoeffer (1906–45), it was the additional moral dilemma of being caught between our Lord's directive to turn the other cheek, thus avoiding any resort to violence, and the equally strong call as a German citizen to pursue justice.

6. For the governments of England and France in the 1930s—watching the growing menace of Nazism in Germany—there was a pull between the apparently irreconcilable commitments of the recent Versailles Peace Treaty—of the commitment to resolve international disputes peacefully, especially against the backdrop of the all-too-recent devastation of World War I—and the commitment to protecting the self-determination of people groups.

7. In twentieth-century America, the debate over abortion took a polarized form around two competing goods: the value of the unborn child and the value of the moral agency and bodily autonomy of the mother—or more simply put, the rights of the child and the rights of the mother.

8. During the 1980s and '90s, those in the leadership of the Soviet Union found themselves torn theoretically between traditional Marxist orthodoxy and a vision of human freedom and well-being that had inspired Marx's writing in the beginning. The tension, much more practically put, pitted the unity and political stability of the Soviet Union against the claims of its citizens to human rights, on the one hand, and against the nationalistic values of its largest republic, Russia, on the other.

9. We are living today in this current moment between the polarized values of individual autonomy over matters of sexual morality and of the free exercise of religion—each claiming to ground their convictions in both the legal authority of the American Constitution and the larger framework of the Judeo-Christian understanding of human flourishing.

Those who have sought in each of these circumstances to point their society or community beyond the unproductive stalemate of polarization have felt the charge from both sides that they are calling for the abandonment of conviction—for a position of lukewarmness, unacceptable compromise, and moral and intellectual timidity. Their task is to reckon appropriately with the weight and legitimacy of the ultimate values represented by both sides of the spectrum, even while inviting individuals all along the spectrum to imagine a path beyond the paralysis of the current polarization, a path that is equally full of conviction and equally committed to the objectivity of the good and the true.[6]

Risking the Loss of Trust in Leadership or an Organization's Integrity

When persons respond to the call to work in middle space, they are risking the loss of trust in their own leadership and potentially trust in the institution with which they are associated. This is no small concern. Leaders have made commitments to a constituency to steward faithfully a set of values. Sometimes this has taken the form of a contract or a covenant. Sometimes it may be in terms of promises to an electorate. Either way, such persons have put their integrity on the line. They have offered to guarantee that what they are now, they will continue to be in the future. Any effort to suggest that a traditional understanding of one of the core values of the institution might need adjustment or further reflection in the light of new circumstances immediately raises eyebrows. Quite understandably. Are the leaders not who they appeared to be when hired? If they are questioning one of the values of the institution, what other values will be questioned? Experienced leaders, with careful and constant communication, may be able to retain the trust of their immediate circle of accountability, but this cannot be taken for granted.

Managing the potential risk of losing the trust of those to whom a leader is most directly accountable is not the only cost to someone seeking to enlarge a community's imagination to see and consider new alternatives. Sometimes there are multiple identifiable constituencies, as in the shared governance model of most institutions of higher education. In these cases, the levels and forms of accountability differ, and the challenge is often to ensure that each constituency hears the same message, as the leader seeks to keep each constituency informed in the ways that are most relevant to their particular

6. For one example of the effort to mitigate the charge that there is unacceptable risk of relativism or abandonment of conviction, see Kevin DeYoung, "Why Reformed Evangelicalism Has Splintered: Four Approaches to Race, Politics, and Gender," The Gospel Coalition, March 9, 2021, www.thegospelcoalition.org/blogs/kevin-deyoung/why-reformed-evangelicalism-has -splintered-four-approaches-to-race-politics-and-gender.

interests. Now, more than ever, there are the much larger, more amorphous, and often invisible constituencies that have been drawn to a leader through networks of loyalty that are not formalized, at least not in any binding way. They are measured by polls or "hits" on the institutional website or contributions to the organization. They include alumni constituencies and prospective students in higher education; they include church attenders and customers, clients, volunteers, and donors in other contexts. These are the constituencies that have fostered the need for directors of marketing within organizations to intentionally measure and manage "brand." They are supported by a growing network of marketing firms that are only too ready to assist in the ongoing tasks of maintaining brand clarity and brand loyalty, as well as in any emergency public-relations challenges that pose an immediate threat to a leader or to an organization.

More than ever since the beginning of the pandemic, all of a leader's constituencies—and especially those with more flexible boundaries—are connected to leaders and their organizations electronically. In this virtual world, the risk of saying or doing something that might damage one's credibility or one's capacity to lead an organization is multiplied exponentially. Long gone is the opportunity for leaders to look their audiences in the eye to assess whether they are truly getting a message across—or to respond immediately to reactions in body language that signal a need for further explanation. In this new digital world, the audience is most often invisible to the leader. Even in those situations of synchronous electronic connection facilitated by various video platforms, the notion of "eye contact" and interaudience feedback is not at all what it used to be. While magnifying the risk of losing trust for leaders, the electronic world has minimized proportionately any reputational risk to members of the constituency. In short, there is no symmetry in leader-audience accountability. Moreover, the immediacy of the electronic world accelerates the potential for a carelessly dropped word, casual comment, or even speculative reflection shared by a leader in a spirit of trust to become a media crisis before he or she even has the possibility of following up with a more complete explanation. Sometimes the damage is beyond repair.[7]

Abraham Lincoln (1809–65) risked his personal credibility and that of his new Republican Party with the Emancipation Proclamation of January 1, 1863. Such a radical move had not been part of his electoral platform when

---

7. The importance, as well as the growing challenge, of building and maintaining trust is explored helpfully in Stephen M. R. Covey, *The Speed of Trust: The One Thing That Changes Everything*, with Rebecca R. Merrill (New York: Free Press, 2008).

he came into the presidency. This was an executive decision, not voted on by Congress, not mandated by the courts. He did not even have the benefit of Gallup polls to test the potential fallout from this decision.[8]

Mikhail Gorbachev (1931–2022) took a risk with his new policies of *glasnost* and *perestroika*—Russian words that soon became part of the world's vocabulary in the 1980s. We all knew the words in their English translation as "openness" and "restructuring." It was Gorbachev's idea that in allowing the Soviet Union to face its past honestly—and to allow for a more efficient market-driven economy, rather than being driven in all areas by considerations of abstract ideology undergirded by vigilant secret police—that all that was truly important in Soviet Russia could be secured. For a few years, it looked promising.[9]

Neville Chamberlain (1869–1940), in an effort to halt the seemingly inexorable march toward another European war so soon on the heels of World War I, took the bold move as Britain's prime minister of initiating contact with Adolf Hitler in the fall of 1938 and inviting a face-to-face conversation about Czechoslovakia. He returned from the consultation with key international leaders at Berchtesgaden, Hitler's mountain retreat outside Munich, and he stepped off the plane in London waving the paper that announced to the world, "peace for our time." He also suggested in reporting on the meetings more generally that Germany's new leader was not as sinister as he had been portrayed. Rather, he was a "good, German gentleman." The moment of triumph was short lived. When, several months later, the Germans marched into Czechoslovakia in direct violation of the Munich Accords, Chamberlain's supposedly brilliant move pointing beyond an impasse of international polarization became the source of derision. Chamberlain's policy of "appeasement" became overnight not the stuff of innovative diplomacy but forever after a byword for naive and groveling catering to bullies that would inevitably, eventually, prove fatal.[10]

---

8. For examples of recent biographies of Lincoln that explore the complexity of his presidential leadership, see Jon Meacham, *And There Was Light: Abraham Lincoln and the American Struggle* (New York: Random House, 2022); Ronald C. White Jr., *A. Lincoln: A Biography* (New York: Random House, 2010); Doris Kearns Goodwin, *Team of Rivals: The Political Genius of Abraham Lincoln* (New York: Simon & Schuster, 2006).

9. For further reading on Gorbachev's efforts to reform the Soviet Union, see William Taubman, *Gorbachev: His Life and Times* (New York: Norton, 2018).

10. For further reading on Chamberlain's dilemma and how his role has been evaluated in retrospect, see, for example, Frank McDonough, *Neville Chamberlain, Appeasement and the British Road to War* (Manchester: Manchester University Press, 1998); John R. Ruggiero, *Hitler's Enabler: Neville Chamberlain and the Origins of the Second World War* (Santa Barbara, CA: Praeger, 2015).

Leaders who risk their reputations and that of their institutions to create new options beyond paralyzed polarization are not all in the past. More recently, Russell Moore, former leader in the Southern Baptist Convention, invested himself in mediating conversations within and outside his denomination in the areas of ethics and public policy, seeking to imagine options that remained true to Southern Baptist theology while also honoring a growing plurality of views within the church itself and within the larger civil society within which the church members functioned. Eventually, the strain on his own credibility was too much.[11] Today, Moore is the editor-in-chief of *Christianity Today.*

Risking the Cohesion That Unites a Support Base

When a person invites a community into conversation about potential common ground beyond their differences, the person is putting at risk many of the practical and psychological features that secure a strong support base. People want clarity and concreteness in order to invest their financial support. People do not give to causes that appear muddled or compromising. Nor do they give their private or foundational support to ideals that are not attached to strategic plans for execution that include specific, tangible, and evidence-based outcomes. Donors want to know that their investments are making a practical difference in the world, not just providing the space, time, and refreshments for endless conversations that may go nowhere. I mentioned earlier my conversation with the leader of an organization seeking to foster a framework of honest dialogue within the academic world that offers an alternative to our current politicized and polarized "cancel" culture. The person, whose anonymity I should respect here, mentioned with some concern his realization that the organization was going to have difficulty raising funds precisely because its goals were more speculative and imprecise than those organizations promising clearer and more concrete outcomes that support a particular political perspective.

Supporters want to know that the institutions they support are clearly on their side—not waffling or trying to placate all sides. I have seen this personally in working with alumni from multiple institutions of higher education. What is most fascinating in such situations is the assumption, voiced from those on both sides of specific controversial issues, that by not lending the institution's support more unequivocally to their side, the institution must

---

11. For an exploration of Moore's creative thinking about middle space growing out of his own experiences, see Russell Moore, *Losing Our Religion: An Altar Call for Evangelical America* (New York: Sentinel, 2023).

certainly be acting out of fear of the censorship of the other side. There is no sense that the issues might actually be more complex.

But, of course, a support base is built around more than money. It also includes the social and psychological benefits, for individual members, of belonging to a community of like-minded individuals. People want to know that their own views are also shared by others, preferably others who are more attractive and powerful in some way or another than themselves. I have watched this in the context of serving on volunteer boards. Yes, the cause matters to some extent, but what keeps people coming back is also the community associated with the cause. When the cause becomes muddled or when there is perceived division of support within the community for the cause or the leader or its accompanying brand, the board members start counting the days until their term is up.

People also like to be part of a community that is associated with a winning cause, not just a clear and concrete cause. This can be an athletic team or a political party or an ideological position. As long as something is clearly at stake and there are clear winners and losers, good guys and bad guys, there will be a sense of unity and togetherness. We do not like "ties," whether in a baseball game or an intellectual debate. We want the intensity of risk, the hope of a clear victory, and the security of belonging to a community that shares a confidence in the significance and the "rightness" of one's cause.

Moreover, evidence suggests that fear of potential loss can bind communities even more effectively and securely than hope of potential gains. We see this phenomenon painfully clearly in the political environment of America today. When fear of loss takes over, it unites a community around the perceived threat and inspires loyalty in anyone who purports to provide safety from that threat. Communities will put support of such protection even ahead of the ideals that purported to create the community in the first place.[12]

12. For an analysis of how political values gradually took priority over religious values in explaining changing religious-group loyalties in America over the past several decades, see Robert D. Putnam and David E. Campbell, *American Grace: How Religion Divides and Unites Us*, with Shaylyn Romney Garrett (New York: Simon & Schuster, 2012). For further reading and reflection on the factors driving loyalties and support in today's America, see, for example, Michael Gerson, "Trump Should Fill Christians with Rage. How Come He Doesn't?," *Washington Post*, September 1, 2022, https://www.washingtonpost.com/opinions/2022/09/01/michael-gerson-evangelical-christian-maga-democracy/; Tim Alberta, "How Politics Poisoned the Church," *Atlantic*, June 2022, 28–42; Pamela Cooper-White, *The Psychology of Christian Nationalism: Why People Are Drawn In and How to Talk across the Divide* (Minneapolis: Fortress, 2022); Keri Ladner, "The Quiet Rise of Christian Dominionism," *Christian Century*, November 2022, 48–52.

All of this is up for grabs when someone threatens to disrupt this framework by asking complicated questions or pointing out complexities in what an organization or community stands for. So the person seeking to convene dialogue on middle ground not only threatens those features that have drawn people to the poles, but faces the challenge of creating a new community of belonging on middle ground without those very features that support, strengthen, and sustain such communities in the first place. It is a daunting risk at best!

The Risk of Promising a Path Forward

When a person has the courage to convene a proactive conversation around the hope of arriving at a path forward beyond polarization, the person cannot promise anything definitively. The very nature of the situation entails that risk. Individuals are being invited to be pioneers and trailblazers, like the Lewis and Clark expedition to explore the American West, the European rulers' search for the Northwest Passage to India and China, or the expeditions to the North and South Poles. The way is not marked, nor arrival at the goal guaranteed.

It is easier for potential participants to hold back and remain passively neutral or curious bystanders at best. The clarity of their certain losses outweighs any potential for gain in joining a new conversation.[13]

We see this risk illustrated daily in the legislative process of democratic governments. It happens within parties when individuals seek to build coalitions around new strategies, with no guarantee that such coalitions will survive the vicissitudes of internal politics. We saw this in the recent leadership instability within the Conservative Party in Great Britain, as successive party leaders sought to inspire party confidence in a unified party strategy for addressing the nation's deepening economic crises. In the process, the country saw a new record set for the shortest term of a prime minister in the history of parliamentary government. Prime Minister Liz Truss served only forty-five days, setting a new record previously held by nineteenth-century Prime Minister George Canning.[14]

The risk is also illustrated whenever someone takes the bold step "across the aisle" to seek to build bipartisan support for a proposal that might

13. See, for example, the article on the preference for passive nonalignment in the context of the Russia-Ukraine conflict: "Developing World Quiet on Putin," *Wall Street Journal*, April 15, 2022, A8.
14. William Booth and Karla Adam, "How Liz Truss Became the Shortest-Serving Prime Minister in U.K. History," *Washington Post*, October 20, 2022.

previously have been associated with one or the other of the parties—or, for that matter, a proposal that invites imaginative alternatives that address previously real or perceived conflicting interests across party lines. Such efforts at coalition building are some of the most familiar examples of working in middle space that we have available. We might choose to follow current examples of such efforts in America to address the impasse around immigration reform or the impasse between religious liberty and the civil rights of the LGBTQ+ community. But we do not know how these situations will turn out—which, of course, only serves in one way to illustrate the risk.

I would invite us, instead, to illustrate the risk with an example drawn from the legislative world of Great Britain, which attempted to outlaw the slave trade and the very institution of slavery itself within the British Empire. Ultimately, the effort succeeded, but it took decades longer than anyone might have expected, and it did not at all follow a preconceived or predictable trajectory. This is despite the fact that significant numbers on both ends of Britain's political spectrum recognized the legal and cultural legitimacy of the two values in conflict—respect for the dignity and autonomy of individual persons and respect for private property. They also recognized the awkward moral unacceptability of allowing the impasse of polarization to continue.

We credit William Wilberforce (1759–1833) with leading the campaign to abolish the slave trade in the British Empire and eventually the institution of slavery itself. He was definitely someone called to work in middle space. He knew that he could not accomplish the abolition of slavery by himself. He also knew the intractable forces that opposed the abolition project. No matter how strong the moral objection to slavery, it was countered by the principle of free trade and the rights of private property—both considered to be as sacred to the British political tradition as the notion of individual freedom. Furthermore, the influence of the economic interests tied to the perpetuation of slavery far outweighed the influence of those opposing the institution—or so it seemed.

Wilberforce—motivated primarily by his moral opposition to slavery itself, as well as by his conviction that slavery was a corrupting influence on the entire civil society of eighteenth-century Britain—positioned himself physically in the center of political power and began building support for the possibility of moving beyond the stalemate that allowed slavery to continue.[15] In 1786,

15. For a developed explanation of Wilberforce's motivation in his own words, see William Wilberforce, *A Practical View of the Prevailing Religious System of Professing Christians in*

he leased a house near Parliament so he would have access to the decision-makers. He joined forces with others like Thomas Clarkson (1760–1846), the Clapham Sect—influential Anglicans who were committed to the moral reform of society—and the Quakers. He cultivated a friendship with William Pitt (1759–1806), the prime minister who, as early as 1788, indicated his intent to raise the question in Parliament about the legitimacy of the slave trade. Even then, there was no clear path forward. Clarkson traveled throughout the country, mobilizing public opinion for such actions as petitioning Parliament. Popular leaders like John Wesley voiced his support to Wilberforce even as he prepared to die in 1791. Nevertheless, even with the support of leading politicians like Pitt, bills on behalf of the abolition cause failed to pass in Parliament eleven times between 1790 and 1805.

In 1806, the Foreign Slave Trade Abolition Bill was introduced. This focused on preventing British traders from bringing slaves into foreign territories. It seemed innocuous enough to the opposition, at least at first. The bill passed Parliament in May of 1806, to be followed in January of 1807 by Prime Minister Lord Grenville's introduction in the House of Lords of the broader Slave Trade Abolition Bill. Coming as a measure from the government in power, it passed with a strong majority in the Lords, despite opposition from peers tied to West Indian trade. There were still no guarantees that it would pass in the House of Commons. The abolitionists rented a house on Downing Street so as to be able to lobby members of Parliament day and night. When the House of Commons took up debate on the bill on February 23, the debate went on for ten hours. Finally, when the House voted, the bill passed overwhelmingly, 283 to 16. Who could have guessed that, after eleven failed efforts? During the debate in the House, Wilberforce, who had invested eighteen years of his life in public advocacy for this cause, received a standing ovation. His investment had been an act of faith. There were no guarantees for him or for all those who supported this work of middle space at any point on the journey; in fact, the road signs along the way pointed in the opposite direction.[16]

Wilberforce lived to see the success of his efforts—at least the first major step, the abolition of the slave trade. It took twenty-six more years until the

---

the *Higher and Middle Classes in This Country Contrasted with Real Christianity*, 6th ed. (London, 1798). See also Kevin Belmonte, *William Wilberforce: A Hero for Humanity* (Grand Rapids: Zondervan, 2007); Stephen Tomkins, *William Wilberforce: A Biography* (Grand Rapids: Eerdmans, 2007).

16. For a general but concise account of the parliamentary abolition of the slave trade, see "Parliament Abolishes the Slave Trade," UK Parliament, accessed October 5, 2023, https://www .parliament.uk/about/living-heritage/transformingsociety/tradeindustry/slavetrade/overview /parliament-abolishes-the-slave-trade/.

institution of slavery itself was abolished in 1833. Many of those who step out into the uncharted territory of middle space never see their work bear fruit, at least not in this world. We might point to Dietrich Bonhoeffer, who was executed in prison during the final days of World War II. His risky actions in middle space dramatically cut short his promising life of pastoral care, seminary teaching, and creative scholarship.

Our Lord Jesus might be judged, from all outward appearances, as the ultimate example of a failed calculation of risk. His lifelong efforts to move his people from all ends of the religious spectrum to a deeper and more imaginative understanding of what it means to fulfill the law—to love God with all one's mind, heart, soul, and strength and to love one's neighbor as oneself—ended on a Roman cross.

So the costs of working in middle space are real. The question is whether there are potential opportunities that outweigh the potential costs. It is to the opportunity side that we now turn.

Imagining the Benefits

Weighing the costs and benefits of seeking to move a community beyond polarization is not a symmetrical task, as I have already noted. The costs are much more visible in the short term; the benefits are most often aspirational and long term. They reflect our hopes, rather than the realities that press in on us urgently in the moment. They are, nonetheless, equally important—or so we are asserting here.

The hopes that invite us to imagine the possible benefits of "middling efforts," which might outweigh the risks of the clearly evident costs, are grounded in a number of assumptions that have already been identified in this book but might be worth reviewing at this point. First, we are assuming that those on the poles—even people of pure intent, flawless moral character, and significant intellectual capacity, who have taken their stand on one pole or another for legitimate reasons of conviction—may have blind spots. As finite human beings, who see from one perspective, and as fallen human beings, who have been affected by the tragic bentness that pervades all of creation, they may not have a complete understanding of the issues at stake. Or to put it another way, they may have truth—even what is often termed "absolute" truth—but they may not have the whole of that absolute truth. When they are invited to conversations in the middle, they are not being invited to give up on their sense of truth, but rather to come to see more fully the truth to which they are committed.

Second, those seeking to host middle space see the value of providing ground for exploration that might permit growth in one's understanding of the truth. It is not simply, as in the first point, that at any one moment we might not see all of the truth. This same middle space allows for new insights or discoveries that might emerge over time.

Third, we assume a fundamental dignity and good faith in those who share convictions about the truth that are not the same as our own. We do not equate a person's moral character or intellectual capacity with their position on an issue. We know that good people can be mistaken and that even people who have worked hard to develop support for their positions can continue to grow.

Fourth, those hosting middle space assume some commitment to pluralism, or the recognition that allowing a measure of legitimacy for diverse opinions is, in the long run, not at all necessarily giving way to relativism. Rather, it can be part of an ultimate commitment to the truth, as society makes space for an appropriate exchange of ideas within the circle of its larger commitments. The space for such a diversity of thought would be bounded in different ways, depending on the situation. American civil society, circumscribed by the Constitution, would have one set of limits for the diversity of ideas appropriate to the civic arena. A church denomination, restricted by a set of doctrines, would have quite another. In either case, the legitimacy of diversity of thought and expression is intended to serve the ultimate good and the ultimate vision of truth undergirding the community—not to undermine the strength or unity of the community.[17] This commitment to pluralism, on whatever scale is deemed appropriate, rests on the assumption that individuals are unlikely to have a complete understanding of the truth and, therefore, would benefit by the best thinking of their community—especially when community members are committed to the same ideals. In this way, we are affirming a view of human beings that reflects both their being created in the image of God and their participation in the effects of the fall.

Fifth, those investing in the work of the convening middle have confidence that the safety of the truth does not rest finally in their hands. They

17. It should be noted here that pluralism is also not at all the same as secularism, with which it is sometimes confused by those on both the right and the left. Secularism is the assumption that religion or claims to truth grounded in religion belong in the private sphere and have no appropriate place in the public arena. Those in more conservative circles are likely to worry that pluralism inherently implies relativism or leads inevitably to secularism. Those in more liberal circles are more likely to worry that a vision of pluralism that allows for the inclusion of multiple religious opinions in the public arena will eventually lead to interference with the constitutional commitment to the separation of church and state.

are not the ultimate guardians of the truth. They are not the final line of defense against heresy or falsehood. Rather, they are in partnership with the God who is the final arbiter and even embodiment of truth. This is a great relief—and one of God's greatest gifts to his children. This grounding of middle work—particularly such work in the public square—in one's spiritual identity provides the passion and conviction that is often associated with the polarizing convictions themselves. As Richard Mouw writes in his article "A 'Middle Way': Lessons for Faithfulness in the Public Square," "The alternatives on both the left and the right have the advantage of generating a kind of spiritual passion. Is there a way to instill that same passion in calling people to cultivate, for example, the spiritual virtues of patience, love of neighbor, respect for differences, and the like, in public life?"[18] One's identity, passion, and motivation must be grounded in a community of convictions larger and more compelling than those on either pole.

It is within this spirit of faith and hope that we imagine the possibilities of gain from working in middle space. The calculation is not, then, a contest between having a firm hold on one's conviction and giving up on one's conviction or softening one's conviction. It is an assessment of whether there is sufficient reason to hope that working in middle space can lead to a deepened sense of conviction about a larger or more complete vision of the truth.

A More Complete Understanding of the Issues at Stake

Perhaps the most obvious argument for being an explorer in middle space is the possibility of coming to a more complete understanding of the truth—either truth in general or the truth about a specific topic in particular. It is simply difficult to imagine that either side contains all the good and all the truth that is to be had on any particular issue. We must make room for growth and a more complete understanding of the truth that either side is seeking to protect. By saying this, we are not at all minimizing the reality of true binaries in this world. We want to affirm the existence and the power of good and evil, right and wrong, true and false. But most polarization in our culture today is not a result of either side doubting these realities. The polarization results more often over matters of strategy for securing what is right or good or true.[19]

18. Richard J. Mouw, "A 'Middle Way': Lessons for Faithfulness in the Public Square," Shared Justice, November 19, 2019, https://archive.sharedjustice.org/most-recent/2019/11/19/a-middle -way-lessons-for-faithfulness-in-the-public-square.

19. I have seen this myself most clearly in the efforts among conservative religious groups to ensure that their constitutional right to religious liberty is respected in the course of the expanding understanding of the civil rights of members of the LGBTQ+ community. While

Part of coming to a more complete understanding of the truth is assuming that there are at least some others, besides those in one's own group, who can be trusted to also come into this middle space in good faith and with trustworthy motives. According to his own testimony, Jonathan Haidt began life as an atheist, utterly opposed to religion in general and Christianity in particular and convinced that religion was a detriment to the flourishing of a humane society. It was in meeting actual people who identified with conservative Christianity, in part, that he realized he was not dealing with alien beings unlike himself—but rather fellow human beings who also desired to see the world with clarity and to be part of an intellectual community committed to that pursuit. But what really changed his mind was his research in social psychology. He discovered that it was those who were most committed to religion, rather than those without a religious commitment, who contributed more to the bonds of civil society. In the course of being open to enlarge his understanding of religion and its impact on society, he discovered that his original convictions had been mistaken.[20] As a result, Haidt has become one of the most passionate supporters in the world of higher education today of bold and open dialogue across difference. His vision in this area led to the founding of the Heterodox Academy, an online network of over five thousand individuals across higher education and around the world, all committed to open and respectful discussion across difference, as long as opinions are supported by evidence.[21]

Daring to venture into true dialogue with one's opponent in middle space can enable one to understand more fully and argue even more effectively for one's position. In order to be in the best position to understand our own convictions, we must understand why intelligent and good people might be drawn to the other side. If we have opted for a particular position on a question without giving serious attention to the case for the other side, we can hardly be in the best position to explain the reasons for our own choices. How do we know our conclusions are anything more than prejudices of our upbringing or our own subculture? It is the importance of understanding the entire landscape of issues on any one topic that motivates standard procedure in preparation for formal debates. Participants

---

all groups share a commitment to the Constitution's provision for both the protection of the dignity of persons and religious liberty, they disagree on which strategies are most effective in ensuring that the right to religious liberty will be protected over the long term. This distinction between shared ultimate commitments and differing strategies is all too often lost in the passionate rhetoric that drives these discussions forward.

20. See Jonathan Haidt, "Moral Psychology's Role as an Aid against Antagonism," *Advance*, Spring 2018, 31–34, https://www.cccu.org/magazine/moral-psychologys-role-aid-antagonism.

21. See the network's website at www.heterodoxacademy.org.

in debating competition routinely prepare without always knowing which side they will be arguing.[22]

I once team-taught an undergraduate humanities class on issues of war and violence with a philosopher and a political scientist. Interestingly, it was right at the point in the early 1990s when the West was indulging in triumphalist rhetoric about having won the Cold War. For a very brief period of time, there actually was public speculation about how we would spend the "peace dividend" that would supposedly result, as we no longer needed such a large defense budget. Needless to say, there was no need to fret about this for long, as the fragile peace of the bipolar world of the Cold War disintegrated almost immediately into the multitude of local conflicts that we have come to accept as normal in this strange and ironically much less settled world of the early twenty-first century.

The early 1990s was a radically different time than the student days of the three professors teaching the class, each of whom had lived through the 1960s. Among the three of us, we had personally witnessed the burning of buildings, the shooting of bystanders during antiwar demonstrations, and the passion of a polarized society fighting a war in Vietnam that few understood. At the very least, any thoughtful, morally sensitive male student agonized during that time about the issues of just war and pacifism and whether Christians should seek conscientious objector status or engage in civil disobedience if they were not eligible for this special exemption. For most of the students of the 1990s, a class on the issues of war and violence was a sleeper, a good time to catch up on a short night's sleep—especially since it met at eight in the morning.

No doubt the professors learned more from that class than many of the students. My colleague in philosophy, a serious ethicist who himself thought deeply about many of the complex issues in the moral world that so often take the form of a dilemma, called himself a "51 percent just war theorist." He went on to say that he was also "49 percent pacifist" and that his understanding of pacifism was what finally made him come down on the side of just war and yet also enabled him to enter productively into dialogue with those on the other side. When we stop seeing the person on the other side as evil or

22. It is the conviction that we can learn most from those who are different from ourselves that drives the thinking of Jonathan Sacks, longtime chief rabbi of the United Hebrew Congregations of the Commonwealth, in both his classic, *The Dignity of Difference*, and his final work, *Morality*, published shortly before his death in 2020. See Jonathan Sacks, *The Dignity of Difference: How to Avoid the Clash of Civilizations*, 2nd ed. (New York: Bloomsbury, 2003); and Sacks, *Morality: Restoring the Common Good in Divided Times* (New York: Basic Books, 2020).

intellectually incompetent, and when we stop viewing the arguments for the other side as simply positions to be refuted or the source of intellectual sport or the context of political posturing, we can imagine the value of engaging in the work of middle space.

It is this exploration of a larger framework for one's own convictions that we see in Michael Bird's *Religious Freedom in a Secular Age*.[23] Contrary to common assumptions that Christians ought to be advocates of a government that would give preferential treatment to their own convictions, Bird makes the case that rather than continuing to fear or fight what he refers to as "secularism," Christians ought to have a greater appreciation of the gifts of this alternative approach to historic Christendom. In fact, he even finds a biblical home for advocating this pluralistic framework as the wisest strategic approach to making space for religious freedom in general and for Christianity in particular.

Thus, when we imagine the potential benefits of venturing into middle space, we do so believing that this will permit an enlarged understanding of our own previous convictions about the truth. Rather than resulting in a diminishment of our zeal, this exploration has the potential to enable us to be even more sure of the gift of the truth that we believe we are called to protect. In a strange and ironic way, this bold move into dialogue reflects the very strength of our confidence in the truth that we have. I think here again of my grandfather's encouragement to me to move boldly into the large world of the free exchange of ideas that he saw before me at the University of Toronto. "Go with what seems to be true; after all, if Christianity is not true, wouldn't you want to be the first to know? You cannot serve the God of truth by protecting yourself from new ideas."

The Possibility of New Options That Honor Both Sides

Venturing out into middle space opens the possibility of imagining options for moving forward that honor the convictions of both sides. These options are not mere compromises that betray the truth of one side or the other. Nor are they the bland averaging of the sum total of the convictions represented by both sides. They do not ask one side to be the loser and the other the winner. They are born out of the convictions that if there are good, intelligent individuals on both sides of a polarization, there is likely to be truth value on

---

23. Michael F. Bird, *Religious Freedom in a Secular Age: A Christian Case for Liberty, Equality, and Secular Government* (Grand Rapids: Zondervan, 2022). See also the review of this book by Natasha Moore, "Secularism Doesn't Have to Be Bad," *Christianity Today*, May/June 2022, 78–79.

both sides that must be honored. The new options emerge from the hope that there could be a win-win alternative that is better for the entire community. They represent the creative thinking that is possible when energy is devoted to loving and searching for the truth more than seeking to prove that "my" position is the full embodiment of the truth. This is what can happen when we care more about the truth than being right.

In John Tomasi's *Free Market Fairness*, we see the results of boldly moving into middle space within the academy and within the author's own field of political philosophy.[24] In this groundbreaking work, Tomasi draws on two thinkers, John Rawls and Friedrich Hayek, who are usually taken to be on opposite sides of the political poles, to consider how we might come to a deeper understanding of the economic conditions that create the greatest opportunity for social justice. In a recent discussion with Professor Tomasi, he used the image of seeking to identify a third "north star" for public policymakers in a world that often seemed to force economists to choose between the north star of Hayek's libertarianism and that of Rawls's communitarian vision of social justice. Seeking to learn from both Hayek and Rawls did not, then, represent an effort to trade in truth or conviction; rather, it signified the daring courage of moving beyond the standard options taken by the tradition to be the only available choices.

All too often, we assume that there are only two sides to a question, not because we have arrived at that conclusion from our own research but because that is the tradition. It is simply easier to continue in the tradition than to step out and challenge it. Furthermore, as we have been noting all along, it takes some independence and courage to resist falling into the framework of either-or thinking when that is the accepted mode of operating. I have referred already to my colleague in philosophy who once commented that he used to think that students who questioned the standard ethical dilemmas—usually women, I might note—just were not "getting" the issues involved. He then realized that it was not that they were obtuse; they were simply pushing to consider how the truth of both sides might be preserved.

Keeping alive the possibility of imagining new alternatives may be one of the best reasons for not splitting off, either formally or informally, from those from whom we think differently. This is difficult, especially when we believe that some ultimate truth is at stake. It no doubt explains the trend we have seen throughout church history for the proliferation of denominations. It takes energy to remain in unity and fellowship with those we believe to be

24. See John Tomasi, *Free Market Fairness* (Princeton: Princeton University Press, 2012).

in error, perhaps even more so with those who believe that *we* are in error. Choosing to opt for more uniformity of conviction may ultimately result in a diminished view of the truth—rather than its preservation. It is this concern that Bishop William Willimon raises in his essay on the recent schism in the United Methodist Church: "The United Methodist Church will be weaker when they [the conservatives] leave: from the loss of financial resources and of a few of our dearest, most vital congregations and our most creative, entrepreneurial pastors. Progressives will also lose some of their most adept, doggedly persistent, Bible-loving interlocutors, leaving them stuck in a denominational echo chamber with an even higher percentage of people who think just as they do."[25]

By citing Willimon, I am not taking a position on the recent schism in the United Methodist Church, nor am I asserting that schism is never a reasonable action among those within an organization who disagree. Rather, I am simply noting the cautionary advice that such an action runs the risk of losing important voices of "loyal opposition" within a community. We often need the animating challenge of dissent to keep us thinking at our best and to keep pushing us toward new possibilities. It takes organizational energy to accommodate dissent, no doubt, but this cost may be worth it when the alternative is an all-too-comfortable complacency in service to a reductionist vision of the truth. Only those who have cared enough to labor long in pursuit of the appropriate balance of truth and unity, which best allows the core mission of an organization to go forward, are in a position to determine when schism is a necessary—if always regrettable—option.

Bold commitment to the imagination of new alternatives for moving beyond polarization also involves each side giving up some claim to be right or in sole possession of the truth. This is difficult, especially when this "rightness" has legitimized political power. Peggy Noonan, speech writer for former president Ronald Reagan and persistent advocate for the imaginative possibilities that can emerge from the often hidden but vigilant work of middle space, illustrates in recent columns both the cost when this work is not done and the rewards that come for the world when it is. In the first instance, we see the ongoing social and personal costs of the legislative impasse on gun control.[26] In the second instance, we see the defusing of the 1962 Cuban Missile Crisis and the retreat from the brink of a very real threat of nuclear war. It took the willingness to imagine how both sides could save face and the humility

25. William Willimon, "The United Methodist Divorce Is a Mistake," *Christian Century*, October 2022, 74–76.

26. Peggy Noonan, "Let Not Our Hearts Grown Numb," *Wall Street Journal*, May 28–29, 2022, A13.

to back off from a win-lose position that enabled a new and more mutually beneficial alternative to emerge.[27]

The importance of imagining new alternatives that move beyond the painful paralysis of polarized choices is seen most powerfully at the practical level of public policy and legislation. This is also where the challenge of working in middle space with integrity is the greatest. It is just easier to create laws or policies that protect one good than it is to create laws and policies that honor multiple goods. When there is an ultimate good at stake—such as the sanctity of life, on the one hand, and the rights of the mother, on the other—it is nearly impossible to imagine a regulative framework that is both faithful to the good and makes room for exemptions. Even the very notion of an exemption is difficult from a theoretical standpoint. If life is sacred, how can that sanctity be violated under any conditions? But even if one could allow for extenuating circumstances at the theoretical level, the practical difficulties of creating such a framework of appropriate exemption are daunting.

It is this difficulty of imagining a legal framework that allows for the honoring and regulating of two ultimate goods that has kept the abortion debate alive for decades. Even after the Supreme Court decision of 1973, *Roe v. Wade*, which recognized the constitutional right of abortion, the debate did not die. In fact, it intensified, fueling partisan animosity in both politics and religion over the next fifty years.[28] One's view on abortion became a touchstone of electability for candidates of both the Republican and Democratic Parties, as well as eventually the ultimate test of whether a nomination to the Supreme Court could expect to be confirmed. This either-or mentality continued to show itself following the Supreme Court decision in June of 2022 to return the regulation of abortion to individual states. We saw it in the one-sided reactions of the public media, in the triumphalism of the right as well as in the apocalyptic cries of the left. We saw it in the world of Christian journalism—the mainline *Christian Century* highlighting the loss of the right of the mother to independent moral agency[29] and the evangelical *Christianity Today* highlighting the scandal of a legal framework that for so long had allowed for the taking of human life through abortion.[30]

27. Peggy Noonan, "Enduring Lessons of the Cuban Missile Crisis," *Wall Street Journal*, October 1–2, 2022, A15.

28. For a comprehensive narrative account of this journey, supported by extensive quantitative data, I refer once again to Putnam and Campbell's *American Grace*.

29. See the lead editorial "Death of a Compromise," *Christian Century*, July 27, 2022, 7, as well as the series of essays under the title "After Roe," *Christian Century*, July 27, 2022, 19–25.

30. Marvin Olasky, "How Americans Got Away with Abortion," *Christianity Today*, September 2022, 58–62.

The June 2022 Supreme Court "Dobbs" decision, while continuing to divide the country, has opened the way to a more imaginative consideration of alternative intellectual positions and legislative options that honor both the good that each side has tried to protect and a framework that appropriately balances the tensions between these goods.[31] Such work is more complicated but in the end has the potential to create a richer and less reductionistic moral framework for both our individual lives as citizens and our collective life as a society. We see this imaginative and agonizing wrestling with the complexity of multiple goods in Allyson McKinney Timm's article "The Right to Life Is an Essential Human Right," where she acknowledges the ultimate sanctity of life but questions the assumption that this right should automatically entail certain costly obligations on the part of a mother. The fact that she is considering the reality of her own family's journey lends both credibility and emotional pathos to the discussion.[32]

We see this imaginative consideration at work in the activism of Kelly Rosati, JD, who has devoted her career to the work of advocating for the sanctity of life. Rather than assuming, however, that being pro-life means that one automatically puts the life of the unborn child over the rights of the mother, she has worked tirelessly to enlarge the pro-life position to include implications for both the unborn child and the mother who is carrying the child. She makes the case that being pro-life is not simply about protecting the biological life of the unborn child, but about ensuring the quality of life that will enable a mother to care for herself and her child once the child is born. Outlawing casual access to abortion is only the first step in being pro-life for Ms. Rosati. A society that is truly pro-life must also be willing to provide health care, childcare, and other resources that make possible a flourishing life for both the child and the mother. This creative advocacy challenges the traditional legislative platforms of both Republican and Democratic Parties. It is not at all a compromise of the concerns of either party—but a call for a new vision of moving beyond polarization that encompasses the convictions of both parties.[33]

31. See Peggy Noonan's reflection on this hopeful possibility in "The End of Roe Will Be Good for America," *Wall Street Journal*, May 7–8, 2022, A13.

32. Allyson McKinney Timm, "The Right to Life Is an Essential Human Right," *Christian Century*, October 2022, 68–72.

33. After working for years as the vice president of advocacy for children at Focus on the Family, Ms. Rosati now heads her own consulting firm, KMR Consulting, which invites clients to this kind of imaginative, practical work that allows them to move beyond seemingly irreconcilable alternatives without abandoning their convictions. For an introduction to her story, see Kelly Rosati, *Wait No More: One Family's Amazing Adoption Journey* (Carol Stream, IL: Tyndale House, 2011).

We see this imaginative consideration at work in the legislative arena in the state of Kansas, where politicians sought to pass the "Value Them Both Amendment" to find a way to protect both mothers and unborn children in the wake of the Dobbs decision. Though it appeared on a state ballot on August 2, 2022, it did not pass. Such efforts to craft legislation that both honors the goods that are at odds in the traditional framing of the abortion controversy and is workable at the level of policy and enforcement will not be easy. But it is part of the hopeful calculation that drives the work of those in middle space, who believe they can do better than just keep the country in ongoing moral unease, having to choose between protecting unborn life and honoring the independent moral agency of the mother.

Sometimes this work of imagining new alternative options begins not in new arguments or new legislation but in a new vision. This is where the arts can play a role—not so much in giving us the new options themselves but in making us contemplate a place beyond our current horizon of thinking and language. The arts can create in us a yearning—a longing, if you will—for options beyond the inadequacies of polarized choices, which motivate us to do the hard work of turning the hunger into actual options. Historian Chris Gehrz contends as much in his blog post praising the work of his former colleague who, as a sculptor, saw the world "at an angle" different from anyone else.[34]

The Possibility of Building Community on Common Ground

By calculating the potential benefits of hosting middle space, we are seeking to honor the reality of the common ground that unites any community, whatever might be the differences that divide the individuals within that community. We are resisting the tendency of single issues to dominate the landscape of politics, theology, or morality such that they obscure the often much larger set of issues or interests that the community holds in common. We are actively working against the kind of short-term passion that can make a community denigrate or jeopardize deep and longstanding bonds of unity in order to resolve one source of disunity. In this case, it is not at all that we are ignoring the importance of the issue that is dividing the community—or minimizing the absoluteness of the convictions on that issue. Rather, we are refusing to allow that issue to count disproportionately when considering what the community has in common.

34. Chris Gehrz, "Seeing the World 'at an Angle,'" *Pietist Schoolman* (blog), September 23, 2022, https://chrisgehrz.substack.com/p/seeing-the-world-at-an-angle?utm_source=profile &utm_medium=reader2.

It is this affirmation of a commonality beyond difference that motivates a commitment to partner in public service projects with religious groups or nonprofits that do not share all of one's particular theological commitments.[35] It is also this affirmation of the importance of all that unites a community in the face of deep difference that motivates a religious community to continue listening to each other, to make room for hospitality, and to be open to the possibility that what is needed is a larger vision of God rather than a better argument for one or another of the polarizing positions on a particular issue.[36]

It is this affirmation of a commonality beyond difference that motivates much of the work of interfaith dialogue in this country and around the world.[37] It is not at all the case that religious differences need to be ignored or minimized. Rather, they are placed within the context of larger and more comprehensive convictions that affirm the possibility of a community that encompasses the differences. It is this confidence in God's love, manifested in Jesus Christ, that motivates and sustains the work of Justin Meyers, who works at the Al Amana Centre in the Muslim country of Oman, under the auspices of the Reformed Church in America's Global Mission. According to Meyers, "So often, we think that to be in the middle means to be moderate, or that in order to mediate, we need to soften our beliefs. That is not my experience. While the term the 'moderate middle' is fairly common, being in the middle does not necessarily equal moderate. We can be in the middle and hold deeply held convictions. It means that while we hold onto our convictions, we need to remain in contact with people on both sides of the conflict and help bridge the gaps between them with the love of Christ."[38]

It is this affirmation of our common humanity, together with the respect due to the dignity of each person as an image bearer of God, that we honor as members of American civil society, when we make space for the protection of the rights of those who would speak and worship and organize in volunteer societies that differ from our own. When we make space for a plurality of ideas and even protect that pluralistic framework, we are not at all ignoring

35. See, for example, Jason Byassee, "My Missional Friendship," *Christian Century*, June 1, 2022, 32.

36. See, for example, Tammie Grimm, "The Necessary Middle," Catalyst, September 12, 2022, https://www.catalystresources.org/the-necessary-middle. See also Samuel Wells, *Humbler Faith, Bigger God: Finding a Story to Live By* (London: Canterbury, 2022).

37. See, for example, the work of Eboo Patel and Interfaith America at https://www.interfaithamerica.org.

38. See Justin Meyers, "What It Means to Live in the Middle and Be a Peacebuilder," *Faithward*, https://www.faithward.org/what-it-means-to-live-in-the-middle-and-be-a-peacebuilder.

the seriousness or absoluteness of our own particular convictions. We are, rather, affirming an equally serious, shared conviction in the context of which there may be room for differences.[39]

The weighing of imaginative, hopeful possibilities against the immediate and concrete risks of moving into the work of middle space seems inherently unbalanced in favor of risk rather than possibility. We should not be surprised. It is the nature of the case. Nevertheless, when we count the factors in favor of braving the risk, we would do well to remember that we are choosing not only for this moment but for future generations. Holding back now, for all the legitimate reasons that we recognize, not only limits options for our own time but also makes it more difficult for those coming after us to imagine that anything might be different. Allowing our hopes to count for more than our fears reflects this responsibility we have to future generations and not simply to our own. It is not an exercise for the laboratory or even the data scientist. The work of weighing the risks and benefits of middle space is the work of practical wisdom, the work of creativity, the work of faith in realities that we cannot see, and the work of partnership in the great cosmic exchange that will someday trade our spirit of heaviness for a garment of praise.[40]

Questions for Discussion

1. Have you ever felt personally the cost of stepping out into middle space? Or the fear of doing so?

2. Can you think of a situation in your own life (e.g., in your family, church, business, or social network) in which you see polarization and have a desire to help your community move beyond it?

39. See Amar Peterman, "Lambeau Field and Civil Society: An Opportunity for Formation and Flourishing," *Common Life*, September 20, 2022. See also Stuart Adams, "The Utah Compromise," Law & Liberty, April 14, 2015, https://lawliberty.org/the-utah-compromise. Adams outlines how the Utah legislature was able to craft legislation that created space within the civil society of Utah that protected both the core civil rights of the LGBTQ+ community and the religious liberty of those with dissenting convictions on sexual morality. The article can also be found on the Alliance for Lasting Liberty's website, https://fairnessforall.org/the-utah-compromise.

40. Isa. 61:3 (KJV). See also biblical references to this exchange in Isa. 55:12–13; 61:1–3. For two recent books that advocate compellingly for a recommitment to the common good of the human community despite all the challenges that it will involve, see Wendell Berry, *The Need to Be Whole: Patriotism and the History of Prejudice* (Berkeley: Shoemaker, 2022); and Sacks, *Morality*.

3. Which of the possible costs and potential benefits seem most relevant to you in this situation?

4. Are there other costs and benefits that have not been suggested so far?

5. What might you do to increase the potential benefits over the likely costs in the situation?

6. Have you ever been on a "pole" and been called out of that space to consider a third alternative? What was most persuasive to you in considering a third alternative?

5

So You Want to Prepare to Work in Middle Space?

As a young faculty member, I prided myself on being efficient and able to get ready for a presentation at a moment's notice. Whether it was class prep or a talk for an admissions day at the college, I was confident of my abilities to get ready quickly. My mentor, a much more seasoned professor—and someone I admired very much—always took much more time than I did even though he had done the same things over and over. I took notice.

It is from this senior mentor that I received two important and memorable lessons in preparation. He was an avid fan of sports and of World War II. If there were "greatest generation" spectators, he would have been one of them. He especially admired the athletes who took time off from their athletic careers to serve in World War II. The legendary Ted Williams (1918–2002), of the Boston Red Sox, was one of these. My mentor told the story (many times!) of Williams coming to the field and working out day after day, even after he was the "Great Ted Williams." According to the story, when he was asked by a custodian why he showed up and worked so hard at practice, even on his own, he replied, "Preparation is everything." (I cannot vouch for the story. I tell it here because my mentor believed it and it shaped his own journey—and mine!)

My mentor was also a philosopher and an admirer of Iris Murdoch (1919–99), the Oxford Platonist who wrote novels as well as philosophy. Perhaps it would be truer to say she always wrote philosophy but sometimes in the form of novels. One of her longer essays was published under the title *The Sovereignty of Good*.[1] Here, she is exploring what it means to be a good person and to do the right thing when life calls for moral courage. According to Murdoch, we cannot be ready for those moments, unless we have been preparing all along to become a certain kind of person. Our capacity for honorable, courageous acts "when the time comes" depends entirely on our "habitual objects of attention" or the "quality of our usual attachments."[2] We have to prepare in advance to become a certain kind of person, if we expect ourselves to do the right or the good thing when the opportunity presents itself. In other words, we cannot cram for the moral life in the way we cram for exams! Preparation is everything.

If we want to be ready for the work of middle space, we have to be preparing to be a certain kind of person so that we are ready when the opportunity comes. There are no special techniques for helping a community of people imagine a future possibility that would call them to leave the confident comfort of their place on the edges to cooperate with others—especially those "others" who might have been on the opposite side of the issue in question. There are no manuals to tell us the "ten easy lessons" or "ten steps" to mastering middle space.

It is a matter of intentionality and availability. I am guessing that there are very few people who set out to be ambassadors of middle space as a lifelong calling. The work of middle space finds us—sometimes for specific moments of our lives, sometimes for prolonged seasons. It is as particular in its character as are the individuals involved. Our task is to be ready for service—to become the kinds of people who can be used by God's Spirit "when the time comes."

There are several aspects of this preparation. While the process is intentional, it is not at all linear. It is a kind of back-and-forth movement of proactivity and reflection—putting ourselves in the position to access resources of various sorts and then spending time in reflection on what we have seen and heard. Finally, this preparation is particular to each individual. It is work that involves the whole person—one's intellectual development, one's spiritual sensibility, one's emotional capacity, and one's ability to embody all of this in concrete situations with particular people. It is the work of seasoning and leaven, to use two metaphors that our Lord Jesus

1. Iris Murdoch, *The Sovereignty of Good* (London: Routledge, 2001).
2. Murdoch, *Sovereignty of Good*, 55, 89.

used. It is not about having something in one's hands to distribute; it is about effecting a change from inside the situation because of the kind of person you have become.

Remembering Your Own Story

The work of middle space begins in the context of one's own story. Chances are, if you are reading this book by choice, you are already attuned to this calling of middle space. If you are reading this book as a text and the work of middle space has sparked your interest, begin by reflecting on your own journey. In either case, it helps to name those elements of your life experience that are now available to be used in service to others.

> What aspects of your story have placed you in situations in which you felt that you did not fit any of the available boxes? (Remember Margaret's story.)
>
> Have there been moments in your life when your questions seemed larger than any of the answers you were given?
>
> What aspects of your life have prepared you to see a situation from more than one perspective?
>
> Where have you seen communities divided in ways that seemed unnecessarily polarized—where it seemed to you that each side had pieces of the truth?

I have already shared with you my own story. I want to share elements of three other stories of individuals who have been effective at moving communities beyond polarization to imagine new and larger possibilities for their life together. Critically, these new possibilities are not a mere averaging of the convictions of those on the poles; nor are they a bland watering down of passion for the truth. Rather, they are born of a passionate commitment to a vision of the truth that is larger than one's own current capacity to see it, along with the courage to engage other truth seekers in the collective work of caring more about the truth than about being right.

After meeting each of these individuals, I wanted to understand how they became involved in the work of middle space. Not surprisingly, none of them went looking for it. But when I asked them how they became involved, their personal stories were a key aspect of the answer. Each story is unique. But you will also see some common elements. Perhaps they will inspire you to see your own story more fully and clearly.

Darryn's Story

Darryn grew up as a "third culture" kid. His parents were missionaries in a context that included missionaries from several denominations. He went to school with "MKs"—that is, missionary kids—from these different denominations. Thus, he learned from early on that people who call themselves Christians do not all think the same way, even on issues that are important to them. Growing up in a different culture also gave him the opportunity to develop friendships with children from other cultures. He learned by experience that people from different ethnic and cultural backgrounds, despite their differences, also had a lot in common. They had similar challenges as human beings—providing for their families, obtaining an education, solving community problems that affected everyone. In this context, he learned not to be afraid of connecting with people who were different. Perhaps most important of all, as an MK, he learned that it was more helpful to talk about Jesus in the context of a person's particular situation than to deliver an abstract message of the good news in a one-size-fits-all approach. He saw himself as a personal representative of Jesus, a kind of ambassador, much as the apostle Paul describes Christians in 2 Corinthians 5. He was simply passing along what he thought Jesus would want to say to the person after hearing their story.

Doug's Story

Doug grew up in the context of a conservative Christian family. He attended a Christian college during years of intense debate in the world of American Christianity about the authority of the Bible—in particular, the use of the word *inerrancy*. Doug studied mathematics and physics and early on came to see differences between the ways that those in different parts of his life went about answering questions or finding what they considered to be significant or certain truth. He saw the power of the rationalist and empirical methods of mathematics and the natural sciences to deliver answers that seemed to give important information about the nature of the world. He also saw the ways that some in his religious tradition used the Bible in a literalist way—no matter what kinds of topics were in question. In particular, he began to feel the tensions between the answers that the Bible gave—when viewed through the lens of inerrancy—and the answers that science and mathematics gave. Not surprisingly, given the larger culture into which his studies were taking him, he came to think of the methods of science and mathematics as more dependable in yielding significant and reliable truth than the methods of looking into the Scriptures.

As a student, he had the good fortune to be mentored by a professor of philosophy who was not at all put off by his questions. Furthermore, Doug's professor wanted his students to think deeply about the contemporary debates over the nature of biblical authority rather than to assume that their own community's understanding of inerrancy was the final word on the subject. The professor took a group of students to hear Karl Barth at Princeton Seminary, where Doug heard the legendary European theologian himself lecture on his views of biblical authority, which had been shaped in a context quite different from the context of the American fundamentalist-modernist controversy. Barth's words were liberating. Through the lecture, Doug was invited to consider a view of God's revelation that included not only the biblical texts but the Word as embodied in Jesus Christ and as proclaimed by the church under the guidance of the Holy Spirit. He came away not less certain of his confidence in biblical authority but with both more confidence in biblical authority and a larger understanding of the nature of that authority.

Doug's studies took him not only into graduate work in the natural sciences but also to graduate studies in theology. He was deeply invested in understanding how the worldview of faith and the worldview of the natural sciences worked together in leading us into truth. He did not want to yield to the assumptions of the modern Enlightenment world that one must choose between loyalty to science and loyalty to religious faith. The more he worked in these two fields, the more he became accustomed to not seeing them in terms of battle imagery but rather in terms of collaborative partnership. They were two different ways of looking at the world, two different methods of seeking valid insight and significant truth on questions that mattered to human beings. The challenge was to understand more clearly what could be seen from each perspective and how each perspective provided value for our journey as human beings in the world. Rather than trying to fit the complexities of the world into the reductionist paradigms provided by either the religion or the science of his early understanding, he allowed his vision of both religious faith and science to grow as partners in his quest for truth about the world.

As someone who could speak the language of both the natural sciences and mathematics and the Christian faith, Doug quickly became involved in discussions about the relationship between science and religion. He became adept at doing the work of translation and interpretation, investing his own credibility in inviting the kind of cross-cultural exchanges that enabled the "friends of science" and the "friends of religion" to understand each other more fully. Eventually, he expanded his use of these same skills of translation and interpretation to the work of interfaith dialogue.

Kelly's Story

Kelly grew up in Wisconsin in the context of middle America, where being an evangelical Christian usually meant also being a member of the Republican Party and being a political conservative on matters of the economy and ethics. Most of the Christians she knew were white, Protestant, and middle class. As a young attorney concerned to protect the historic rights of Christians in America, including a pro-life position on abortion, she became involved in such organizations as the Christian Legal Society and Focus on the Family.

Then her husband's position called the family to Hawaii. Hawaii was not Wisconsin. She learned what it felt like to walk into a McDonald's for lunch and be the only white person. She learned that deeply devoted Christians were involved in both Republican and Democratic Party politics. For the first time, she met Christians who were at the same time leaders in their local churches and leaders of the local trade unions. In her advocacy work, she also met Roman Catholics whose views on such moral issues as the sanctity of life had been developed over centuries, including advocacy not only for the life of the unborn but for human flourishing at all stages of life. She found herself at one point in the fascinating but somewhat curious position of serving as a lobbyist for both the Hawaii Family Forum and the Roman Catholic Church. As the first person in her family in that multicultural position, she had to learn quickly without the benefit of models or mentors. To her great joy, she found that working on the two assignments together made her a better advocate for each of her clients. The precision of her legal training and the clarity of her evangelical pro-life convictions on behalf of the unborn were deepened by the rich and complex tradition of Catholic moral teaching going back centuries to such philosophers as Thomas Aquinas (1225–74) and extending to the more recent history of Catholic social thought represented by such activist-thinkers as Dorothy Day (1897–1980).

In Hawaii, Kelly encountered Christians who were as committed to working at Christian health centers for the poor as to working at crisis pregnancy centers for young women without other means of family support. Their Christian faith did not call them to the political right or the left, but to causes in both traditions that seemed to fit with the teachings of the gospel. It was in Hawaii that she began to see how much her understanding of the gospel of Jesus Christ had been shaped by her Midwestern culture rather than by the teachings of the Scripture. The experience was liberating for Kelly, and it led her into an ever-larger vision of being pro-life that she calls "whole life." To be pro-life, for her, meant being for human welfare and flourishing at all stages of one's journey.

As you can see, Darryn, Doug, and Kelly have quite different stories. One grew up in the context of full-time missionary service outside the United States; one was shaped by the questions of the American academy; one by the context of Christian political activism. Their interests were not at all the same. Their training was quite different. And the causes that invited them into middle space were not at all alike.

But their stories all have common elements. They all found themselves in some way or another in places where others did not think or act the same as they did. They saw people—good people, whom they respected—who did not all think the same or in the same way they had been brought up to think. They all were brave enough to keep asking questions—to care more about serving God with their full range of gifts than about earning the approval of any one of the individuals who might have been watching them.

As you reflect on your own story, you may want to think about experiences in your own journey that put you in a context in which good people you respected did not all think the same way about matters you considered important. What were the convictions that enabled you to process their various perspectives without necessarily believing that you had to choose among their positions or accept the totality of any one of their perspectives? Were the matters on which there was disagreement concerns within your family, issues of church doctrine or policy, or issues at some level of your civic community? What motivated you to want to be an agent of hospitality in these moments, to draw the parties beyond a polarized framework for the discussion? If you acted on that desire, how did you go about seeking to create the space for the dialogue?

While the process of preparing to be an agent of pointing a community beyond polarization is not at all necessarily a linear process, if you are reading this book and motivated to do this work, considering your own story is a promising starting point.

Developing Your Own Philosophy and Theology of Working in Middle Space

While I am not at all suggesting that you must have a fully developed philosophical and theological framework before you begin this work, it will be helpful if you have begun to reflect on a general theoretical framework that provides you goals, principles, and boundaries even as you begin this work. Your theoretical framework may begin at the level of intuitions and assumptions—beliefs upon which you have operated your entire life without even thinking about them. But as you enter into this space, it will be useful to you and to those with whom you are working if you are able to articulate these beliefs. Then, of course, your framework will grow in clarity and strength as it is informed and tested by the work of middle space itself.

First of all, you will need some transcendent goal toward which you are inviting your respective community to move when considering your invitation to move out of its current position of conviction. Is it a larger vision of the truth? Is it a goal that you believe will encompass their differing convictions about the truth—that will be more important in some way than the cognitive convictions that are the source of their current division? For example, could it be love in the case of a family? Could it be the kind of unity that Jesus describes in John 17 if you are speaking to a church? If you are dealing with a civic matter, is it a vision of pluralism that invites different positions to coexist in the service of a larger goal?[3]

Second, you will need some regulative principles or standards of judgment that you are able to offer to your conversation partners to help them see that their position may not be the final word. They will need to be convinced in some way or another—besides force—that there is a better approach to the situation in question or a higher goal to be served than the convictions to which they are currently holding so tightly. Are you giving them stronger arguments? Or are you enabling them to see something they have not seen before? Are you sharing stories that expand their capacities to empathize more fully with others?

Thirdly, you will need some framework that allows people to see that they are not betraying the loyalties that took them to the poles in the first place. Usually this involves some vision that allows them to see that arriving at the truth does not all depend on them. This can be a greater appreciation for the work of the Holy Spirit as suggested in the Gospel of John, chapters 14–17. It can be inviting people to make a distinction between their own clear conviction that there is truth to be discerned in a particular situation and their own limited capacity to find that truth by themselves. In other words, as we have noted in other contexts in this book, people who are gathered at the poles

---

3. In this regard, I will mention once again two recent books that I have already noted and add a third that helps to inspire the large humane ideals in which this work of middle space is most productively grounded. See Jonathan Sacks, *Morality: Restoring the Common Good in Divided Times* (New York: Basic Books, 2020); and Wendell Berry, *The Need to Be Whole: Patriotism and the History of Prejudice* (Berkeley: Shoemaker, 2022). Given the central—and pain-filled—role of race in the American context, it would be critical to understand how the Black church is processing America's story, so I recommend Walter Earl Fluker, *The Ground Has Shifted: The Future of the Black Church in Post-racial America* (New York: New York University Press, 2016).

need to be reassured that in considering other views of a situation, they are not being plunged into relativism.

Fourth, you will need a framework that convinces them of the dignity and value of others who do not share their view—or a way of distinguishing between the individuals who hold a particular perspective and the views themselves. How might good, well-meaning people, morally sensitive and even intelligent people not share one's own view?

In summary, you need a picture that allows people to move beyond a simplistic binary approach that sees the world in terms of good and evil, truth and falsehood—without landing them in the abyss of relativism. They need to see how it is possible to speak truth without necessarily needing to assume that their dissenters speak falsehood. They need to know that they can be motivated by a desire to be right without inherently assuming that those on the other side have suspicious or conspiratorial motivations.

This is not an easy picture to paint, at least not in a way that speaks compellingly to the audience. We are well trained in our modern Western world to see things in terms of either/or. Our court system, our approach to logic, our two-party political system, the twentieth-century framework of the Cold War, the tendency to see our society as either religious or secular, and even the dominant worldviews in our society[4] all reinforce this tendency to see ourselves and those like us on one side of a great divide between truth and falsehood, good and evil.

The resources are readily available to invite people beyond this binary framework—in a way that allows them to retain their belief in absolute truth—but it takes time to enable them to see this. You will want eventually to have your own words for this middle space—a space that is safe but not passive or complacent, that is animated by a deep passion for the truth but open to seeing one's own perspective as one part of this truth rather than a complete understanding of the truth. Increasingly, as we have already noted, the word *pluralism* is being used to describe the creation of a space that allows for both the animated pursuit of truth and the coexistence of multiple opinions, even deeply held opinions, by individuals who are seen to be both intellectually competent and morally serious. The boundaries of this pluralism will, of course, be different depending on the context. For example, within a civil society like the United States of America, the boundaries of pluralism are determined by the Constitution, as interpreted by the judicial system. The Constitution, especially the first ten amendments that we know as the Bill of

4. See, once again, Robert D. Putnam and David E. Campbell, *American Grace: How Religion Divides and Unites Us*, with Shaylyn Romney Garrett (New York: Simon & Schuster, 2012).

Rights, sets up the framework of rights and privileges that are guaranteed to those within the civil society and that must be respected by all others within that society. There may well be a different set of boundaries that applies to a particular voluntary society within that larger civil framework. This might be a church or a particular corporation or an educational institution. At any given moment, we might be operating with some convictions that are worked out within the boundaries of a particular voluntary society, such as a religious denomination, and others that are worked out within the framework of the larger civil society.[5]

As you begin to develop your own language for this convening space, you have a rich library of resources to draw upon. We have also discussed the ways in which the Scriptures themselves create this space that allows for confidence in the truth but at the same time leaves space for moving beyond a prooftexting approach to applying that truth. We see this in the way God speaks to his people through the stories of the Old Testament. We see this in the tradition of the Wisdom literature, especially in the Psalms and Proverbs. There is room within a commitment to obedience to exercise judgment about how to apply the truth in different contexts: to see which principles we ought to draw on and in what proportion to speak in each situation. We see in the Scriptures not only a vision of the truth delivered in propositional terms that must always be considered, but an approach that requires the exercise of practical judgment or wisdom in knowing how to enable the truth to be effective in particular situations. We see this again in the New Testament, as we watch our Lord embody the truth in numerous individual conversations, rarely using the same set of words and often speaking in parables or stories that invite questions and engagement in order to understand what is being affirmed.

We also have available to us the thinking of those who have gone ahead of us in reflecting on a theoretical framework for this work of middle space. We do not have to reinvent the wheel. In addition to the three general works I mentioned earlier in this section, I will add several more specifically focused resources I would recommend as you begin to build your own philosophical framework.

Professor Richard Mouw, longtime professor of philosophy and later president of Fuller Seminary, has modeled in his life and in his writings a way of

---

5. Of course, one of the most contentious sources of current polarization within our society is determining where certain particular issues should be housed and which boundaries should apply. For example, to what extent is the question of abortion to be determined by boundaries shaped by moral and religious convictions that are applied to an entire civil society, and to what extent is it to be determined as a matter of private conscience within a more pluralistic legal framework that makes room for a greater range of moral or religious considerations?

embodying both deep conviction and the earnest pursuit of the truth, on the one hand, and gracious civility and humility, on the other. Drawing on his own theological journey, which included time in communities of the Wesleyan and Reformed traditions, and drawing on his study of the Dutch theologian and politician Abraham Kuyper (1837–1920), Mouw provides for us an inspiring and accessible resource. While the theme of "convicted civility" is woven throughout all of his writings, we see it developed intentionally in his book *Uncommon Decency* as well as in his more recent autobiography, *Adventures in Evangelical Civility*.[6] Mouw's work provides not only a sound theological framework for this work of convening middle space but also examples drawn from his own work in sustained dialogue between conservative Christians and the Jewish community and between conservative Christians and the Church of Jesus Christ of Latter-day Saints. The work inspired by Professor Mouw is now continued within the framework of the Richard John Mouw Institute of Faith and Public Life at Fuller Theological Seminary.[7]

John Inazu is the Sally D. Danforth Distinguished Professor of Law and Religion at Washington University in St. Louis. He brings his training in legal theory as well as his background as a Japanese American, his earlier career in government, and his experience in campus ministry through InterVarsity to two works that are "musts" for anyone seeking to develop their own framework as Christians living and working in a civil society. His *Confident Pluralism* provides a legal framework, grounded in the constitutional Bill of Rights, that establishes space for difficult conversations on everything from politics to religion among citizens from different backgrounds, all grounded within a framework of mutual respect and human dignity.[8] Furthermore, his book also makes the case that Christians can enter boldly into that space with their own religious convictions, while also—consistently with those convictions—making space for those within the civic framework who do not share their beliefs. The outworking of this thinking is made even more practical in the book he recently coedited with Tim Keller, a former pastor at Redeemer Presbyterian Church in New York City.[9]

As Christians, we can be grateful for significant allies from other religious traditions who enlarge our understanding of an imaginative middle space that

---

6. Richard J. Mouw, *Uncommon Decency: Christian Civility in an Uncivil World*, 2nd ed. (Downers Grove, IL: IVP Books, 2010); Mouw, *Adventures in Evangelical Civility: A Lifelong Quest for Common Ground* (Grand Rapids: Brazos, 2016).

7. See the institute's website at https://www.fuller.edu/mouw-institute.

8. John D. Inazu, *Confident Pluralism: Surviving and Thriving through Deep Difference* (Chicago: University of Chicago Press, 2018).

9. Timothy Keller and John Inazu, eds., *Uncommon Ground: Living Faithfully in a World of Difference* (Nashville: Nelson, 2021).

mediates between the stereotypic Western paradigms of what is religious and what is secular. Given the pervasively dominant—and sometimes inappropriately intolerant—role of Christianity in shaping European culture from the time of Constantine (ca. 272–337) to the seventeenth century, it is no accident that much of the Enlightenment's suspicion of religion as a source of reliable knowledge and its hostility to religious interference in the political realm is directed at Christianity in particular. It is understandable historically that since the time of the Protestant Reformation in the sixteenth century, religion became increasingly privatized within the Western tradition.[10] Because of this, Christians in the Western tradition have had to be especially cautious when defending the legitimacy of religious voices in the public square, lest they seem to proffer special pleading or suggest a return to a kind of Christian triumphalism.

At this moment of growing cultural diversity in the West, there are many new citizens and participants in civil society who have not been shaped by traditions that have asked them to compartmentalize their religious convictions within a private sphere, separate from the public arena of intellectual and cultural engagement. As Christians, we benefit from the work of several thinkers from other religious traditions who are offering compelling and accessible articulations of the importance of creating space in the public square for voices thoughtfully informed by their religious traditions. It is humbling to realize that, over the centuries, we as Christians have often not granted those in these same religious traditions the respect that their voices are now creating for the Christian faith.

We have already met in the course of our discussion Rabbi Lord Jonathan Sacks (1948–2020), chief rabbi of the United Hebrew Congregations of Great Britain and the Commonwealth from 1991 to 2013, who wrote and spoke extensively over the course of his career on the importance of honoring those who think differently from oneself based on their common human dignity and supported by their respective religious traditions. His *Dignity of Difference* was published in 2003, shortly after the shocking events of 9/11 seemed to lock the Christian and Islamic traditions into irreconcilable and perpetual conflict. In this work, he outlines the basic arguments that are developed subsequently through his BBC talks and through various books, culminating in his final book, published posthumously as *Morality*.[11]

10. For a compelling historical account of how the Reformation itself contributed to this growing privatization of religious conviction and the secularization of the public square, see Brad S. Gregory, *The Unintended Reformation: How a Religious Revolution Secularized Society* (Cambridge, MA: Harvard University Press, 2015), and the more accessible version of this argument developed in Gregory, *Rebel in the Ranks: Martin Luther, the Reformation, and the Conflicts That Continue to Shape Our World* (New York: HarperCollins, 2018).

11. Rabbi Jonathan Sacks, *The Dignity of Difference: How to Avoid the Clash of Civilizations*, 2nd ed. (London: Bloomsbury, 2003); Sacks, *Morality*. See also his *From Optimism to*

We have also already mentioned two American scholars from the Muslim tradition, Eboo Patel and Asma Uddin, who have established from a Muslim perspective an intellectual foundation for a vibrant role of religion in the public space as an aspect of respecting human diversity in general. For both Patel and Uddin, the confinement of religion to the private sphere both forces individuals to live less holistic lives and deprives public discourse of critical moral and theological insights. By not making space for the integration of religiously inspired voices within a framework of public pluralism, both our individual persons and our social discourse are made more reductionistic and less fully human.

Patel, a child of Muslim immigrants from India, felt as a young adult in the American university context the existential oddity of separating his religious identity from his ethnic identity. He soon became a champion of making religious diversity an aspect of general diversity training within the American educational context, especially in light of growing cultural diversity in the American experience. While the separation of church and state has been part of the framing convictions of the American Constitution since the earliest days of the country's founding, the fact that most of America's immigrants from the 1600s through the 1900s had come from countries rooted in some form of Christianity meant that the social fabric of American society was, in practice, predominantly Christian. Patel believes that American society would be richer given both a deeper understanding of all the religious traditions of its citizens and a more integrated relationship of each person's religious convictions and that person's overall worldview. Eboo founded the Interfaith Youth Core, now Interfaith America, to promote the work of interfaith understanding as a building block of pluralism both within America and around the world. You can read his story in *Acts of Faith*.[12] In *Out of Many Faiths*, Mr. Patel develops the case for the critical importance of religious diversity for understanding America as a country and for understanding the unique potential this country has for modeling a religious diversity that enriches rather than divides nation states and societies throughout the world.[13] While all Patel's writings are accessible to a broad audience, he has provided a handbook for those interested in engaging others in interfaith thinking in *Interfaith Leadership*.[14] For his latest thinking, see his *We Need to Build*.[15]

Hope: Thoughts for the Day (London: Continuum, 2004), and his *To Heal a Fractured World: The Ethics of Responsibility* (New York: Schocken Books, 2007).

12. Eboo Patel, *Acts of Faith: The Story of an American Muslim, the Struggle for the Soul of a Generation* (Boston: Beacon, 2007).

13. Eboo Patel, *Out of Many Faiths: Religious Diversity and the American Promise* (Princeton: Princeton University Press, 2018).

14. Eboo Patel, *Interfaith Leadership: A Primer* (Boston: Beacon, 2016).

15. Eboo Patel, *We Need to Build: Field Notes for Diverse Democracy* (Boston: Beacon, 2022).

Asma Uddin, also a Muslim American, is trained as a lawyer and practices in the area of religious liberty. Just as Patel's work in the world of education has helped to legitimate space for those of faiths other than his own, so Uddin has defended America's tradition of religious liberty for those of all faiths. Her writings have especially addressed our current cultural moment in America, a cultural moment in which Americans have felt threatened in particular by the Muslim faith in the context of the 9/11 attacks and the subsequent military conflicts that have so often been framed in religious rhetoric. These lingering fears from the early part of the century have been exacerbated by concerns over the threat of increased immigration—especially the ways these concerns have been weaponized in our polarized political context. Both of her books, *When Islam Is Not a Religion* and *The Politics of Vulnerability*, provide valuable background in understanding not only the legal and cultural framework that has shaped America's civic structure, but also the growing challenges to basic assumptions of human dignity necessary to promote a healthy and vibrant pluralistic civic policy.[16]

Finally, as part of preparing one's own theological and philosophical framework for hosting productive conversations that point beyond polarization, I would encourage one to become acquainted with the tradition of *covenantal pluralism*. This term has been made popular in the philanthropic world in recent years by the Templeton Religion Trust, which has sought to make the notion the philosophical foundation of its own commitment to cultivate human flourishing throughout the world. The notion includes, in brief, both the conviction that religion is a key aspect of human flourishing and the conviction that religion in general—but especially the religions in the Abrahamic tradition—provides the most helpful foundation for creating and sustaining a pluralistic framework in which multiple religious voices can flourish for the common good. Templeton's particular articulation of this tradition is outlined on its website;[17] it is also articulated in *The Routledge Handbook of Religious Literacy, Pluralism, and Global Engagement*.[18]

Long before the Templeton Religion Trust began formulating its understanding of the tradition of covenantal pluralism, Rabbi Irving Greenberg (b. 1933) began outlining a theology of pluralism grounded in the Jewish tradition of covenant. Whereas this theology began explicitly within his own

16. Asma T. Uddin, *When Islam Is Not a Religion: Inside America's Fight for Religious Freedom* (New York: Pegasus Books, 2019); Uddin, *The Politics of Vulnerability: How to Heal Muslim-Christian Relations in a Post-Christian America* (New York: Pegasus Books, 2021).

17. See https://www.templetonreligiontrust.org.

18. Chris Seiple and Dennis R. Hoover, eds., *The Routledge Handbook of Religious Literacy, Pluralism, and Global Engagement* (London: Routledge, 2021).

tradition, he ultimately asserts that it provides a framework that applies to all those who are created in the image of God—thus a framework that applies to the entire human community.[19]

While one's theological and philosophical framework for the work of middle space will continue to develop over the years, these works provide a starting place. What is most critical, however, is not to think that one must have everything figured out at the theoretical level before taking steps to put one's theory into practice. The very nature of hosting a community of dialogue with the potential to move beyond polarization involves imitating our Lord in seeking to embody truth and grace in our personhood. We cannot give out truth or grace in the abstract. It must be mediated through our lives. For this to happen, we must step out to put our theory into practice, even as we grow in our theoretical understanding of our work and develop helpful language for describing this work to those we invite into a new community of dialogue and exploration.

Putting Theory into Practice

Finding a Community of Kinship

Working in the middle can be a lonely place. We have noted already that you will be vulnerable on both sides. You will be criticized, and you will wonder sometimes if what you are doing is making a difference for good—or whether you are simply engaged in wishful thinking. Furthermore, just about everything you do in the middle requires a judgment call. You rarely know in the midst of a decision that you have done the right thing or taken the action that will be most productive in the long run. For all these reasons, you will want to seek out a community of kindred spirits—no matter how small. You will need safe space, where you can talk about what is happening, seek advice, and get feedback on ideas that you want to try. You will need a place where you can be encouraged and renewed. In short, you want to find a set of individuals you can trust and among whom you experience the sort of winsome magnetism that will also draw others away from the poles in this cultural moment.

Unfortunately, it may not be easy to find such a community, at least not at first. Those who work in this middle space do not wear name tags or sport a logo that signals to you a friendly face. There is no list of members that you

19. See Ira Bedzow, "Rabbi Irving (Yitz) Greenberg and His Theology of Covenant," Academia.edu, https://www.academia.edu/15032033/Rabbi_Irving_Yitz_Greenberg_and_His _Theology_of_Covenant.

can look up on the web. Nor is there a secret handshake or a specific professional organization for those seeking to invite others beyond polarization. Furthermore, the very nature of this creative, countercultural work means that the people you may most want to meet will not look at all like you or have the same background. This community of common ground, as we might call it, will be noted for the particularity—even idiosyncrasy—of its members. You may even find these kindred spirits intimidating at first. Chances are, they will be mature, highly individuated people who have opinions about the world that you do not share. In fact, they may be individuals whom, at first glance, you are tempted to categorize as some kind of "other." I have done that myself on several occasions during this journey, only to find out later—fortunately—how mistaken I was.

Finding this community of kindred spirits will be itself part of the adventure to which you are committing yourself. You will learn to recognize each other gradually. You will want to listen carefully for clues. Are these persons curious? Are they ready to ask you questions as opposed to telling you what they think—or what *you* ought to think? Do they share your desire to imagine a future beyond polarization? Do they see complexity and ambiguity as they speak about various issues? Do they allow you to speak to them? Do you feel welcomed and at home in their presence? Chances are, these individuals have met suffering somewhere along their journey and have learned to make friends with sadness, to use a phrase I learned from my husband. Their hopefulness about the world has most likely been wrested from struggle. They have been shaped by some sort of adversity, not by a life that has met all their expectations.

You may be fortunate enough to find some of these individuals in your church or in a Bible study. But know that this community of middle space will include those who do not share your faith. They may have the same questions about you that you have about them. So just as you are listening for clues from others, you will want to send out search signals yourself. That may include referencing certain controversial issues to test the reaction. Or it may include referring to a particular author or book or blog that you read recently. You may cross paths with them at a conference.

But the most likely place to find individuals who will eventually become part of your community of colleagues in this work of middle space is where the work is being done. For what these kindred spirits have in common is the work they seek to do, the bridges they seek to build, and the space for healing and conversation they seek to make available to others. And in those spaces, you will find not only kindred spirits but those who are further along in the journey, those from whom you can learn the craft, as it were. Once you have met a few of these individuals, your network of connections will grow naturally and even exponentially as these individuals introduce you to their own network of connections. You will soon find yourself in the center of a lively community of kindred spirits that you could not possibly have arranged for yourself.

Becoming an Apprentice

As you have clearly figured out by now, there are no textbooks or guidebooks for the work that you are preparing yourself to do. There are no graduate programs or academic certificates that you can complete. This work of middle space is work that you learn by doing. If you want to do this work well, you seek to make yourself an apprentice to someone who has worked at the craft longer than you have.

Depending on where you are in your journey, you may already have contacts in place that can lead you to such an apprenticeship. (Of course, I am not at all talking about a paid apprenticeship. I am thinking of volunteer work, at least at first.) If you are new to a community, you may want to ask around and volunteer in several places to find out where you are most likely to find a good match. Kelly Rosati, one of the individuals you met earlier in the book and whose story you read earlier in this chapter, has suggested that if you find yourself in a new place or simply want to become involved in a more active way in a place you have lived for a long time, you may want to seek out nonprofits that are associated with both the right and the left. Become acquainted with those in your town or county who are supporting a wide range of causes.[20] In doing this, you will learn the lay of the land in your community. You will find out who has the passion to be involved in volunteer work, and you will no doubt meet some of the individuals you will want to invite into the conversations of middle space. All the while, even as you are learning about others, you are also making yourself available to be known. You have the opportunity to establish yourself as someone who is known and trusted for your curiosity, your convictions—coupled with your posture of grace—your ability to listen, your humility, and your passion to imagine new possibilities for the common good of the community.

As you are becoming acquainted with those organizations known for their work on the two sides of the political spectrum, you are also listening for clues about organizations or individuals in your community who are already imagining new options for the common good—and with whom you might wish to be more involved.

20. Kelly Rosati, interview by Shirley Mullen, November 2, 2022.

Finally, because of the internet, you are able to contact those on a national and international level who are doing this work. The internet can be a resource, certainly, for making connections and finding resources virtually, but it can also lead you to those in your own community with the same mind and heart that you have.

As we have already made clear, while your own personal and theological reflection is important in preparing you for the work of middle space, there is no substitute for getting involved at the practical level. You learn to embody this work—instead of simply thinking about it—by watching it being done. The good news is that there are growing numbers of individuals and organizations in every arena of society who are taking the risk of leaving the safety and security of the poles to venture into middle space. I will introduce you to some of those I have encountered in my own journey. I am not at all suggesting that this is an exhaustive list of organizations and arenas in which you might become involved. I am sharing this particular list for three reasons. First, I want to illustrate the wide range of hospitable middle spaces that are being created throughout our society. While this work of the redemptive middle is not getting as much media attention as the ongoing polarization, it is working like the salt and leaven that our Lord spoke of. Like salt, it is seasoning the communities in which it is at work with the flavor of hope. Like leaven, it is introducing an active agent of imagination. I am encouraging you to find the area of engagement that calls on your gifts and that engages your interests and passions. Second, I want to suggest that by beginning to identify yourself with the cause of convening redemptive middle space, you, too, will begin making connections and building your own network. Each person you meet knows someone else, and bit by bit, you are contributing to the strengthening of the collective impact of this proactive work. Third, I am hoping to show that one person can make a difference. Many of the organizations discussed below began because one person saw a need for change and an opportunity to do something imaginative. Perhaps you will be inspired to explore a call that you never imagined possible—to dare to move out to a life as large as God's calling because others have dared to do that ahead of you.

The World of the Church

We are well aware of the impact of polarization within the church. The media seems all too willing to keep us informed about the contentions within the country's mainline denominations as they seek to work through their particular theological divisions on key social issues, most especially questions related to marriage and the ordination of members of the LGBTQ+

communities. We have seen divisions within the Presbyterian Church (USA), the Episcopal Church, and more recently the United Methodist Church. Each has taken a particular form—and the Methodist Church's breakup is still being worked out. There are issues of endowment to be settled and church property ownership to be renegotiated. It is not unlike a divorce. It is always painful and often public. It makes the news, and unfortunately, it all too often serves only to reinforce the larger culture's skepticism about the credibility of the Christian message in the twenty-first century, at least the credibility and trustworthiness of the organizations associated with that message. It may still be respectable and fairly common to be "spiritual," but it is increasingly less popular to be a member of the organizational church—most especially not one that is associated with the conservative or evangelical tradition.

The politicization of American Christianity over the past half century has been well documented. Especially since the founding of the Moral Majority in the 1980s, one's political position on certain social issues is a better indication of one's religious convictions than the other way around.[21] The public's stereotyping of religion based on one's voting patterns hit a new level of notoriety after the news that 81 percent of white evangelicals had voted for Trump in 2016 and retained that loyalty even into the 2020 election and beyond.[22]

What we do not hear about as often is the work going on behind the scenes seeking to invite denominations, evangelical organizations, and individual congregations to imagine new possibilities shaped primarily by the gospel of Jesus Christ rather than the terms of American politics. This is not easy work, but it is beginning to bear fruitfulness in hope.[23]

21. We have noted multiple times in this regard the work of Robert Putnam and David Campbell in *American Grace*. See also Kristin Kobes Du Mez's statistics on declining church membership in her book *Jesus and John Wayne: How White Evangelicals Corrupted a Faith and Fractured a Nation* (New York: Liveright, 2021).

22. See, for example, Sarah Pulliam Bailey, "White Evangelicals Voted Overwhelmingly for Donald Trump," *Washington Post*, November 9, 2016, https://www.washingtonpost.com/news/acts-of-faith/wp/2016/11/09/exit-polls-show-white-evangelicals-voted-overwhelmingly-for-donald-trump/; Justin Nortey, "Most White Americans Who Regularly Attend Worship Services Voted for Trump in 2020," Pew Research Center, August 30, 2021, https://www.pewresearch.org/short-reads/2021/08/30/most-white-americans-who-regularly-attend-worship-services-voted-for-trump-in-2020/; Tom Gjelten, "2020 Faith Vote Reflects 2016 Patterns," NPR, November 8, 2020, https://www.npr.org/2020/11/08/932263516/2020-faith-vote-reflects-2016-patterns.

23. See, for example, several books that came out in 2022 advocating for strategies at the denominational and congregational levels for moving the church beyond polarization: Robin W. Lovin, *What Do We Do When Nobody Is Listening? Leading the Church in a Polarized Society* (Grand Rapids: Eerdmans, 2022); Gary B. Agee, *That We May Be One: Practicing Unity in a Divided Church* (Grand Rapids: Eerdmans, 2022); Pamela Cooper-White, *The Psychology of Christian Nationalism: Why People Are Drawn In and How to Talk across the Divide* (Minneapolis: Fortress, 2022).

Let me illustrate. At this moment, the same triad that mobilized in the 1940s to offer a third alternative to the poles associated with fundamentalism and the social gospel—the triad of interdenominational association, evangelical media, and evangelical higher education—is now at work to offer an alternative vision of Christianity to the polarization that we see today. In the 1940s, this collaboration resulted in the founding of the National Association of Evangelicals, the launching of the publication *Christianity Today*, and the strengthening of institutions of Christian higher education that could provide training for a new generation of scholar-teachers and pastors to support this work of a third way. The goal was to create a community of Christians— including both clergy and laity—who could speak the languages of American fundamentalism and mainline Christianity and offer a bridge-building model of cultural engagement informed by Christian orthodoxy. This new imaginative alternative became known, somewhat ironically from today's standpoint, as evangelicalism.[24]

While the story of this partnership among the National Association of Evangelicals, *Christianity Today*, and various institutions of evangelical Christian higher education has been anything but seamless or smooth—or even always moving in the same direction—this same triad of associations is coming together in this moment of renewed polarization to imagine new possibilities of an appropriate third way. The current leaders of these organizations— Walter Kim of the National Association of Evangelicals, Timothy Dalrymple of *Christianity Today*, and Shirley Hoogstra of the Council for Christian Colleges and Universities (CCCU)—are seeking to be active agents of bridge building, cultural translation and interpretation, and imagination, both within their respective organizations and within the culture at large.

We see this commitment in the establishment by *Christianity Today* of a new Public Theology Project led by editor-in-chief Russell Moore. We see it in the discussions at the National Association of Evangelicals of the possibility of creating a center to cultivate greater understanding among member denominations of the ethical and social issues of concern to the larger culture. And we see it in the CCCU partnering with bodies outside traditional evangelical circles that share common concerns about protecting traditional understandings of religious liberty in our society.[25] To be sure, this commit-

---

24. The story is well told by George Marsden in his several works on American religious history. See especially George M. Marsden, *Reforming Fundamentalism: Fuller Seminary and the New Evangelicalism* (Grand Rapids: Eerdmans, 1987); Marsden, *Fundamentalism and American Culture*, 3rd ed. (Oxford: Oxford University Press, 2022).

25. See the Fairness for All archives at https://1stamendmentpartnership.org/category/fair ness-for-all/.

ment has been controversial within these organizations themselves—as the imaginative, redemptive work of middle space often is. The work requires constant attention to countering partial truths or real and potential misunderstandings within one's constituencies and among those outside one's constituencies. But it is also beginning to establish a new coalition of individuals who can support and encourage one another in providing a hopeful version of Christian faithfulness for this moment in our country's story. It is to be hoped that once again, as in the 1940s, American evangelicalism can be an agent of surprising and redemptive hope for our culture rather than an agent of divisiveness.

The work of redemptive middle space is not only going on at the level of national organizations. It is going on at the level of individual congregations. You have already met Darryn Scheske, who along with his wife, Loree, serves as joint senior pastor of Heartland Church in Fishers, Indiana.[26] The church began in 2001 to focus on reaching those who did not know Christ. As you can learn from the church's website, its goal is to "love people well, lead them into a transforming relationship with Jesus Christ and launch them out to change the world." At first glance, it could sound like a typical mission statement for any evangelical church in the world. In conversations with Pastor Darryn, however, it soon becomes clear that the work of this church is anything but typical and certainly not stereotypical. Introducing people to Jesus is only the first step. The church wants to train people to be as bold as Jesus was in reaching out to those who would not otherwise join his community; in the modern context, that includes recent immigrants who are part of religious traditions outside Christianity. In addition, Heartland wants to create partnerships with those in the city who share its commitment to the works of mercy and empowerment, not only for those within their own religious communities but for all who bear the image of their heavenly Father. The several thousand people who gather each week in one of the thirteen congregations that have grown out of the original dream are testimony to the fact that the gospel of Jesus Christ is still offering new possibilities for redemption and hope.[27]

At a recent board meeting of the National Association of Evangelicals, I learned of another pastor who is drawing on his particular story to craft imaginative alternatives that point his congregation beyond the alternatives that our culture and the congregation's own tradition had laid out for it. Kevin McBride is the senior pastor of Raymond Baptist Church in Raymond, New

---

26. See Heartland's website: https://www.heartlandchurch.com.
27. Darryn Scheske, in conversation with the author, October 20, 2022.

Hampshire.[28] His is a smaller congregation, reflecting in part the different cultural space of evangelical Christianity in New England. But the redemptive, imaginative work of middle space is the same. And Pastor Kevin, like Pastor Darryn, has found the resources for this holy creativity in his own story. Earlier in his life, he was trained as a scientist—in aerospace engineering, to be specific. He worked in industry, doing the research behind the creation of ever more precise and effective nuclear weapons. At some point, he came to believe that his gifts should be used in ways that offered the promise of constructive hope for the world rather than the potential of more efficient destruction.[29] He went to seminary and prepared to become a pastor. During the pandemic, Pastor McBride drew on his knowledge of the natural sciences, as well as his connections and the credibility afforded by his educational credentials, to invite his community to imagine interpretive possibilities concerning the natural sciences and religion that were different from the polarized options available in social media. (As I learned from my grandfather long ago, in God's economy, nothing is wasted.)

These are only a few examples of the current work within the world of conservative Christianity calling the church and the culture beyond polarization. But this is not the only context in which individuals might become involved in our culture doing the work of middle space.

Higher Education

Heterodox Academy

In the world of higher education at large, Dr. Jonathan Haidt, professor of moral psychology at New York University, has cast a vision for an organization that intentionally cultivates dialogue across the spectrum of polarization, a polarization that has come to characterize the academy in recent decades. He had been concerned about the perceived—and sometimes real—threats to free speech and academic freedom on our college and university campuses growing out of the emerging culture of political correctness, the trend toward making classrooms "safe spaces" (in which professors had the burden of ensuring that students were not offended), and the tendency to "cancel" speakers with potentially controversial messages. The primary conviction grounding the work of the Heterodox Academy is expressed in its logo: "Great minds don't always think alike."[30] The overall goal of the primarily online organization is to

28. See the church's website: https://www.raymondbaptistchurch.com.
29. Kevin McBride, in conversation with the author, October 5, 2022, Flourish Conference, National Association of Evangelicals, Nashville, TN.
30. See the academy's website at www.heterodoxacademy.org.

reaffirm the values of open inquiry based on evidence, wide-ranging diversity of opinions, and civility of style. The fact that the organization has five thousand members from all over the globe—from all stations within the academy and from across the disciplines—suggests a hunger for just such a platform. This middle space, bounded by specific rules of engagement rather than particular convictions of content, has so far welcomed speakers and writers from across the full range of the political spectrum, including those from both faith-based and more pluralistic academic contexts. It is too early to tell exactly what impact this platform will have on the academy at large or on the larger culture—or even whether it will be perceived as truly providing space that transcends the politicization of academia. Recently, after attending one of the organization's in-person conferences, I heard the concern voiced that the Heterodox Academy would simply become part of the polarization itself—but this time, by favoring conservative perspectives on such issues as race and gender equity, in reaction to the perspectives from the left that are seen to dominate most discussions on diversity and inclusion. This is certainly a possible outcome, but it is also part of the risk that any middle work must assume. Those on one side are able to dismiss the work by labeling it as part of the "other."

Professor John Tomasi, longtime professor of political philosophy at Brown University, has recently assumed the leadership of the organization, recommitting its work to cultivating both free inquiry and social justice, thus seeking to point beyond the poles of "truth" and "social justice" that have divided the academy in recent years.[31]

It is my hope that this is an arena in which Christians in the academy will choose to participate. There is certainly nothing explicitly Christian or religious motivating the work of the organization. One might even suggest that this is simply the reinvigoration of the Enlightenment framework that all too often ended up equating the dominant values of European culture and society with all that was rational, "enlightened," and most truly and universally "human." In that process, knowledge claims not perceived to be grounded in logical or empirical categories—including revelation, many historical and other narrative texts, and personal experience—were given short shrift. Thus, while the limitations of Enlightenment values could reemerge in the context of the Heterodox Academy, this need not happen. There is room within the language, structures, and stated values of the academy for a wider range of perspectives and more intellectual and cultural diversity than what regrettably came to characterize the dominant culture of the modern academy. In this

---

31. See, for example, John Tomasi, "Standing up for Social Progress," *Heterodox: The Blog*, January 4, 2022, https://heterodoxacademy.org/blog/standing-up-for-social-progress/.

moment, there is opportunity for Christian intellectuals, both from within and outside the formal academy, to share their perspectives. At the very least, this would complicate and enrich the current stereotypes that Christianity is always aligned with conservative politics! This would be of service both to the academy itself and to the larger culture.

National Collegiate Athletic Association: Common Ground

While much more narrowly focused than the Heterodox Academy, Common Ground, working out of the NCAA Office of Inclusion, is another example of a platform within the academy that seeks intentionally to imagine alternatives beyond polarization. In this case, the polarization is the perceived—and sometimes very real—clash of values between conservative faith communities and the LGBTQ+ community. The goal of Common Ground is to imagine ways of thinking, as well as policies and practices, that would enable students from all across the spectrum of politics to participate together as athletes in a community of competition characterized by dignity and mutual respect. In short, Common Ground calls for a focus on what unites those committed to the thriving of student athletes rather than on what divides them. The organization makes no effort to change the convictions of those who participate; in fact, precisely the opposite. Common Ground seeks to imagine and to create on college campuses spaces within the context of athletics that cultivate mutual respect among students across differences of various kinds. Furthermore, the organization wants to train student athletes in practices of dialogue and community building that enable them to be agents of translation and bridge building well beyond their world of athletics.

Common Ground illustrates what can happen when individuals dare to step out and intentionally seek dialogue with those who come from different perspectives. This is exactly what has happened. The organization has its roots at an athletic conference where representatives of a Christian organization and an LGBTQ+ organization were advertising their work side by side in the display space. The representative of the LGBTQ+ organization ventured over to speak with the representative of the Christian organization and to invite them to talk about their differences—and their common commitment to promoting the well-being of student athletes. Out of this came a series of conversations, sometimes hosted at NCAA headquarters, sometimes on college and university campuses.[32] The conversations have invited the sharing

---

32. My colleagues and I hosted one of these convenings on our campus at Houghton College, now Houghton University. See the report of the meeting at https://ncaaorg.s3.amazonaws.com/inclusion/commongnd/Nov2017Inc_CommonGround3Report.pdf.

of personal stories, the clarification of various perspectives, and a commitment to the common values of human dignity, respect for individuals, and above all the well-being of student athletes. Such conversations are grounded in the concreteness of relationships among professional colleagues who at some point become friends. When these colleagues see each other as persons rather than as representatives of abstract causes, there is room for collective imagination of new alternatives that point beyond polarization.[33]

Interfaith Dialogue

Interfaith America

We have already met Eboo Patel. His organization, Interfaith Youth Core—now Interfaith America—has been a model for engaging all sectors of the culture in the important work of promoting understanding across religious differences, as well as between secular and religious visions of society in general. As a Muslim American, Mr. Patel has worked diligently to enlarge the traditional understanding in America of the constitutional notion of the separation of church and state, together with its accompanying assumption that expressions of religious convictions and religious loyalties are appropriate only in private contexts. He has challenged the notion that religious diversity is necessarily a source of division within the larger society, promoting instead the positive value of religious diversity for a democracy. Twenty-first-century immigrants to the United States often come from parts of the world that have not shared the impact of the Reformation and Enlightenment traditions, which resulted in the privatization of religious conviction and the assumption that the separation of church and state implies both the removal of religious considerations from the public square as well as the commitment to be free of an established religion in the political realm. By promoting an expanded understanding of diversity to include religious identity, Interfaith America has not only made room for a more holistic understanding of new immigrants who practice religions other than Christianity; it also opened the door to more explicit expressions of the Christian faith among traditional Christian communities. Interfaith America works intentionally with college and university campuses across the range of the higher education landscape—including

33. For another example of an organization working in middle space within the academy, consider BioLogos (https://biologos.org), which is working to cultivate dialogue across the faith-science divide. For examples of work being done on individual campuses, consider the Center for Faith, Justice, and Social Engagement at Houghton University (https://www .houghton.edu), which seeks to cultivate dialogue about the concerns of both social justice and biblical orthodoxy; see also the Henry Institute at Calvin University (https://calvin.edu), which promotes dialogue and reflection about the intersection of the Christian faith and public life.

public and private, secular and faith-based schools—grounding their dialogue in a common understanding of what they share as institutions of higher education committed to the cultivation of civil discourse, the dignity of all persons, and the flourishing of a pluralistic and liberal democratic society. Interfaith America invites students from these institutions to imagine that a democracy that allows its citizens to openly articulate the moral and religious foundations that ground their most fundamental convictions (and that encourages this openness across the full range of religious perspectives) will actually be stronger and more vibrant than one that is shaped only by the dominance of one religious perspective or a secular perspective.

The organization's Bridging the Gap initiative is an excellent example of its proactive programming among college and university students to cultivate greater understanding across difference. This program pairs an institution from the conservative evangelical tradition with one that comes from a pluralistic or even secular framework, and it invites students from these two institutions to engage over a period of time in discussions and practical cooperative efforts designed to promote greater understanding not only of their differences but also of what they share in common.[34]

Kaufman Interfaith Institute

Dr. Douglas Kindschi is the longtime director of the Kaufman Interfaith Institute at Grand Valley State University.[35] The Kaufman Institute focuses primarily on cultivating religious diversity and cross-cultural understanding within the region of West Michigan. It does so by building connections with various institutions of higher education, churches, and community organizations. The institute was recently recognized by the Aspen Institute on the occasion of the tenth anniversary of the latter's Religion and Society Program.[36] Dr. Kindschi brings together in his leadership the skills of bridge building across difference from his earlier experience in navigating the tensions between the worldviews of the natural sciences and of conservative faith communities. As he explained in our recent conversation, the secret in either case is to invite people to articulate the unspoken assumptions that are shaping their most fundamental convictions, to bring a spirit of humility and curiosity

---

34. For further information about Bridging the Gap, see https://www.interfaithamerica.org /programs/bridging-the-gap/.

35. See the institute's website at https://www.gvsu.edu/interfaith.

36. See the report of the Kaufman Institute's work: Mary Vandergoot, Charles Honey, and David Baak, *Building Interfaith Bridges: West Michigan's Journey toward Principled Pluralism*, ed. Tuhina Verma Rasche (Washington, DC: Aspen Institute, 2022), https://www.gvsu.edu /cms4/asset/843249C9-B1E5-BD47-A25EDBC68363B726/building-interfaith-report-fin-rev.pdf.

to the conversation, and to realize that while they may have part of a true understanding of the world, they may not have a complete understanding of the truth.[37] Again, as we have seen in each of these examples of potential contexts for apprenticeship, one of the core ingredients is to invite communities to imagine possibilities for moving beyond binary understandings of the world—in whatever context that dualistic thinking might occur. It is not a question of becoming "relativist" or "subjectivist" about the truth. It is a question of letting go of one's fears enough to imagine a larger and perhaps more complex vision of the truth than one had previously perceived.

The Nonprofit World

There is a wide range of examples of imaginative middle work being done in the nonprofit world. I will mention only three with which I am familiar. In these arenas, we see clearly how much difference one person can make. It is in these often smaller organizations where you might most easily locate a master journeyman for your apprenticeship.

Equal Justice USA

Equal Justice USA is a national organization seeking to transform our justice system from one that organizes around punishment to one that organizes around healing and restoration.[38] Sam Heath heads up a branch of the organization that builds partnerships specifically with the world of evangelical Christianity.[39] In a recent conversation with Mr. Heath, I learned that he became convinced that something needed to change in our justice system when one of his good friends was imprisoned.[40] Sam visited regularly and came to believe passionately that our justice system could be more effective than it is. These convictions were only solidified as he watched the series of racially inspired events that unfolded in his hometown of Charlottesville, Virginia, in 2017. His convictions were grounded initially in such generally humane values as the inherent dignity of the individual. At some point, he realized that his own Christian faith provided deeper reasons not only for his convictions about how humans should be treated—even when they commit violent crimes—but also for his convictions about what would most likely bring about their redemptive restoration to the community. A successful classroom teacher of

---

37. Douglas Kindschi, in conversation with the author, November 3, 2022.
38. See the organization's website at https://ejusa.org.
39. The website of the branch, called EJUSA Evangelical Network, can be accessed at https://evangelical.ejusa.org.
40. Sam Heath, in conversation with the author, November 21, 2022.

high school history, he had already been trained as an educator. He and his wife became convinced that God was calling him to use his gifts to make a difference in our society's justice system.

Sam became aware of the work of Equal Justice USA through a mentor at his church. When he discovered that the organization was looking for someone to mediate its vision to the evangelical Christian world, he realized that his own journey had prepared him ideally to do this work of middle space. He could speak both the language of the modern Western tradition (of human rights, justice, and social responsibility) and the language of the Christian gospel (of sin, grace, and redemption). He also saw the potential of bringing together a set of concerns about the justice system—so often associated with the political left—and connecting it to the core convictions of the conservative evangelical community—so often associated with the political right. I was inspired by the thoughtfulness that Sam brought to everything he did—and he is only thirty-six years old. He promises to be a leader among the next generation of individuals called to work in middle space.

Parity NYC

Parity NYC is a national nonprofit that hosts convening space among persons of faith and individuals from the LGBTQ+ community—with specific focus on changing cultural attitudes toward LGBTQ+ youth.[41] Rev. Dr. Marian Edmonds-Allen is the executive director. She brings to her current work a background shaped by time spent in the corporate world; pastoral work, especially in the context of elder-care chaplaincy; her academic training at both Western Theological Seminary and Eden Theological Seminary; and her own personal experiences. Even while remaining involved in the practical work of providing shelter for LGBTQ+ homeless youth, she is deeply invested in promoting a third way among those who see the protection of religious liberty as incompatible with the protection of the civil rights of the LGBTQ+ community. She writes and speaks often on the potential for a richer understanding of religious freedom to make space for both the concerns of conservative faith communities and the civil liberties of the LGBTQ+ community.[42]

I met Rev. Edmonds-Allen in the context of a gathering in December 2021 in Salt Lake City hosted by the Church of Jesus Christ of Latter-day Saints.

41. For more information on Parity NYC, see https://parity.nyc.

42. Samples of her writing are available on the Parity NYC website. She is currently completing her doctoral dissertation at Eden Seminary, which is provisionally titled "Covenantal Pluralism and Mission: Evidence for Healing the LGBT and Faith Divide."

Participants came from a wide range of conservative faith communities (I happened to be representing the Council for Christian College and Universities) as well as organizations representing the concerns of civil rights for the LGBTQ+ community. The goal of the gathering was to further the possibility of securing legislation at the national level that could both provide for an expansion of LGBTQ+ civil rights and also protect the religious freedom of those who retain more traditional understandings of sexual morality. Rev. Dr. Edmonds-Allen stood out in that gathering for her fearless graciousness and generous, welcoming spirit toward all those in dialogue. She is proactive in ensuring that all participants are heard and treated with dignity. Furthermore, she seeks to move communities that may not agree fully at the ideological or theoretical level to focus on their common commitments to ethics and to practical projects that promote the well-being of the larger community.

Again, without in any way minimizing the differences among the participants at the gathering, she inspired the group by her example to dare to imagine alternative ways forward beyond the current, seemingly polarized options.

KMR Consulting

I am including KMR Consulting because of its CEO, Kelly Rosati. You have already met her. Whereas KMR Consulting works with clients on a broad range of projects, Ms. Rosati's expertise as a convener of middle space grew out of her background in advocacy for the concerns of families and children. She has worked over the years in such capacities as vice president of community outreach for Focus on the Family and as an advocate for children on behalf of institutions both with the evangelical and Roman Catholic traditions. Ms. Rosati is well acquainted with those across the full range of the political spectrum who care about family well-being. I recently heard her speak at the Flourish Conference, sponsored by the National Association of Evangelicals, on the abortion issues in the wake of the June 2022 Dobbs case. Her presentation surprised everyone in the audience (including me) who had grown up with the traditionally polarized perspectives of the abortion debate. Pro-life concerns for the unborn child have consistently been pitted against the rights of the mother, whether those rights are understood in terms of biological autonomy over her own body or her autonomy as a moral agent to make whatever decision she deems right for herself without the interference of the law. From the beginning of her talk, it was clear that Ms. Rosati was proposing a much more imaginative and comprehensive vision of being pro-life, one that encompassed the concerns of both child and mother—not simply in the context of a pregnancy but over a lifetime—and one that also encompassed the traditional concerns of the political left and right. Her advocacy for a "holistic human dignity perspective" cuts across any simplistic or narrowly polarized understanding of what it means to support the flourishing of children and families in this country.[43]

Social Space

The work of convening dialogues that move beyond polarization is not always formal or even narrowly organizational. In the Bay Area, Teresa Goines, a graduate of one of our nation's evangelical colleges and a former corrections officer working with young offenders on probation, imagined and founded a restaurant and supper club run by youth who are at the same time being trained in all the aspects of restaurant management.[44] The program includes opportunities for the development of life skills and leadership as well. Realizing this vision required Ms. Goines to cultivate conversations with sectors of our society that do not often find common ground—the business community and those who work with at-risk youth. Her persistence has resulted in a program that has inspired admiration throughout the Bay Area and beyond.[45]

The Arts

The arts in general invite creative and imaginative collaboration. Seeing with new eyes is more valued in this context than one's political or ideological perspective. Having said that, the arts have often been cautiously viewed by those on the conservative end of the political spectrum precisely because creativity is harder to regulate through policies and formal rules. (Plato's suspicion of the arts in *The Republic* casts a long shadow in the Western tradition!) Furthermore, the arts are often viewed as a luxury in our society, as a pastime for those individuals who can afford it. They are certainly not assumed to be among the practical courses of study for students who wish

43. I highly recommend that you check out Rosati's website (https://kmrconsulting.net/) both for a more complete understanding of her thinking and for the personal and organizational connections to which it will direct you.

44. See https://www.oldskoolcafe.org.

45. Ella Chakarian, "Old Skool Cafe's Founder and CEO Teresa Goines Leads by Example," *San Francisco Magazine*, April 20, 2021, https://sanfran.com/teresa-goines-old-skool-cafe -profile.

to make a successful living in our society. Consequently, the arts are often among the first programs to be cut when budgets are tight in elementary and secondary schools. They are also among the first courses to be cut in any effort to make a general education curriculum more efficient and "relevant" in our colleges and universities.

It is in this context that I introduce you to Thrive Collective, a program in New York City that seeks to "empower students and schools to thrive" by cultivating participation in the arts.[46] Founder Jeremy Del Rio grew up in New York City under the tutelage of his parents, who continue to work in ministry in the most underserved parts of the city. He took his academic training at New York University and worked for a time in corporate law at Dewey Ballantine in New York City—that is, until 9/11 redirected his priorities to relief work at Ground Zero and gave him a new vision for making a difference in the world. I met Jeremy in the same context in which I first met Kelly Rosati, at the Thrive Conference of the National Association of Evangelicals in Nashville in October of 2022. Jeremy was placed at my table for breakout sessions, and before I knew anything about his work, I was struck by his thoughtful and creative application of the Scriptures of both the Old and New Testaments to the concerns of contemporary society. He spoke at the conference, drawing on what he had learned from watching his father evangelize parts of New York City that most ministries viewed as too dangerous. He was, in effect, sharing how he had served as an apprentice to his father and how that apprenticeship had shaped him in such a way that he returned to continue this creative, imaginative work of social transformation rather than spend his career in the more predictable, conventional world of corporate law.[47]

Political Advocacy

There are opportunities for apprenticeship in the work of political advocacy at all levels of our society—local, state, and national. I will focus here only on several at the national level that have shown themselves especially adept at convening conversations that not only draw together participants from both ends of the political spectrum but also result in imaginative options for moving beyond the current polarization—options that are not possible without the active engagement of those from all parts of our divided society and culture.

46. See https://www.thrivecollective.org.
47. For a more complete account of Mr. Del Rio's impressive work, see his biography on the Thrive Collective website.

The AND Campaign

Justin Giboney, a successful African American attorney engaged in the local politics of Atlanta, dreamed of an organization that could bring together Christians from across the political spectrum to promote the common good. The AND Campaign, founded in 2015 by Mr. Giboney and several colleagues, affirms that it is possible to imagine alternative paths forward that include a commitment to both biblical truths and social justice—or the two values of "conviction" and "compassion."[48] Giboney has made it his priority to serve as a translator or interpreter between white evangelicals, associated stereotypically in the public mind with the values of Trump Republicanism, and the community of African American Christians, who have more often been associated in contemporary politics with the Democratic Party. Wherever he speaks and writes, he is inviting Christians and citizens of goodwill more broadly to imagine a vision of American politics that moves beyond the entrenched alternatives of the current Democratic and Republican Parties. Mr. Giboney, while remaining grounded in Atlanta, is increasingly drawn into national discussions in both the political and religious spheres. For example, he has agreed to serve on the board of directors for the Council for Christian Colleges and Universities. In this context, he provides invaluable perspectives from the experience of the African American church to this historically predominantly white organization of evangelical colleges and universities, which is seeking to become more culturally diverse. He is also able to provide insight on the CCCU and its educational commitments to those on the political left who might pigeonhole it more narrowly on the far right of the political spectrum because of the current cultural understanding of the term *evangelical*.[49]

The National Immigration Forum

The National Immigration Forum cultivates conversation among those across the full range of the political spectrum who have concerns about our country's approach to immigration.[50] It seeks to invite creative approaches

---

48. See https://andcampaign.org for more.

49. The work of the AND Campaign is described more broadly in the book *Compassion (&) Conviction*. This book brings together the authors' rich and varied experiences as Christians working in the political realm to provide practical advice for those who wish to become more involved in this critical work of middle space, informed by both their Christian faith and their desire to promote a healthy civic society. See Justin Giboney, Michael Wear, and Chris Butler, *Compassion (&) Conviction: The AND Campaign's Guide to Faithful Civil Engagement* (Downers Grove, IL: InterVarsity, 2020).

50. See https://immigrationforum.org.

both to policy issues and to the care and flourishing of the immigrants in our communities. At a time in our society when immigration has been a polarizing political issue, to say the least, the forum has continually created contexts in which those from conservative theological traditions, such as the Wesleyan Church and evangelical organizations like World Relief and the CCCU, can be in dialogue with those from the broader American political community to imagine options for immigration reform, for the care of newly arrived refugees and other immigrants, and for the education of the broader American society concerning immigration issues.

1st Amendment Partnership

1st Amendment Partnership, under the leadership of CEO Tim Schultz, seeks to protect religious freedom for all faith communities in our society and to promote greater understanding of the value of religious freedom for all Americans.[51] The organization has been particularly active in recent years in mediating between groups that believe that religious liberty is simply a euphemistic cover for the protection of bigotry on matters of race and LGBTQ+ rights, on the one hand, and traditional faith communities that seek to ensure the protection of their traditional understanding of sexual morality amid rapid cultural change, on the other. 1st Amendment Partnership has convened conversations that include both those from conservative faith traditions (including evangelical, Roman Catholic, Jewish, and Church of Jesus Christ of Latter-day Saints traditions) and those representing the interests of the LGBTQ+ community (including delegates from American Unity Fund, Parity, and state advocacy groups) to imagine legislative alternatives to approaches that seek to advance LGBTQ+ rights at the expense of traditional religious convictions (e.g., the Equality Act) or that protect traditional understandings of sexual morality at the expense of the LGBTQ+ community (e.g., the Defense of Marriage Act). The organization has worked tirelessly among interest groups from across the political spectrum, as well as with legislators from both major political parties, to cultivate greater mutual understanding and to imagine legislation that guards the essential, nonnegotiable elements of the civil rights of all Americans—even when those rights are perceived to be in tension.

The credibility of the 1st Amendment Partnership has grown through its legislative advocacy but also through its educational efforts embodied in Faith Counts, its web-based program that cultivates greater understanding of the

---

51. See https://1stamendmentpartnership.org.

value of faith for the common good of all Americans, whether or not they are members of particular faith communities.[52]

Summary and Conclusion

In this section, we have only scratched the proverbial surface of the options available at all levels of our civic life for seeking out an apprenticeship in the work of calling communities beyond polarization. As you prepare both theoretically and practically to be a host of this redemptive, courageous middle space, I would also encourage you to become acquainted with those in the online community who are actively engaged in this work. I would include such voices as Chris Gehrz, a historian at Bethel University who regularly posts on his blog, "The Pietist Schoolman" (https://pietistschoolman .com); Kristin Kobes Du Mez, a historian from Calvin University (https:// kristindumez.com); Michael and Melissa Wear, who bring their experience in Washington political life to their newsletter *Wear We Are* (https://wear weare.substack.com/); David French, editor of *The Dispatch* (https://thedis patch.com/newsletter/frenchpress); and historians John Fea from Messiah University, Eric Miller from Geneva College, and Jay Green from Covenant College, who jointly give leadership to the range of voices featured in *Current* (https://currentpub.com). These are only a few of the available voices you can access easily online. My list here is admittedly weighted toward historians, given my own discipline, and to those within the Christian community who are engaging the concerns of the public square. My main point here is to suggest that you find your own community of online dialogue that provokes and refines your own thinking without taking up an inordinate portion of your day.

Finally, I would refer you to one recent book by Samuel Wells, vicar of St. Martin-in-the-Fields in Trafalgar Square, London. In *Humbler Faith, Bigger God*, Wells draws on his own prolific writing and wide-ranging reflection on various topics related to living authentically as a Christian in the context of the twenty-first century.[53] His goal in this work is to invite the Christian community to ruthlessly honest engagement with ten classic and contemporary

52. For other examples, consider the Center for Public Justice (https://cpjustice.org), which engages Christians from across the political spectrum in concerns of public policy and education, and the International Justice Mission (https://www.ijm.org), which seeks to call together people from across the political spectrum to attack human trafficking from the standpoint of national and international law.

53. Samuel Wells, *Humbler Faith, Bigger God: Finding a Story to Live By* (London: Canterbury, 2022).

critiques of the Christian faith—and in that process to seek out a "constructive vision for a renewed Christian faith."[54] The format of the work provides a helpful model for framing the dialogues you might wish to convene in the coming months and years.

Questions for Discussion

1. Reflect on where you believe you are best prepared already to participate in and to convene conversations that move beyond polarization.

2. What audiences do you feel most and least comfortable engaging in potentially controversial conversations?

3. What issues do you believe you are best and least prepared to engage?

4. Have you formulated a set of potential questions that invite authentic and deep engagement with issues—rather than superficial or stock responses? And how do you move a person or group beyond the surface?

5. How will you test alternative possibilities to determine whether they are simply bland averages of the controversial aspects of a particular issue—or whether you have truly arrived at an alternative that advances a situation beyond polarization?

54. Wells, *Humbler Faith, Bigger God*, 4.

Concluding Thoughts

The Persistent Call to a Courageous Middle Space

Judging by the continued preoccupation in the national media with the 2020 presidential election and its aftermath and the already-ubiquitous speculation about the 2024 election, polarization in our country is not disappearing anytime soon. Nor is it leaving the church or our communities or our families. We have become used to it, almost comfortable with it. At least we know what to expect, and no one is surprised.

It is not just polarization about one thing. The concerns about LGBTQ+ rights continue to divide us. We saw this division clearly in 2022 in the efforts by some to secure legislative support for the 2015 Supreme Court decision in *Obergefell v. Hodges* to legalize same-sex marriage throughout the United States. In the summer of 2022, this legislation had strong bipartisan support in the House of Representatives. This proposed legislation would have not only replaced the 1996 Defense of Marriage Act but also made no provisions for traditional protections for the concerns of religious liberty embodied formally in the Religious Freedom Restoration Act (RFRA) of 1993. Thanks to nearly a decade of behind-the-scenes relationship building across political, religious, and ethical differences, there was already in place a network of legislators, educators, religious leaders, and faith-based humanitarian leaders—from both inside and outside the LGBTQ+ community—who understand the potential costs to society at large of passing the proposed legislation without also attending to the concerns of religious liberty. As a result of the tireless collaborative work of this network, the Respect for Marriage Act passed by the 117th United States Congress in late 2022 included not only explicit affirmation of existing religious freedom legislation such as RFRA but also language that declared the intellectual and ethical legitimacy of respecting those in the society who support traditional views on marriage. There was to be no equating support for traditional marriage with bigotry. The Respect for Marriage Act, as passed, was a testimony to the critical importance for our liberal democracy of the work of the courageous middle.

It also highlights the challenges of such work. There was no hint in the title of the bill, nor in much of the media attention following the passage of the bill, nor in the Washington celebrations of the bill's passing to suggest the rich complexity that characterized the actual content of the bill. The bill was treated in the public sphere as a victory for the interests of one side, not a victory for the protection of civility and mutual respect in the context of a pluralistic liberal democracy. This was so much so that some who had been part of the coalition building that resulted in the religious liberty protections in the final bill, were criticized publicly by their conservative colleagues for attending the administration's event to celebrate the bill, thus supposedly betraying—or at least appearing to betray—the moral values of the traditional evangelical community. I witnessed such an exchange myself.

The complex story that led to the passage of this legislation may never be fully known to more than just a few of the characters in the narrative.[1] But that is the nature of the work of the courageous middle. It is always an act of faith offered in hope and without any guarantee of success. Who would have guessed that the years of building trust across difference would ever truly bear fruit for the common good? This work is most often humbling work that cannot be defended or even fully explained.

We know that LGBTQ+ rights are not the only issue dividing the country. Abortion has once again become a major topic for discussion and debate. The Dobbs decision did not resolve the division of the last fifty years; in some ways, it enlarged the arena of the discussion. Now it is not only a key issue in national politics but in the politics of each of the states in the union. We continue to be torn on issues of climate change, foreign policy, immigration, and how to stabilize the economy. In the meantime, the international context continues to become ever more complicated and uncertain. We yearn almost wistfully for the days of the Cold War when at least we supposed we knew the rules of engagement.

---

1. While I certainly do not purport to know the entire story, I have been privileged to watch this legislative journey unfold over the past decade through service on the following boards: Council for Christian Colleges and Universities, National Association of Evangelicals, and 1st Amendment Partnership. It was a special honor to be present at a small delegation sent to thank Senator Susan Collins (R-Maine) for her critical role in the final stages of the legislative process.

As we have discovered in our explorations so far, polarization has its useful purposes. It serves to highlight the key tensions at issue in any discussion. It continues to keep alive the notion that there is "right" and "truth." I do not believe that most people would choose a world in which it was widely accepted that everyone arbitrarily chooses his or her own truth. Despite the strains of relativism and subjectivism that have persisted throughout history, most recently in certain quarters of the postmodern movement, we do not function in daily life as if fairness and justice are utterly relativistic. This is the point to which C. S. Lewis draws attention in the early pages of his classic, *Mere Christianity*.[2] Nor would we prefer a world in which the truth was simply dictated in monolithic form from a top-down authoritarian voice.

Yes, polarization has certain values in this moment. It provides new contexts in which people are able to satisfy their need to belong—at a time when some of the more traditional communities of belonging, like family or church or local service clubs, are not functioning as smoothly as we might wish. It provides the security of being "right" at a time when moral clarity is hard to come by. And polarization creates communities of certainty in the midst of the confused plethora of authorities. When we don't know who to trust—and when even science has failed to provide clear answers in the recent pandemic—we know that there will be those on the poles who will save us the challenge of having to deal with complexities and ambiguities in isolation or in our own strength.

Yes, polarization has its uses. But it is continuing to exact a cost—certainly on many of our personal and professional relationships but also in our capacities as a society to work as efficiently and creatively as we need to, given the overwhelming challenges we are confronting at this time. There is still too much time spent trying to build coalitions in Washington and to craft legislation that has even a remote chance of passing both houses of a polarized Congress—even when there is general bipartisan support for dealing with the concerns. (Perhaps getting to constructive immigration reform would be the best example of this!) There is still too much time spent by leaders in the church and in the nonprofit world navigating their polarized constituencies and communicating in ways that do not lose one side of their support in the very process of reassuring the other side.

We may not be able to solve polarization as an abstract problem. It is not that sort of thing. As we have already acknowledged, polarization is not just about one issue; there are multiple polarizations on a wide range of issues, some overlapping but some existing on their own.

2. C. S. Lewis, *Mere Christianity* (New York: HarperCollins, 2015), 1–8.

But we need to keep conversations going across the chasms that divide the various poles existing throughout our society. We need to keep alive the hope that it is possible to come up with alternative proposals and visions of the truth that point beyond the paralysis of entrenched, binary options. Furthermore, these alternatives need to be fueled by the same passion and conviction that exist on the poles. As we have said repeatedly, these alternatives cannot be bland averages of the current competing options. Nor can they be grounded in relativism or subjectivist views of the nature of truth and how we arrive at our beliefs. These alternatives must be built on the same commitment to truth that exists on the poles. They must be informed by the research and knowledge claims that continue to be compelling among those of goodwill and competence from both poles.

The difference will not be that these alternative proposals are less committed to seeing the truth about the world or less willing to look honestly at the issues involved. The difference will be that these alternative proposals are shaped by a community of individuals who are more concerned about seeing the truth than they are about being right. They are more willing to wrestle with the complexity and ambiguities of issues than in arriving at simple (often simplistic) sound bites that can be the stuff of Twitter feeds or that can fit into a one-line campaign slogan. They have the humility to admit they do not have the entire truth at the moment; they are willing to listen to other viewpoints, to wait, to be patient until things become clearer. In the meantime, they allow the clarities to provide guidance in interpreting and weighing those aspects of a situation that are not yet clear. Most of all, this group is confident that the final arbitration of the truth is not in their hands. It is in God's hands—however one understands theologically the working out of God's purposes in this world. They can rest in the comfort that it is not their job alone to rescue the world. They know that someone with a much broader perspective than theirs has already promised to make all things new and has simply engaged us as partners in that redemptive operation.

This book is intended to inspire a group of individuals who will commit themselves to be agents of this activist and attentive hospitality wherever they find themselves. For some, this may be in their family. For others, it may be in their workplace or their church. For some, it will be occasional work, prompted by specific conversations or particular contexts. For others, this might become the work of their calling at least for a season of their journey.

It is hoped that this book is the beginning of a long-term conversation, not the end. We want to remain open to learning from our past about what God might be calling us to do or be in the future. While we do not want to be mired in the past—neither past triumphs nor past regrets—our past can almost always inform us helpfully about those strengths and weaknesses that we are able to offer to our communities and to God as the occasion requires.

We want to continue to grow in our understanding of the many ways that God speaks to us through the Scripture—not just in those areas that come to us propositionally but in those parts of the biblical text that teach through narrative example, that cultivate in us a larger vision of who God is, even when we cannot fully capture that vision in words. We want to continue to grow in knowledge of God and of the world—and in the practical wisdom of how to apply that knowledge in the particular circumstances of our lives. Above all, we want to grow in our imitation of the Lord Jesus Christ, embodying in our finite ways that full incarnation of grace and truth that is described for us in John 1 and that we see lived out in the pages of the four Gospels.

We want to continue to cultivate both the discernment and the boldness required to engage productively in the conversations of middle space. These conversations must never be about us—but must suggest at least the possibility of moving a community forward beyond polarized paralysis and unproductive binary thinking. There will never be guarantees, but working in the company of kindred spirits can help us work with both minds and hearts informed by love and grace rather than by fear or power.

In all of this, we must submit to the knowledge that the results of the work will often be invisible. The work itself will be like the salt and leaven of the parables of Jesus. It will provide seasoning and ensure that things are not as they would be without it. But we will not be able to measure that impact, nor will we be able to record it on a reporting form for some measurable evidence of outcomes. Furthermore, the impact may not be immediate. It is all an investment of faith. We may never live to see the results of our labor in a particular situation or in the lives of individuals for whom we have served as models. Occasionally, we might hear back from someone—or think we see what might have happened without our efforts. But mostly, we must leave the results in God's hands.

In the course of our commitment, we will come to be part of a community of kindred spirits, both within and outside the circles of our Christian community. This will be a community of highly individuated people—curious, creative, and most likely even intimidating at first. They will add an element of adventure and richness to our journey that we could hardly have bargained for. They will also help us know when we are enjoying the idiosyncratic nature of our work too much. After all, just because we are taking risks to move into uncharted territory—just because we are being criticized by those on both sides—does not, by itself, mean that we are on the right path.

Furthermore, we will have the confidence—always carefully, cautiously, and humbly shared with others—that we are in the company of those throughout the history of the world who have sought to listen first to God's voice, to move beyond the ready alternatives available by the establishments of our time—no matter how intelligent and well-meaning they might be. We will keep in mind that we are playing before the audience of the great "cloud of witnesses" of Hebrews 12—not the audiences that surround us in our daily lives.

May God give us wisdom and grace to apply well what we have read to our lives and in our world in the days ahead.

Index